Mark Dall and Noble C. Hatfield

Commercial Leases for Restaurants and Franchise Operations

SECTION OF REAL PROPERTY | TRUST & ESTATE LAW

ABA
Defending Liberty
Pursuing Justice

Cover design by Tamara Kowalski/ABA Design.

Printed in the United States of America.

22 21 20 19 18 5 4 3 2 1

Library of Congress Cataloging-in-Publication Data

Names: Dall, Mark, author. | Hatfield, Noble C., author.
Title: Commercial leases for restaurants and franchise operations / Mark Dall and Noble C. Hatfield.
Description: Chicago: American Bar Association, [2018] | Includes index.
Identifiers: LCCN 2018008399 (print) | LCCN 2018012090 (ebook) | ISBN 9781641051521 (E-book) | ISBN 9781641051514 (pbk. : alk. paper)
Subjects: LCSH: Commercial leases—United States. | Franchises (Retail trade)—Law and legislation—United States. | Rent control—United States. | Leased departments, concessions, etc.—United States.
Classification: LCC KF593.C6 (ebook) | LCC KF593.C6 D35 2018 (print) | DDC 346.7304/3462—dc23
LC record available at https://lccn.loc.gov/2018008399

Discounts are available for books ordered in bulk. Special consideration is given to state bars, CLE programs, and other bar-related organizations. Inquire at Book Publishing, ABA Publishing, American Bar Association, 321 N. Clark Street, Chicago, Illinois 60654-7598.

www.shopABA.org

Contents

Preface

In auto racing circles, insiders joke that the quickest way to make a small fortune in the sport is to start with a large fortune. The same wry observation can be made of restaurants. They too are expensive and risky endeavors. Restaurants are labor-intensive, capital-intensive, and largely dependent on the whims of a capricious public. While these challenges are beyond the lawyer's purview, there are two areas in which the lawyer can substantially increase his client's chance of success or at least minimize the risk of failure. The first is the review and negotiation of the lease of the premises where the restaurant will operate. Unless the client is a strong national or regional operator, the client will be subject to the terms of the landlord lease, which, as might be expected, is oriented in favor of the landlord. In most states, the lease is the law, so the client will have to rely on the four corners of that document to enforce its rights and determine its obligations. It will be the lawyer's job to read the lease carefully so he can identify and evaluate the risks that the client assumes by signing the lease, to explain these risks clearly and succinctly to the client, and then to attempt to negotiate changes to the landlord lease that will enable the tenant to maximize success.

The second area in which the lawyer can contribute is the review and negotiation of the franchise agreement if the client pursues that option. Many people prefer investing their time and money in a proven concept or one that is fastgrowing and offers the best potential return on investment. Purchasing a franchise can give restaurateurs a head start in terms of brand recognition, marketing, consistency of food quality, and service. Rather than relying on trial and error, the franchisee can tap the expertise of its franchisor to build a successful restaurant. The franchise agreement is, in essence, a business plan for the franchisee. However, signing a boilerplate franchise agreement is not necessarily a recipe for success. Much to their chagrin, individuals or retirees who dream of being their own boss may become disillusioned once the attorney explains the mandatory directives the franchisee must follow. In addition, there are royalties and other fees that must be paid to the franchisor. Often the franchise agreement is negotiated contemporaneously with the lease, but regardless, the attorney must harmonize the two documents so that adherence under one document does not cause a violation under the other.

This book is a guidepost for the lawyer who negotiates restaurant leases and franchise agreements. It identifies the major issues and potential resolutions for problems that both of the authors have faced in their combined seventy years of legal experience. It is the authors' fervent hope that the clients of the attorneys who read this book can avoid the fate of Mike in Ernest Hemingway's classic *The Sun Also Rises*, who, when asked how he lost his fortune, responded, "Two ways. Gradually and then suddenly."

About the Authors

Mark Dall has been practicing law since 1978. He is admitted to practice in both Indiana and Arizona. Since 1984, he has worked as a real estate attorney for the largest shopping center developer in the United States, with a focus on retail and restaurant leasing. He has made presentations on commercial leasing to various continuing legal educations programs, including the International Conference on Shopping Centers, the National Business Institute, and the Indiana Continuing Legal Education Forum. He is the coauthor of *Commercial Retail Leases and Outlot Purchases*, which was first published by the American Bar Association in 2014.

Noble Hatfield has been practicing law for over 25 years and is admitted to practice in Indiana. He obtained his JD in 1992 from Indiana University School of Law – Indianapolis (cum laude) and his Master of Science in Industrial Administration (MBA-style) degree from Krannert Graduate School of Business at Purdue University in 1976. As an attorney, he continues to focus on strip center development and leasing and has extensive enclosed mall background. Prior to earning his JD, he worked in the printing field, including owning his own business. Currently, he is co-owner of 3 fast-casual franchised restaurants. He is the coauthor of *Commercial Retail Leases and Outlot Purchases*, which was published by the American Bar Association in 2014.

PART ONE

Restaurants

The portion of this book pertaining specifically to restaurants will be unique in the sense that it will deal primarily with issues that are not typically covered by the standard landlord-oriented lease form. The focus will be not so much on what is in the lease, but what is generally not in the lease. A host of questions will be raised for the parties to consider so that they can determine which of these issues need to be addressed for their particular deal. The scope of this part of the book will divided into four parts: (a) computation of rental charges, (b) operational issues, (c) construction issues, and (d) lease exhibits. The section on rent computation will deal not only with the application of traditional rental charges to a restaurant lease but also lesser-known rental charges that may be buried in the lease. The section on operations will address issues that generally arise after the restaurant has opened for business, such as hours of operation, maintenance obligations, and trash removal. The section on construction will consider issues that primarily arise prior to the opening of the restaurant, such as the scope of work, who will perform it, and payment for such work. The discussion on lease exhibits will examine issues that are external to the restaurant premises but often critical to the success of the restaurant, such as no-build zones, parking, access, and visibility. Following these four sections of the book will be a compendium of lease clauses that may pertain specifically to restaurant leases. These clauses are illustrative of the concepts discussed in the restaurant section of this book but are by no means model clauses. As in any lease, language must be carefully tailored to meet the specific needs of the parties and the business deal. For a general discussion of lease clauses that are common to most retail leases, the authors refer you to their previous book *Commercial Leases and Outlot Purchases*, which was also published by the American Bar Association. Except for specific applications of those clauses to restaurant leases, no extensive discussion of those concepts is included in this book.

In the context of these chapters of the book, it is necessary to define what the authors consider to be a "restaurant." In its most basic sense, a restaurant is a retail establishment that primarily offers food and beverage service to the general public for immediate consumption. Within this rubric are subcategories of restaurants. The most prevalent form of restaurant in the United States is the fast-food restaurant. For discussion purposes, the authors define a fast-food restaurant as one using precooked or preheated standardized ingredients that are served to the customer in a packaged form for either eat-in or takeout. Fast-food restaurants often use a drive-through where the customer orders and receives and pays for the order through a service window. There is also the table-service restaurant, which, for our purposes, refers to a restaurant where food or beverage orders are taken from the customer at the customer's table, the food or beverages are delivered to the customer at the customer's table, and a check is delivered to the customer at the customer's table. A fast-casual restaurant is a relatively new category that is wedged between a fast-food restaurant and a table-service restaurant. It differs from a fast-food restaurant in the sense that it generally offers higher-quality food with an emphasis on healthy and fresh rather than frozen or processed ingredients. The customer has more variety in terms of both preparation and choice of ingredients as compared to a fast-food restaurant. Prices will be somewhat higher than the price points for fast food. The fast casual restaurant differs from the table-service restaurant in that the order is usually taken, delivered, and paid for at a counter. A food court tenant generally will be either a fast-food restaurant or a fast casual restaurant. The unique feature of a food court tenant is that it shares common seating with other food establishments. While some restaurants effectively blend aspects of each of these subcategories, these distinctions will be noted only where relevant to our discussion. Otherwise, the generic term *restaurant* will be used. Finally, our treatment of restaurant uses will be primarily focused on those restaurants located in an enclosed shopping mall, lifestyle center, or strip center. The emphasis will be on how the restaurant must integrate its construction and operation into a retail project with multiple and often competing uses. Nonetheless, many of the observations made here are equally applicable to freestanding uses.

An important factor that must be kept in mind are the significant distinctions between a retailer and a restaurant operation. In most instances, the financial investment in a restaurant dwarfs the investment in a retail space of similar size. Restaurants require a longer lead time for design, permitting, and construction. Labor costs are also much higher for the restaurateur as they must employ more people, especially if it is a table-service restaurant. The inventory of a restaurant must turn over more quickly since operators cannot offload a day-old hamburger to an outlet mall. A restaurant may have unique concerns regarding parking, trash removal, and hours of operation. The ability to finance the leasehold improvements may raise issues that are not commonly dealt with in a retail lease, such as leasehold financing and progress payments on construction allowances. To the extent these differences are recognized at the outset and addressed in the lease negotiations, it will minimize misunderstandings during the lease term that could jeopardize the ultimate interests of the landlord in collecting the rent and tenant in making a profit.

Chapter 1

Computation of Rental Charges and Rent Offsets

Base Rent

The essence of a commercial lease is that the tenant pays the landlord for the right to occupy a particular space for a specific period of time. The most common term for this occupancy charge is *base rent*. Sometimes it is referred to as minimum rent, fixed rent, or rent. The letter of intent or proposal letter will set forth the initial base rent and the method of computing increases. During the preliminary negotiations for the deal, the tenant should be cognizant of the different ways in which these increases can be implemented. The simplest method is that the base rent increases annually by a fixed percentage. For example, "the base rent increases on each anniversary of the rent commencement date by 3%." Another alternative is that the increases are staggered over a number of years. Thus, the base rent might remain fixed for the first three years, increased by a certain amount for the next four years, and then increased again for the last three years. The first example enables the landlord to obtain rent increases quicker. This may be important for debt service or, if the landlord is a public company, for showing consistent growth in earnings. The latter example gives the tenant some breathing space before it must adjust to higher occupancy costs. Inadequate capitalization is the reason most restaurants fail in the first few years; so if money is projected to be tight in the early years of operation, then the staggered increases might be preferable.

The base rent also might be adjusted based on the increase in the consumer price index (CPI). The CPI method can be either the sole method for computing rent increases or an alternate computation. If it is an alternate computation, then the rent increases are based on the greater of the fixed increases or the increase in the CPI. If the CPI is used, it is essential that the lease establish which index is applicable. The most common indexes are the CPI-U (for all urban consumers) and the CPI-W (for urban wage earners and clerical workers). These two indexes will not necessarily result in the identical level of increase.

For example, according to the Bureau of Labor Statistics website, during calendar year 2014, the CPI-U increased 0.8% while the CPI-W increased 0.03% during the same time period. The CPI-U is a broader measure. Social Security cost-of-living adjustments are based on the CPI-W. If the CPI is used as a method of computing rental increases, it is important to determine the relevant base period. For example, the initial release date for the CPI for January 2015 was February 26, 2015. They are generally six weeks behind before the initial estimates are released. If the tenant's rent is due to increase in January 2015 based on the increase in the CPI for calendar year 2014, that figure would not be known until February 26, 2015. This would entail a reconciliation of the rent charges. To avoid this result, the parties could agree to use the increase for the period from November 2013 through November 2014, those figures likely being available in December 2014. The lease should also specify that these initial estimates are final, binding, and conclusive since the Bureau of Labor Statistics revises these initial estimates. As with horseshoes and hand grenades, close enough should be good enough.

Some leases use a rent stabilization clause to adjust the base rent. While it can take many forms, the most common version of a rent stabilization clause is that the base rent is increased periodically by the increase in the sum of the base rent and the percentage rent payable by the tenant in a preceding period. This sum is often referred to as "effective rent." For example, if the base rent in the first lease year was $100,000 and the tenant paid percentage rent in the amount of $20,000 for that first lease year, then the base rent would automatically increase to $120,000 for the second lease year. Sometimes this rent stabilization is an annual adjustment, but it can also be staged (e.g., every third lease year or a one-time increase halfway through the lease term). If base rent is increased periodically rather than annually, the rent stabilization can also be the average effective rent over a period of years or it can exclude some years altogether. Rent stabilization can be used in connection with any of the foregoing methods of increase to maximize the base rent potential.

For option periods beyond the initial lease term, there can also be some additional wrinkles. Some leases provide that base rent for an option period will be based on the so-called "fair market rental value" of the premises at the time the option to renew is exercised. This method is fraught with difficulties. In the authors' experience, the parties rarely agree upon this value without third-party intervention. The tenant thinks the base rent is too high, and the landlord thinks the base rent is too low. Thus, it is essential that the lease contain a procedure for resolving this difference of opinion. A well-drafted clause will stipulate that if the parties are unable to agree upon the fair market rental value within 30–60 days after receipt by the landlord of the tenant's exercise of the option to renew, then the parties will submit to some form of binding arbitration. They can invoke the rules of the American Arbitration Association, or they can use a more informal procedure where each party selects an experienced commercial real estate broker or appraiser within the area where the shopping center is located. If the latter is chosen, then those two brokers attempt to reach a fair market rental value; if they are unable to do so within 30–60 days, they select a third broker. The third-party broker can resolve this issue in a myriad of ways, so it is important that the precise method be outlined in the lease. The third-party broker could be given discretion to determine an independent fair market rental value, and that determination could be binding on the parties. The third-party broker could be required to invoke the "baseball" option where it must choose one or the other of the two original appraisals of the fair market rental value. The third-party broker could be required to eliminate any original estimates that deviate by more than 5%, for example, from its own appraisal and then average the remaining appraisal with its own. The parties are limited only by their own creativity. The key point is that the lease should not simply say "fair market rental value" without establishing some mechanism for determination.

Percentage Rent

There are numerous other rental charges of which the tenant must be aware, including percentage rent, taxes, common area expenses, utilities, and pest control. An exhaustive treatment of these charges is beyond the scope of this book, but the authors would refer the reader to their prior publication mentioned earlier, which deals with these issues in great detail. Still, a cursory review is in order as it pertains to restaurants.

In many commercial retail leases, the tenant will be required to pay percentage rent. The tenant is obligated to pay the landlord, as an additional form of rent, a portion of its gross sales generated at the restaurant. Usually the percentage rent is computed over a base figure called the sales breakpoint. A natural sales breakpoint is computed by dividing the base rent by the percentage rent rate. For example, if the percentage rent rate is 5% and the base rent is $50,000, then the natural sales breakpoint would be $1,000,000. The tenant would pay 5% of its annual gross sales in excess of $1,000,000 to the landlord as percentage rent. An artificial or unnatural breakpoint is one that is determined by some other method devised by the parties. The artificial breakpoint could be lower or higher than the natural breakpoint. There could also be a stepped-up artificial breakpoint where the percentage rent rate is one figure between two breakpoints and the percentage rent rate increases or decreases for sales over that upper breakpoint. For example, "5% of annual sales between $1,000,000 and $2,000,000 and 6% of annual sales above $2,000,000." It is important that the tenant recognize how the breakpoint is computed in the lease so that it can budget accordingly for this additional rental payment. The percentage rent rate can be an important factor too in the tenant's rental charges. For food court tenants, the percentage rent rate can vary from 10% to 15% of annual sales, while for fast casual and table-service restaurants, the percentage rent rate often ranges between

5% and 7%. The discrepancy is usually attributable to the simple fact that fast casual and table-service restaurants have higher operating expenses, such as labor and input costs for food and beverages.

The tenant should also confirm that the percentage rent is computed on "adjusted gross sales" rather than "gross sales." Most leases contain some boilerplate exclusions from gross sales, such as sales taxes, exchanges of merchandise between stores, and refunds to customers. The percentage rent should be computed on this adjusted figure since that is the monetary amount actually retained by the tenant from sales. Our focus will be limited to identifying exclusions that are either unique or significant to restaurants. The most common exclusion for restaurants is tips paid by customers to the tenant's employees. As long as this money is retained by the employee, the landlord will agree to this exclusion. However, some fine dining restaurants pay a salary to their experienced wait staff and retain the tips themselves. In that case, these tips should not be excluded since that is profit to the restaurant operator.

A variety of tipping that has gained some popularity on both the East Coast and West Coast is what is known as "revenue sharing." Many restaurants have found it increasingly difficult to retain the kitchen staff, especially cooks and chefs. When restaurants are busy, the servers make more money but the line staff does not. To remedy this situation, some restaurants have added a "food administrative" charge of between 3% and 5% to the price of the meal and beverages. This amount is paid directly to the kitchen staff so that they share in the bounty. From the landlord's point of view, it could be argued that this is nothing more than a wage and therefore a cost of doing business since the charge is mandatory. Thus, the landlord would not want to exclude it from gross sales. From the restaurateur's perspective, it is another form of tipping which, as long as it is paid to the kitchen staff, should be excluded, especially if tipping the service staff is excluded. As with the case of tipping, the compromise may be to exclude it to the extent the charge is paid to the kitchen staff.

Many upscale restaurants also offer complimentary or discounted meals and beverages to certain customers. These exclusions are often capped at 2%–3% per year. If the meal is discounted, then the lease should be clear about whether the cost of the entire meal is excluded or only the portion is discounted. If a customer brings in a coupon and gets 20% off his entrée, then the remainder of the bill should be included as a sale. To avoid tracking all of these discounts, the aforementioned cap on overall discounted sales per year is often implemented. Both the landlord and the tenant have an interest in driving business to the restaurant, and a discounted meal or a "buy one, get one free" meal can be a very effective form of advertising.

Fees paid to credit card companies for processing transactions pose a sticky problem. From the landlord's perspective, these fees, which can range from 1%–5%, are a cost of doing business and should not be excluded. However, given the significant cost that tenants must absorb in paying these fees, the tenants are often adamant that they be excluded. They argue that many sales would not occur if the customer had to pay in cash. With the advent of mobile payment, this problem is likely to loom larger in the future. If the point becomes a deal breaker, then an annual percentage cap of 1%–2% is often the solution.

Some tenants want to exclude the cost of employee meals from the gross sales calculation. To the landlord, this is another form of compensation, i.e., wages, and would object to its exclusion, especially if the employee had to pay for some portion of the meal. As a practical matter, the cost of employee meals is often minimal. Table-service restaurants may want to exclude costs incurred with respect to valet parking. Some landlords may consider this a cost of doing business as well and are unwilling to exclude it from gross sales. The sale of gift certificates is usually excluded from gross sales as long as the redemption of any gift certificate, whether purchased at the restaurant or elsewhere, is included in gross sales. Bad debts are another exclusion that is often vigorously negotiated. The tenant wants to exclude all bad debts from gross sales since it never received the money from the fraudulent credit card charge. The landlord, however, does not want to subsidize bad credit practices. As with many of the other exclusions, a common ground is often an annual percentage cap on these bad debts. However, if the landlord does agree to exclude any portion of bad debts from the gross sales, then any subsequent recovery of those bad debts should later be added back into gross sales. Many restaurants, whether fast-food, fast casual, or table service, offer catering services. The lease should clearly address whether these sales are included in gross sales. Increasingly popular are food delivery services, such as Uber Eats where a third party delivers food prepared by a restaurant. In that case, the tenant should be permitted to exclude the amount of the delivery charges paid to the third party. If the landlord will not permit an unlimited exclusion of these delivery charges, then the parties should agree on a suitable cap that can be excluded on an annual basis.

The tenant may also want to exclude sale of obsolete or used restaurant equipment since its primary business is selling food and beverages. A few enterprising restaurant operators provide third-party advertising space on its menu. Presumably this would be included in gross sales unless specifically excluded. Some tenants may have vending machines on their premises. If operated by the tenant, then all of these sales would ordinarily be included in gross sales. However, if a third-party vendor operates these machines, then at least the commissions paid by the vendor to the tenant should be included in gross sales.

The advent of e-commerce sales at shopping centers has and will continue to affect restaurant leases. Many restaurants and ridesharing companies offer to deliver to the consumer's home or business meals that are prepared at the restaurant. As with internet sales at brick-and-mortar retailers, the landlord will assert that since the meal originated at the restaurant, it should capture the sale for percentage rent purposes. In most cases, the proceeds from these e-commerce sales go directly to the restaurant that prepared the food, which further bolsters the landlord's case that the sale occurred at the restaurant.

The restaurant may assert that the sale would not have occurred if it was not delivered to the consumer's home or business and therefore it was made simply as a convenience to the customer. The customer did not show up at the shopping center, so no sale would have been made but for the delivery service. The landlord will counter that these delivery sales are no different in form and substance from a carryout order where a customer might call in by phone and pick up the meal at the restaurant. Complicating matters would be where the customer uses a mobile app to order the meal and then picks it up at the shopping center. Is that different from ordering by phone? How does one assess the motive of the customer? Was it an impulse buy when the customer was at the shopping center, or did he intentionally order it off-site and simply pick it up on the way to another destination, such as an airport or on the way to a business appointment? The pick-up case seems stronger for the landlord since the customer had to make the effort to show up. In any event, it is clear that there are no simple solutions to the treatment of internet sales in the restaurant sector, and these issues are likely to multiply in the years ahead as e-commerce becomes a major, if not primary, means of conducting transactions between customers and shopping-center based businesses, especially in major metropolitan areas.

In some cases, delivery sales are a "loss leader" to encourage customers to build loyalty with a restaurant. The margins are very thin as opposed to a customer who consumes at the restaurant, so the restaurant may attempt to exclude them entirely from gross sales. Another vexing question may arise where a national chain has its own web-based application and orders are made to a central clearinghouse and then transmitted to the restaurant. The parties may have to investigate whether the chain allocates these e-commerce sales to the local restaurant. As with many other exclusions, a cap on such exclusions may satisfy both parties. However, the landlord would still want the restaurant to report all of these delivery sales as gross sales at the restaurant while allowing the tenant to exclude those orders generated from the internet, or some amount thereof, for purposes of paying percentage rent. Even if the tenant is required to include in gross sales the entire sale price of the meal, the tenant should exclude third-party delivery charges from the sale price since that is no different than paying UPS or FedEx to deliver a package of soft goods to the customer's home.

A unique twist on the delivery-to-consumer concept is where a third-party delivery service takes the order on its phone lines or web-based application and transmits the order to the restaurant; the restaurant prepares the food; and the delivery service delivers the food, bills the consumer, and then pays a percentage of the proceeds to the restaurant. The restaurant should provide in its lease that in such transactions, only the amount actually paid to the restaurant is included in gross sales for percentage rent purposes since it is to some extent subsidizing the sale.

As with most issues on a lease, exclusions from gross sales often revolve around the negotiating strength of the parties. The intent here is to make the parties cognizant of certain exclusions that may be applicable for restaurant tenants and of the dichotomy between reporting a sale and paying on a sale. To maximize the rental value of its real estate, the landlord will want to include as much as possible in gross sales so that it can advertise that the shopping center does "x" sales per square foot even if it does not collect percentage rent on some of those sales.

Ancillary Lease Charges

In addition to base rent and percentage rent, the tenant will often be required to reimburse the landlord for some share of the real estate taxes, common area costs, and insurance premiums for the shopping center. While these charges are not unique to restaurants, they can be significant outlays and must be factored into the tenant's analysis of the total occupancy costs the tenant must pay for leasing the premises. The most prevalent form of computation for these charges is a "true" pro rata charge where the tenant's share of these expenses is determined by dividing the square footage of the premises by the gross leasable area of the shopping center and then multiplying that percentage by the total expenses for a particular charge. In this case, if the tenant occupied 1,000 square feet and the gross leasable area of the shopping center was 100,000 square feet, then the tenant's share of the tax bill, for instance, would be 1%. A "modified" pro rata charge often excludes certain tenant spaces from the gross leasable area of the shopping center (e.g., anchor stores or separately assessed parcels) and determines the tenant's share not on the basis of the gross *leasable* area of the shopping center, but on the basis of the *leased or occupied* area of the shopping center. This can be a significant difference. Let's use the above example but assume that 80% of the gross leasable area of the shopping center is leased and open (80,000 square feet). Using the modified pro rata calculation, the tenant's pro rata share would be 1.25%. Over the course of a 10- to 20-year lease, this can be a substantial increase in expenses. Going one step further, a tenant with significant leverage may be able to negotiate a first-year cap on these expenses or an annual cap on increases based on a fixed percentage or on the change in the CPI.

Some landlords eschew the pro rata computation for all or certain charges and instead establish a fixed amount for the first year and then base annual increases on a specified percentage. For example, "the common area charge for the first lease year shall be $5 per square foot of floor area in the premises and increase annually on the first day of each subsequent lease year by 5%." This method is utilized more often for common area charges since the landlord has more control over those expenses than it does taxes or insurance. However, it can be used for any charge if that is the agreement of the parties. The fixed charge does provide certainty and eliminates disputes and audits. At the same time, it may not reflect the actual increases in expenses. The parties must balance the certainty of the charge against the risk that the charge may be greater or less than the actual expenses. A modified version of the fixed charge is to establish a base amount for the first year and stipulate that the tenant pay increases over that base amount. Before the tenant gets too excited and thinks it has wrung a valuable concession from the landlord, it should be noted that this base amount is usually already rolled into the base rent.

Some states and municipalities impose sales taxes on rent or assess occupancy taxes on rent. The tenant should be aware of these taxes since they may be passed through to the tenant. These taxes are over and above ad valorem property taxes for the shopping center. Most often the landlord is the "collection agency" for the taxing authority so that these taxes will be invoiced by the landlord. For a tenant with strong negotiating power, it may be able to offset these taxes against their percentage rent obligations under the lease or have these taxes added to the sales breakpoint over which they pay percentage rent.

Utilities and HVAC Charges

The lease should also clarify who provides utility services to the premises and who pays for such services. In many instances, the tenant will obtain utility services directly from the utility company and will pay for its consumption, utility deposits, connection fees, and meter fees directly to the utility. If utilities are interrupted, the tenant will contact the utility company directly to restore them. At some shopping centers, some or all utilities are included in common area costs. If this is the case, the tenant should determine whether increases in utility charges are subject to an overall negotiated cap on increases in common area costs or if they are excluded from that cap. For a lease with a cap, it would not be unusual for a lease to provide that "common area costs will not increase more than 5% per annum, exclusive of utilities."

Too many leases and lease reviewers overlook or gloss over the sections of the lease that pertain to utilities; this is a major mistake since the consumption of utilities will be a major expense for a restaurant. It is crucial that the tenant understand who installs and maintains the utility lines; whether the utility is provided by the utility company or the landlord; and, if provided by the landlord, how the tenant's consumption is calculated. If the restaurant space is metered directly, the tenant should determine whether the existing utility lines are adequate or must be upgraded. If new lines are necessary, the tenant should determine whether the tenant or the utility company will install them. In some cases, the landlord may install and charge the tenant back for these installation costs. From the restaurant's perspective, direct metering by the utility company is the preferred approach since the tenant can monitor and control its individual consumption as opposed to being part of a pool with other tenants where the engineering formulas for allocation require the expertise of an electrical engineer to decipher. A simple question to ask is who the tenant calls if, for example, its electricity or gas service goes out. If it cannot be clearly ascertained from the lease language, then the tenant should insist on more clarification in the lease.

In some jurisdictions, the landlord may be permitted to purchase utilities (e.g., electricity, water, or gas) at a wholesale rate and resell them to the tenants at a retail rate. Often this charge includes an administrative fee for billing and may include a facilities upcharge to reimburse the landlord for maintenance of utility lines outside the premises. The tenant should clearly understand the components of any utility charge that it must obtain from the landlord. Some tenants object to the landlord manufacturing a profit center out of utilities, but unless the tenant has strong negotiating power, it is a losing battle for the tenants; the landlord often has a significant investment in the utility infrastructure at the shopping center and wants a return on it. However, those tenants with substantial bargaining power may be able to negotiate the elimination of these administrative fees, access fees, fire detection service charges, and similar fees. If the lease does not provide otherwise, the tenant should request that the charge not exceed what the tenant could have obtained from the utility company if the tenant had obtained service directly from the utility company. If the landlord accommodates this request, the landlord may draw a distinction between the "rate" the tenant could have obtained and the "cost" the landlord must pay. Due to natural or human-made disasters, utility costs could spike temporarily and the landlord would want the right to pass those temporary surcharges through to the tenants. If the landlord is supplying a utility to the tenant, the lease should specify whether the charge to the tenant is based on a meter reading or an estimate of consumption based on load calculations.

Restaurants are heavy users of utilities, especially electricity, water, and gas, so it is essential that the tenant understand how and what they are being billed for. If the tenant must purchase utility service directly from the landlord, the tenant should inquire whether applicable law or utility company regulations permits installation of a test meter or check meter to verify the landlord's calculation of the charge. This test meter is run over a period of time (e.g., 30 days) on a periodic basis so that the tenant can compare its consumption as shown on the check meter against the landlord's determination. As long as the landlord approves of the criteria for the check meter, the check meter reading is conclusive.

In addition, the tenant may request the right to have the landlord's books and records for utilities audited by a qualified engineer to determine whether the charge was calculated appropriately. Some landlords use models to determine estimated consumption, which may not reflect actual usage. These estimated charges may not be "trued up" for years. In cases where the model understates the cost of consumption, the tenant could be in for an unpleasant surprise and find itself liable for substantial arrearages. To avoid this, the tenant should attempt to add a clause that prevents any undercharges from being billed within a certain time period after the end of the calendar year in which the charge was incurred (e.g., 12–24 months). If the restaurant is an "endcap" or a freestanding building, the landlord may want the tenant to contract directly with the utility companies for service since the demand loads of the restaurant may exceed the capacity of the utilities that the landlord's system could provide.

Most of the above-mentioned discussion applies to HVAC charges as well. The HVAC charge is more prevalent in the enclosed mall setting. The landlord may operate a central plant for the entire shopping center or within particular zones of the enclosed mall. The charge is generally based on either an engineering formula set forth within the lease or a pass-through of actual costs plus an administrative fee. Given that most restaurant tenants will not have the expertise to evaluate the computation of the HVAC charge or be willing to pay for outside consultants, it is not uncommon for the restaurant operator to ask for either a fixed first-year charge or an overall cap on annual increases. After the first year of operation, the landlord and tenant should have adequate information upon which to project future charges.

The tenant should understand all components of the HVAC charge. It generally includes the cost of utility service, which can be based on bulk or retail costs, projected maintenance costs of the system, amortization of the initial purchase or major investments in the central plant system, and a special load calculation for heavy users, such as restaurants. Restaurant ovens can generate a great deal of heat compared with a shoe store, so the calculation may allow the landlord to upcharge the restaurant for excessive load. It may also adjust the charge based on additional hours of operation since many restaurants remain open past normal mall hours. Some restaurateurs located within enclosed malls may find it more cost effective or more convenient to install their own HVAC units for their operations. That way, the tenant can control the temperature within the premises at all times, ensure adequate cooling capacity even during peak hours or hot weather conditions, and avoid surcharges assessed by the landlord for operating beyond the mall standard hours. For a tenant with strong leverage, the landlord may pay for the cost of the HVAC unit by installing the unit itself or paying a construction allowance to the tenant to defray the cost. Of course, if the tenant operates its own HVAC unit, it generally bears the risk of repair, maintenance, and replacement.

Unique Charges for Pad Deals

A few issues may be unique to pad deals. Since the building constructed on the pad is generally not physically connected to another structure, the pad tenant may be able to obtain a separate tax parcel for the pad. In this case, the tenant would pay the taxing authority directly for all property taxes assessed for the land and the improvements on the pad. If the pad is not initially treated as a separate tax parcel, the lease should specify whether the landlord or the tenant will pursue separate assessment and at whose expense. Until such time as the separate assessment is obtained, the tenant pays its share of the property taxes the same way the inline tenants pay. If a separate assessment is obtained, the tenant should be required to provide the landlord with proof of payment of each installment of taxes within a reasonable period of time after the due date. The landlord does not want to find that a tax lien has been filed or that a tax sale is imminent because the tenant did not pay the property taxes when due. Some taxing authorities will tax the improvements on the pad separately but not the land underneath the pad. In this case, the tenant would pay all of the taxes attributable to the improvements at the assessed amount on the tax bill and a pro rata share of the taxes for the land based on the ratio of the acreage of the pad to the acreage of the larger tax parcel.

Additionally, if the pad has its own dedicated parking areas, the tenant may not be obligated to pay the landlord for any common area expenses other than a "ring road" maintenance fee. In this case, the tenant would be responsible for the maintenance of the parking spaces and landscaping on the pad at its expense; the landlord would not have any maintenance obligations in this regard. However, since ingress to and egress from the pad uses the access points from the rest of the shopping center property, the tenant would be expected to contribute toward these maintenance costs via a ring road or comparable fee. This is often a fixed charge with annual increases since it is difficult to separate these expenses from the other common area costs. Even if the tenant does not maintain the parking on its pad, at the very least, the pad tenant's common area costs should be limited to exterior common area costs so that the tenant is not subsidizing the cost of, say, HVAC service provided to the shopping center.

The most important point in this discussion of computing ancillary charges under the lease is that the tenant must clearly understand how these charges are determined. Many letters of intent or deal proposal letters simply say "pro rata" without defining what that means. If the landlord quotes an estimate for these charges, the tenant must understand how that estimate was determined. The tenant may want to request evidence of past charges over a period of years so that it can gauge the accuracy of the landlord's estimate. Otherwise, it could face an unpleasant surprise when it receives the first invoice or a year-end reconciliation statement.

Rent Abatements, Offsets, and Termination Clauses

From the landlord's perspective, the cardinal rule of commercial retail leases is that the rental stream is sacrosanct. The investors in the shopping center rely on the income generated by the rent to provide an expected rate of return from their initial capital investment. In addition, this rental income is often pledged as security to repay the debt service on any mortgage encumbering the shopping center. If the shopping center is owned by a publicly traded real estate investment trust, then Wall Street investors and analysts project future income streams based on the rents set forth in the leases. Furthermore, the landlord is not an ensurer of the tenant's success. It has provided a space from which the tenant can operate its business, as well as common area amenities. It cannot guarantee that the tenant's business will never be disrupted. As a result, landlord-oriented leases explicitly state that the tenant has no right to abate rent for any reason.

Of course, the tenant views matters differently. At the very least, it will expect that the landlord will not act or fail to act in any manner that interferes with the tenant's ability to operate its business from the premises. The tenant may seek some form of rent abatement if a disruption to its business occurs that is within the control of the landlord. Not all tenants will have the bargaining power to negotiate these concessions from the landlord. For those that do, there are some basic guidelines to consider.

Some tenants ask for rent abatement if utilities to their premises are interrupted. Under only two circumstances will a sophisticated landlord agree to this. The first is when the utility service was directly supplied by the landlord. Some landlords purchase utilities from a utility company at a wholesale rate and then redistribute the utility to the tenant at a retail rate. In this sense, the landlord acts as the utility company. If in the lease the landlord has contracted with the tenant to provide a utility to the premises but fails to do so, this is a breach of the lease. An equitable remedy may be to grant an abatement of rent. This remedy may forestall an expensive lawsuit as to whether the landlord breached the lease or constructively evicted the tenant. The landlord may create an exception for acts of force majeure, such as a flood, a hurricane, a tornado, or another act of God or similar events that are reasonably contemplated to be beyond the reasonable control of the landlord.

The other circumstance where rent abatement may be warranted is if the utility interruption is caused by the negligence, intentional misconduct, or breach of the lease by the landlord. Under this circumstance, there is some direct culpability on the part of the landlord for the disruption to the tenant's business. For example, if the landlord or its agents negligently cut a utility line, shutting off electricity to the premises for a sufficient period of time that the tenant could not operate, then some form of rent abatement may be warranted.

In any case of interruption to utilities, the landlord generally requires a material disruption to the tenant's operation before it will agree to abate rent. If the gas service is interrupted for an hour and the tenant cannot use its ovens during that period of time, the landlord is unlikely to abate rent even though the tenant may have lost its lunch business for the day. Furthermore, the landlord does not want to be in the position of abating rent for an entire day based on a temporary disruption or, even worse, prorating the rent on an hourly basis. Most landlords will require the disruption to be so severe that the tenant is unable to open for business for at least one business day, if not more. Tenants will be reluctant to close the business entirely if there is some opportunity to salvage sales for that day. For this reason, closing the restaurant entirely for a period of time until the utilities are restored is some proof that the disruption was material. Some landlords will agree to abate the rent retroactively while others may insist that the abatement apply prospectively.

Any discussion of rent abatement must define what rent is being abated. It could be all or some portion of the base rent or base rent and ancillary rent (e.g., taxes, insurance, common area expenses, and utilities). Alternatively, the tenant could be permitted to pay percentage rent for those days of utility interruption where it operated only a part of the day. If the landlord is adamant that it will not abate rent for a utility interruption or insists that it will agree to an abatement only if the tenant is closed for a substantial period of time (e.g., one week or more), then the tenant can protect itself by obtaining business income insurance. Depending on the terms of the policy, the tenant is reimbursed for its lost revenues, thereby ensuring that it has sufficient funds to pay its rental charges under the lease. Some landlords will permit rent abatement only to the extent not covered by the tenant's business income insurance. Conversely, the landlord can protect its rental stream by obtaining rent loss insurance so that it is able to pay its debt service notwithstanding the loss of income from the utility interruption.

A casualty involving the restaurant or the shopping center may also give rise to rent abatement. If lightning strikes the restaurant and the building burns down, then most leases will abate the rent entirely (or at least that portion of the rent not reimbursed by insurance) until the earlier of the date the landlord (or tenant, as the case may be) rebuilds the premises or after a specified number of days from the date of the casualty. Some leases provide that tenants must continue to pay taxes notwithstanding any casualty on the theory that neither side wants the property to be foreclosed upon at a tax sale.

The more difficult case is where only a portion of the premises is damaged. For example, a broken water pipe may flood part of the restaurant, but if that portion can be closed off and the remainder can operate in a reasonable manner, taking into consideration safety and health concerns, the rent may not be abated entirely. Instead, it may be abated based on the square footage damaged or on the disruption to the tenant's business. Of course, abating rent based on square footage can have pitfalls. The kitchen might be 10% of the square footage of the restaurant, but if that portion is inoperable due to the casualty, then, effectively, the tenant cannot operate. An abatement of 10% would be wholly disproportionate to the loss actually suffered by the tenant. To address this situation, the tenant would want rent abated on an equitable basis to the extent the casualty impaired its ability to operate. While "equity" is an elastic concept, it is frequently used in leases to address these types of situations. Often the parties will look at comparable sales (e.g., the average of sales for the week or month immediately before the casualty) for the measure of damages.

The rent abatement clause should also address the situation where the restaurant is not damaged but other portions of the shopping center are. If a wing of a shopping center is closed due to a casualty, such as fire or flood, the main means of access to the restaurant might be impaired or eliminated. If the restaurant is part of a vibrant entertainment component with theatres and other restaurants and a substantial portion of that component is closed, then the tenant would expect some abatement of rent until the area reopens. Most customers do not want to walk past construction trailers and scaffolding to go to a restaurant. The number of possibilities is too numerous to contemplate in this discussion. However, it is a contingency that every restaurant tenant should consider in its lease negotiations. An abatement based solely on physical damage to the restaurant may leave the restaurant in the unenviable situation of paying rent on a space that is functionally inoperable.

Similar concerns apply to a condemnation or taking of all or part of the premises or shopping center. Obviously if the entire premises or shopping center is taken by eminent domain, then the lease will terminate and there will be no further rental obligations due. However, if a portion of the premises is taken or a portion of the shopping center is taken, then a determination must be made as to what portion, if any, of the rent should abate. With respect to a taking of a portion of the premises, it will generally be based on the loss of square footage or the loss of utility or fair market value of the portion taken. The lease should address when the rent abates. Does the abatement commence when the taking actually occurs, or does it abate when the parties exercise any right to terminate the lease based on the degree of the taking? Unlike an abatement of rent for a casualty, an abatement of rent for a condemnation will usually be permanent for the remainder of the lease term. The main exception would be if there is a temporary taking or if the area taken was replaced, such as replacing parking that was taken with parking that is contiguous or comparable. For most food court and inline tenants, these questions are more theoretical than real.

As a practical matter, the outlot on the periphery of the shopping center is most likely to be impacted by a taking of its premises. The taking authority may need a portion of the outlot premises for road widening, installation of traffic signals, utility relocation, or entrances to the shopping center. Often it is not a physical taking of the building but rather a taking of parking or access points that are material to the outlot occupant. For this reason, the restaurant on the outlot should address these types of takings as well so that the tenant can abate rent. It can be couched in terms of a "material" taking or if parking is reduced below a certain number of spaces or if the taking affects a protected zone defined in the lease. By way of example, the compensation for reconstruction of curb cuts and replacement of landscaping may pale in comparison to the loss of key parking spaces directly in front of the restaurant. Another means of addressing these takings from the tenant's perspective is to add lease language that a taking is material if it impacts the tenant's business as reasonably determined by the tenant. In some situations, the landlord will not provide any abatement of rent if the outlot tenant is reimbursed for the loss of value by the taking authority. The landlord does not want the tenant to "double dip" by receiving both rent abatement and an award that presumably compensates the tenant for the damage that triggered the rent abatement.

Closely related to abatement of rent is the concept of rent offsets. Often these terms are used loosely in a lease, but they represent two different issues. An abatement occurs when the tenant's obligation to pay full rent is reduced. In other words, a condition occurs that triggers a reduction in rent. The tenant is not in default for not paying the full rent because a lower rent becomes the contractual rent for that period of time. As long as the tenant is paying the contractual rent, it will not be in default for failure to pay the full rent. Under an offset, the full rent is due but the tenant is owed money by the landlord, which the lease specifically permits the tenant to credit against the full rental payment.

Most leases provide that there is no right to offset against rent unless expressly stated in the lease. A tenant should never unilaterally offset moneys owed by the landlord to the tenant against the rent stated in the lease unless the landlord specifically consents to such arrangement or unless the lease explicitly allowed the offset. Since the covenant to pay rent is often set forth in a lease as a separate and distinct covenant by the tenant, the tenant could put its leasehold at risk by withholding a portion of the rent from its payment to the landlord. Usually the tenant will be limited to its remedies at law or in equity, which means going to court.

The two most frequent situations where a tenant will request a right to offset are in its exercise of self-help remedies under the lease and reimbursement for an unpaid construction allowance. Landlords are very reluctant to grant tenants the right to perform an obligation of the landlord and to allow the tenant to offset those expenses against the rental charges otherwise due as discussed above. For those select tenants able to wring this concession out of their landlord, several limitations typically apply. First, the landlord will require the tenant to provide ample prior written notice of the failure of the landlord to perform a specific lease obligation and an adequate opportunity to rectify the failure. Most landlord leases will provide that the landlord be given a minimum of 30 days from receipt of written notice within which to perform the landlord obligation or such additional time as is reasonably required provided the landlord promptly commences to cure and diligently pursues the same to completion. The tenant may consider limiting the period of time within which the landlord may cure to a specific amount of time, such as 90 days before the tenant can intervene. Landlords often limit the ability of the tenant to "cure" or perform the landlord's obligations to repairs and maintenance within the premises, such as a leaky roof, but as with most issues under a lease, this can be amplified to cover areas, such as maintenance of common areas or even payment of the landlord's taxes or debt service in rare instances. If there are numerous potholes where the restaurant customers park, this may impact the traffic to the restaurant, so the tenant may insist on the ability to repair if the landlord does not. The landlord may be amenable to a right of self-help within some specified critical zone in the common areas as opposed to a blanket right to make repairs anywhere in the shopping center.

Even if the tenant has the absolute right under the lease to perform a particular obligation of the landlord, the right to offset must be specifically permitted by the lease. The landlord may limit this right of offset by providing that it may in good faith challenge whether the obligation was in fact the landlord's, whether the exercise of the right of self-help was necessary under the circumstances, and whether the cost was reasonable. The tenant should require the landlord to make these first two challenges during the initial 30-day period rather than allowing the tenant to exercise its self-help rights before questioning the tenant's right to do so. These limitations severely restrict the tenant's right to offset, in which case the tenant's only effective remedy is to seek judicial relief. Some landlords may go one step further and provide that there is no right to offset until the tenant has obtained a final, nonappealable judgment in its favor and the landlord has failed to pay such judgment within 30 days thereafter. Of course, tenants should recognize that this remedy is not much better than being required to take the landlord to court before exercising self-help rights. Rent offsets are anathema to landlords, and they want to make it as difficult as possible for the tenant to invoke. As a result, most tenants will trigger a right of self-help and offset only in extreme situations.

For an unpaid construction allowance, a tenant may be more aggressive in insisting on a right of offset. After all, the landlord promised to pay the tenant a certain sum of money toward the leasehold improvements as an inducement to enter into the lease. This is especially true for restaurants, where the construction costs are usually much higher than for the ordinary retail merchant space. The tenant may be relying on the landlord to fund its construction through installment payments or in a lump sum. The work will not get done on time or sometimes at all if the contractors are not paid when due. Liens may get filed on the shopping center, and the tenant may be placed in default for the imposition of these liens. Contractors may walk off the job until paid. The tenant may have pledged the construction allowance to its lender in order to secure funds to complete the tenant's cost of the leasehold improvements. While landlords often view these construction allowance as reimbursements to the tenant after the tenant has paid for the work in place, as a practical matter, many restaurants rely on this source of funds to replenish funds so that they can pay the next construction draw or, in the case where the allowance is in one lump sum, restore its operating capital.

The tenant should confirm that the payment terms in the lease are consistent with its payment to its contractors. Most landlords will want between 10 and 30 days within which to make the payment to the tenant after submission of the required documentation. If the landlord does not pay on time, then the tenant may be required to provide written notice of the failure to pay, in which case the right to offset would be triggered if the landlord did not pay within a shorter period of time after receipt of such notice. The tenant may also want to protect itself by requiring the landlord to pay interest on any late payments since the tenant was deprived of its use of that money. The basis for the interest calculation should be expressly set forth in the lease, such as 8% per annum, or 2% per annum over the prime rate of interest then charged by a specific bank or as announced in *The Wall Street Journal* or comparable publication.

It cannot be overemphasized that the right to offset for the unpaid allowance must be expressly permitted by the lease. The tenant cannot just assume that it is unfair for the landlord to hold onto the money while the tenant is required to fork over the rental payments. As noted previously, the lease will generally provide that the obligation to pay rent is independent of all other lease obligations. It would be small consolation for the tenant to prevail in a court of law for breach of contract against the landlord but lose its lease because it asserted a right that was not allowed by the lease. Even if tenant has the right to offset, it may take an undue length of time to reimburse itself, which in turn impacts the tenant's cash flow. For example, if the landlord has agreed to pay a construction allowance in the amount of $1,000,000 and the tenant's annual rent is $300,000, it will take the tenant longer than three years to recoup the amount of the allowance. If the tenant is concerned about timely payment of the construction allowance, it could require the allowance to be paid into an escrow account with a third party, such as a title company. The payout of the escrowed amounts would mirror the lease requirements so that the tenant would always be assured of timely payments. Alternatively, it could require the landlord to secure the landlord's obligation to pay with a letter of credit upon which the tenant could draw down if payments were not made as required.

Co-Tenancy

A co-tenancy clause is a provision pursuant to which the tenant is permitted to pay a reduced rent unless some combination of certain occupants and a specified percentage of the gross leasable area of the shopping center is open for business. The tenant has bargained for a contractual rent based on certain expectations of occupancy at the shopping center. If these levels are not met, then the tenant's projections of sales may be wholly disproportionate to the total rental charges payable under the lease. The reduced rent can cushion the blow resulting from these lost sales. Additionally, the co-tenancy may be an inducement for the tenant to open before the desired level of co-tenancy is achieved, such as in the case of a new shopping center. It may also serve as a motivation for the landlord to achieve the occupancy level or else face a loss of rental income. In general, co-tenancy clauses fall into one of two categories: opening co-tenancies and operating co-tenancies.

An opening co-tenancy is generally granted only when a new shopping center is being constructed or a major redevelopment or renovation of an existing shopping center is underway or "is in process." In an opening co-tenancy, the tenant has no obligation to pay full rent from the date it first opens its doors for business until the requirement is initially met. In some instances, the tenant may not even be required to open for business prior to that time. The latter case may be problematic to both landlords and tenants. The landlord does not want to create a situation where one tenant does not have to open until another tenant opens and that tenant's opening in turn is contingent upon a third tenant opening. It could create a domino effect where no one is obligated to open or pay rent, which would be a disastrous circumstance for the landlord. For this reason, most landlords will require the tenant to open for business even if the opening co-tenancy has not been met. Some rent is better than no rent.

Having the ability to delay its opening may be an illusory right for the tenant. It has built and fixtured its restaurant and hired and trained its staff but then must wait until the co-tenancy is met to open its doors? It will be difficult to retain staff if they are not being paid, and the tenant will not want to pay the staff unless it is generating income from the restaurant. In addition, a dark restaurant can have ominous implications for the public's perception. If the tenant is required to open even though the opening co-tenancy has not been met, the restaurant may want to delay its initial opening so that it does not fall within a so-called blackout period. As with some retailers, restaurants may prefer to open for business during certain seasons. For a restaurant in the Snowbelt, opening in the dead of winter may not be an opportune time. For a restaurant in the Deep South, opening when the snowbirds have arrived may be ideal. These blackout periods must be spelled out in the lease in order for the tenant to invoke them. Of course, if the tenant does open within this slack season, the lease must clearly state whether the tenant must pay full rent or can pay reduced rent until the opening co-tenancy has initially been met.

The constituent elements of the opening co-tenancy will be deal-specific. If the restaurant is located near a theatre that is being constructed, it may want to tie its opening co-tenancy to the opening of the theatre due to the synergy of the two uses. Patrons of the theatre may want to have dinner before or after the show. Even though it may seem counterintuitive, the tenant may want its opening co-tenancy linked to a certain number of other restaurants also opening. A cluster of restaurants offering a variety of cuisines can draw more traffic than just a single restaurant. If the restaurant is a fine dining table-service restaurant, it may want its opening co-tenancy tied to a fashion anchor department store or specific fashion tenants since a certain income level of shopper may frequent both. With the increasing demand by patrons for entertainment uses at shopping centers, restaurant tenants should be cognizant of other proposed uses that would complement its use. Skating rinks, bowling alleys, laser tag galleries, and museums, to name a few, could be co-tenants. Community colleges, hotels, office buildings, and hospitals could also generate substantial ongoing traffic to the restaurant. The tenant should engage the landlord in a dialogue as to the planned offerings for the shopping center whether it is a regional enclosed mall, lifestyle center, or strip center. With the emergence of e-commerce, many landlords are looking to repurpose shopping centers with non-traditional uses, some of which may be particularly beneficial to restaurants in terms of foot traffic.

The more traditional opening co-tenancy will be phrased in terms of some combination of a certain number of anchor tenants and a specified percentage of the gross leasable area of the shopping center being open for business. For example, the lease might provide in a four-anchor store shopping center that "not less than three anchor stores" and "not less than a specified percentage of the gross leasable area of the shopping center" must be open for business before the initial co-tenancy is satisfied. Landlords will rarely agree that all anchors and 100% occupancy must be achieved, so the restaurant will need to negotiate a number that offers sufficient assurance that it is opening at a time when the shopping center is viable. The parties should be cognizant of whether the co-tenancy applies to the entire shopping center or just a portion. If there are four anchors in the shopping center but the one closest to the restaurant is not ready to open, then the fact that three other anchors on the other side of the parking lot are open may be of small consolation to the restaurant. Moreover, if 80% of the gross leasable area of the shopping center is open but only 40% of the wing where the restaurant premises are located is open, there may not be sufficient customer traffic for the restaurant. Generally, the larger the shopping center, the more likely it is that the opening co-tenancy will be tied to a defined area of the shopping center.

The lease should identify any areas or types of tenants that are excluded from the gross leasable area component of the opening co-tenancy. Of course, the tenant should always attempt to exclude its premises from the computation. The anchor stores will often also be excluded from the computation of the gross leasable area definition, especially when there is a separate anchor store component to the co-tenancy. The parties may exclude outparcel tenants (i.e., those not physically connected to the enclosed mall or the base building of the strip center), office or service-oriented uses, residential units, and governmental agencies. If the lease is silent, then it can be assumed that the landlord can include temporary tenants or so-called "pop-up" stores in the calculation in order to inflate the co-tenancy. The tenant should be wary of such omissions and clarify whether such tenants qualify. A common demarcation is to provide that a permanent tenant is one whose lease term is at least one year. Unless the term *gross leasable area* is limited to "retail," the landlord will have wide discretion to determine what types of uses count toward the co-tenancy requirement.

The lease may provide that the reduced rent automatically applies from the date the tenant opens. Alternatively, the lease may provide that the landlord has a grace period either from the tenant's opening or from notification by the tenant that the opening co-tenancy has not been met before the reduced rent is triggered. The tenant should carefully review how the provision is written so that it does not lose the benefit of the reduced rent because of its failure to provide the requisite notice. Even if the tenant is required to provide affirmative notice of its election to invoke the reduced rent, it can attempt to negotiate language that the reduced rent is retroactive to the date it initially opened for business. If this is permitted, then the lease should clarify whether any overpayment will be refunded or offset against future rental obligations. The tenant may not know on the date it opens whether the co-tenancy was met, so it will pay the full rental charges until the determination is made. Most landlord leases do not permit many offsets against rent, so the tenant would not want to risk a lease default because it thought it could offset its overpayment against future rent.

The reduction of rent generally takes one of two forms or a combination thereof. The most common approach is that all base rent is abated, and in lieu thereof, the tenant pays a percentage of its monthly gross sales. The percentage can be either the contractual percentage rent rate or a different figure. If different from the contractual rate, it could be higher or lower. The landlord would like to recapture some of its lost base rent, so it may insist upon a higher percentage rent rate during the co-tenancy period. The tenant may counter with a lower rate than the contractual rate because it is unsure as to how the failure to meet the co-tenancy will affect its business. The tenant certainly does not want to be in the position where it pays more than the full rental charges during the co-tenancy period. The tenant's sales might unexpectedly explode due to the lack of competition. For this reason, the tenant may want to insert a clause that in no event would the co-tenancy rent exceed the full rent that would have been due but for the co-tenancy violation. Otherwise, it creates a windfall for the landlord.

The other common way to structure reduced rent is to provide that the tenant will pay a percentage of the full rent (e.g., 50%) until the co-tenancy is satisfied. As noted above, some leases provide that the tenant will have the choice to pay either this reduced full rent or a rent based on a percentage of sales. The tenant should add a provision that it will pay the lesser of these two figures. Whether written as reduced full rent or as percentage rent only, the lease might also provide that the co-tenancy rent is in lieu of all or most ancillary rental charges under the leases, such as taxes, common area expenses, and insurance. The landlord may insist that the tenant pay consumables charges, such as utilities and trash because the landlord will often not have control over those expenses. The right to pay co-tenancy rent should be conditioned upon the tenant being open for business and not in material default beyond any applicable cure period during the co-tenancy period. If the tenant is in default, the landlord may have a clawback provision where the full rent is reinstituted retroactively.

The landlord or its lender may insist upon a sunset clause if the opening co-tenancy is not met within a specified period of time. The landlord cannot afford for the tenant to pay this co-tenancy rent for the entire lease term. At some point, the tenant must make a decision. Either it can make money even though the opening co-tenancy was never met or it must walk away from the lease. The tenant will be forced under the sunset clause to either terminate the lease or waive the opening co-tenancy and commence payment of full rent. Generally, the tenant will be required to make this election within 12–24 months after the tenant initially opened for business. If the tenant terminates the lease, then the lease may provide that the landlord must reimburse the tenant for the unamortized cost of its leasehold improvements less the unamortized cost of any construction allowance paid to the tenant by the landlord.

Unlike an opening co-tenancy which, by definition, occurs only at the start of the lease term, an operating co-tenancy condition can occur at any point during the lease term. If the lease provides both an opening co-tenancy and an operating co-tenancy, then the lease should contain a supremacy clause where in the event of a conflict, one or the other prevails. In most cases, the opening co-tenancy would prevail until the sunset clause was triggered. If there is no sunset clause, then the need for the supremacy clause becomes even more critical since the rent remedies may be different.

Many of the same considerations for the opening co-tenancy are applicable to an operating ongoing co-tenancy. However, there may be some distinctions. The landlord may insist upon a cure period before the tenant can invoke the co-tenancy rent. It can be as short as 30 days or as long as one year. The most common periods are between 6 and 12 months, with landlords insisting on longer periods to replace anchor tenants. The replacement periods for anchor tenants generally falls within a range of 18 months to 2 years. This gives the landlord sufficient time to replace the lost tenants. The lease should specify whether the period begins from the first day the operating co-tenancy was not met or from some specified date following the date the tenant notified the landlord that the co-tenancy was not met.

The landlord may also impose a sales test before the tenant can pay the co-tenancy rent. The landlord wants some proof that the tenant has been harmed financially, and the most common metric is a demonstration of a decline in sales. The parties compare the sales for the cure period against the sales for a comparable period of time before the operating co-tenancy condition occurred. For a restaurant tenant, the percentage decline in sales is usually less than the percentage rent decline for retail tenants. Restaurants have much higher overhead than retail stores so it would not take as much a decline to turn a profitable restaurant into an unprofitable one. While a retailer may be able to absorb a 10%–15% decline in sales, the restaurant tenant may be able to absorb only a 3%–5% sales decline.

If part of the ongoing co-tenancy is an anchor tenant requirement, then the lease should address replacement of a closed anchor. The landlord will want maximum flexibility. If the vacant anchor occupied 100,000 square feet, it may not be possible to find another 100,000-square-foot tenant. For that reason, the landlord may want to provide that the replacement anchor need occupy only a designated portion of the space. It may provide that only the ground floor area need be occupied if the anchor operated on multiple levels. The landlord may want to use some of the vacant anchor space as additional "small shop" space for retailers or some combination of big-box retailers and small shop space or even nonretail uses, such as apartments, offices, and hotels, and count that area once it is open as a replacement anchor. Even if the replacement anchor definition is based on occupancy of certain minimum square footage, the restaurant tenant may want to disqualify certain types of uses as constituting a replacement. For example, if a full-price theatre vacates its premises and is replaced by a discount retailer that may not drive the same degree of traffic to the restaurant as did the theatre. Likewise, a sporting goods big-box retailer may not be an adequate replacement for an upscale fashion department store. The possibilities are limitless, but the parties should make clear what or what does not qualify as a replacement anchor.

Curiously many leases do not address how the tenant documents a co-tenancy condition. It is rare that the landlord would expressly grant the tenant the right to audit its books to determine whether a co-tenancy condition has occurred. More often than not, the tenant must rely on a certification from the landlord as to whether the applicable co-tenancy has been met, and that certification will be binding and conclusive absent fraud or manifest error. In those instances where the landlord agrees to provide some documentation, the landlord will usually limit the tenant requests for documentation to not more than once a year because the landlord does not want the tenant to engage in a fishing expedition and because it can be time-consuming to assemble the information. The tenant will often be required to demonstrate a prima facie case rather than simply asserting that the co-tenancy has not been met (e.g., noting that specific anchors are not open or that a certain square footage of the small shop space is vacant). As noted above, the landlord response may be simply a yes or no certification. However, some leases may require the landlord to provide a summary or spreadsheet of (1) the total number of anchors open for business and the square footage they occupy, (2) the gross leasable area of the shopping center less the square footage of the anchors, and (3) the gross leasable area actually occupied as of the date of the summary. Usually the landlord will be given a designated period of time to respond before the tenant may invoke its rights. The landlord may also be required to notify the tenant when the co-tenancy has again been met, together with an updated verification statement, so that the tenant knows when full rent must resume. In all cases, the landlord will require the tenant to sign a confidentiality agreement so that the information is not disseminated to third parties (e.g., other tenants).

Chapter 2

Operational Issues for Restaurants

Defining the Use

Surprisingly, many use clauses do not describe the permitted restaurant use in any significant detail. It is not uncommon for a use clause to permit "the operation of a restaurant." At the outset of the lease term, it may be clear to the parties what type of restaurant will be operated from the premises, but later this use may morph into a different type based on a variety of factors such as customer preferences, competition, and demographics. In a food court, most landlords will not grant an exclusive, so it is essential that the use be clearly defined. Otherwise, the tenants may cannibalize each other's sales. Often this objective is accomplished by limiting the food and beverage items to those set forth on a menu attached to the lease. Any changes to the menu must be approved by the landlord. Some tenants will seek to modify this approval right by stating that any approval shall not be unreasonably withheld, conditioned, or delayed or by permitting tenant to add items that are customarily offered nationwide by that chain or are required by the franchisor. The landlord wants to provide a variety of cuisines for customers of the shopping center, and it does not want to be involved in refereeing disputes as to who can sell what in the food court. Additionally, the landlord may have granted exclusives elsewhere in the shopping center, and it does not want to discover that an American cuisine fast-food operation has converted to an ethnic cuisine restaurant that now violates some other ethnic cuisine restaurant's exclusive. In those rare instances when the landlord grants an exclusive to a food court tenant, it is generally limited to other operations in the food court.

Many food court operators focus on a particular cuisine, so the landlord may also restrict the food court operator's menu or use to those "primarily featuring (e.g., 50% or more of its food menu items) a certain defined cuisine." Although this is not a cure-all, it would presumably prevent a Chinese restaurant from converting to a Mexican restaurant. The national chains are always refreshing their menus, so it is not easy to define or police the permitted use. For example, if the use clause of an Italian fast-food operator permits the tenant to sell breakfast items, can it sell a breakfast burrito since a burrito is typically regarded as Mexican in nature? Vice versa, can the Mexican food operator sell "Mexican pizza" since pizza is usually regarded as Italian? Can the Japanese fast-food operator sell fish tacos?

The parties may agree that some percentage of the menu items can deviate from the original menu without landlord consent. For example, an Italian food operator might be permitted to offer other menu items "so long as at least ninety percent of its menu entrée items are Italian in nature." This gives the tenant or its franchisor some flexibility in adapting to changing times without infringing on other food court operations. When using terms such as *primarily* or *incidental*, the parties should ascribe a percentage so that there is no misunderstanding as to the scope of such terms. Sometimes there will be a specific prohibition against selling certain items (e.g., individual slices of pizza or hamburgers). The point of this discussion is to emphasize that the parties need to focus on the use clause during the lease negotiations. Concepts evolve over time. Neither party wants to sue or be sued because of sloppy drafting in the lease.

Fast-casual and table-service restaurants generally will not agree to be restricted by a menu. The typical fast-casual restaurant operates on the premise that the customer can personalize his or her order from a variety of ingredients. This is one of the factors that differentiates a fast-food restaurant from a fast-casual restaurant. For this reason, the use clause often will include an illustrative list of menu items (e.g., "primarily for the sale of tacos and burritos" or "pizza, calzones and pastas"). The fast-casual operator has more discretion in terms of preparation and offerings, although most adhere to a specific type of cuisine. The principal concern for the landlord is that the use cannot violate any exclusives or other restrictions applicable to the shopping center. If the landlord agrees to a broader use clause with the fast-casual operator, then it should add language to the use clause that any future changes cannot duplicate any other uses in the shopping center or violate any exclusive of which Tenant has been given notice. Sometimes the parties will attach an exhibit delineating the existing exclusives.

Often a national chain will seek the right in the use clause to change its use to another "lawful use." This clause should be a red flag for the landlord. Lawful use does not necessarily mean "restaurant use." If the fast-casual concept does not work at the shopping center, then the fast-casual operator will attempt to broaden his or her ability to assign the lease or sublet the premises by having the ability to offer the premises to traditional retailers. If the landlord cannot eliminate the right of the tenant to change his or her use, then at the very least, the change should be limited to "any other lawful restaurant use that does not violate any exclusives, restrictions or prohibited uses applicable to the shopping center." In addition, the landlord will generally attempt to condition any change of use upon its prior written consent. The landlord will want this consent to be determined in its sole discretion because it wants maximum flexibility to determine the appropriate tenant mix in the shopping center, but the parties might negotiate a reasonableness standard.

Regarding the pecking order, the table-service restaurant has the broadest use clause. These are often national chains or signature chef restaurants that are in great demand. They do not expand as rapidly as fast-food or fast-casual restaurants, and they often insist on broad latitude for their offerings. Such a restaurant might propose a use clause that says, "for the operation of a fine dining establishment with table service and bar." Nothing in this description suggests that it is a steakhouse. The challenge for the landlord is to balance the need and desire for this particular restaurant against the landlord's need to control uses in the shopping center. A community may support only one high-end steakhouse in a particular market, and every landlord will be competing to attract this tenant, so leverage becomes critical. The landlord may have made some financial concessions to the signature restaurant and does not want the restaurant converted to a lower-quality operation. Many of the proposed compromises for the fast-casual restaurant would be applicable here as well.

In addition, the big chains may attempt to define their core business as "the intended use" or "the initial use." They may operate several concepts and want the right to change the initial use to another food concept without the landlord's consent. The initial concept may not work or may not be as profitable as first anticipated. Since the chain has already invested in both the buildout and the staff, a conversion to another food use may be a relatively easy transition for them. Before granting carte blanche to the tenant, there are numerous factors for the landlord to consider. How often will the tenant be permitted to change concepts? The tenant will want the unlimited right to change concepts, but it may be in the landlord's interest to limit the number. Repeated change over at a restaurant does not present an image of stability for the shopping center. Further, the landlord may be negotiating with another restaurant to bring a new food concept to the shopping center, but that new operator may be reluctant if an existing tenant has or is in the process of converting to that use.

Language must be inserted into the lease that no change of use can violate other exclusives or duplicate other uses, and the landlord will want sufficient advance notice of the proposed change so that it can investigate whether the new concept will violate these restrictions or interfere with its ongoing leasing activities. For certain uses, it may be difficult to define what constitutes a duplication of another use. A varied menu cuisine (e.g., The Cheesecake Factory menu), by definition, can offer almost anything, and that could be interpreted to violate an ethnic menu cuisine (e.g., Italian, Mexican , Chinese, and Thai) unless there is a prohibition against certain food items or a limit on the number of specific entrée, appetizer, or dessert items. A limitation on the trade name may be in order if the tenant changes its use so that the tenant does not hold itself out to the public in a manner that would be perceived as duplicative of another use. For example, "Jay's Turf and Surf" implies that seafood is a major menu item even if the only seafood items on the menu are breaded shrimp and fish and chips. The landlord should reserve the right to approve any change of a trade name. Of course, a national restaurant tenant will not agree to allow a landlord to approve its trade name.

If the landlord agrees to this language, then it must address when the use can change and what types of changes will be permitted. If the tenant has a right to terminate the lease due to insufficient sales volume after a certain period of operation (e.g., five years), then the landlord may insist that the tenant operate for that initial or intended use at least through that date. Similarly, if the landlord has given a construction allowance to the tenant to be applied toward the leasehold improvements, the landlord, at a minimum, wants to recoup that investment in the minimum rent charged under the lease. So it may require the tenant to operate for the initial or intended use through that date. If the restaurant is a national chain, it may have other concepts it would like to implement if the initial use did not succeed. Sometimes these other concepts will be specifically included as permitted changes, or certain ones may be specifically excluded in the lease if that food category is adequately filled elsewhere in the shopping center. In any case, any change of use permitted without the landlord's consent must be subject to any existing exclusives or restrictions of record.

Restaurants offering a varied menu cuisine pose a thorny problem. Since by their nature they have limitless offerings, it would be easy for the landlord to lose control over the type of restaurant being operated from the premises. Sometimes the parties address this issue by providing that the premises will be used "for the operation of a typical XYZ restaurant offering a varied menu cuisine consistent with the menu offered nationwide by other XYZ restaurants," but this does not solve the problem. Food items that were not contemplated at the outset of the lease term may suddenly appear on the tenant's menu much to the chagrin of the ethnic fast-food, or fast-casual restaurants in the shopping center.

The landlord must be cognizant of any existing exclusives granted to other tenants in the shopping center. Perhaps it can restrict the offering of certain menu items that are protected by an existing exclusive or restrict the offering of such menu items to incidental sales, but the latter involves policing menus on a regular basis. It could prohibit the tenant from changing or expanding its menu in a manner that would duplicate other food uses in the shopping center or that violate prohibited uses delineated in other leases or in reciprocal easement agreements with the anchor tenants. It could specifically prohibit certain categories of food or beverages (e.g., ice cream or fruit smoothies). It could define the varied menu tenant's use in terms of the operation of its main competitors (e.g., "offering a varied menu consistent with restaurants such as the ABC restaurant"). Of course, this assumes that the ABC restaurant menu remains static over time.

There are no easy answers to this dilemma. If the landlord had sufficient foresight, it would have excluded restaurants of certain size from any exclusive it granted or limited the area of the exclusive zone. This way, a 5,000-square-foot tenant offering a varied menu would not be considered a competitor to a 2,000-square-foot. Fast-casual restaurant or a food court tenant that specialized in a particular type of cuisine. Even if there are no exclusives at the shopping center, the landlord and the shopping center customers want a diverse selection of food to choose from and it can be very difficult to thread the needle so that variety is available but at the same time the tenants are not sapping sales from each other.

On a continuum, landlords want the use clause drafted as narrowly as possible whereas the tenants prefer that it be written as broadly as possible. It must be emphasized that the attorneys for both sides should not simply copy and paste a use clause from a LOI or deal proposal letter; the brokers or leasing agents who negotiated that letter may not have contemplated all of the permutations that could occur. The attorney's role is to evaluate the risks, assess the effect of the use clause on other clauses in the lease, and anticipate likely scenarios caused by changed circumstances (e.g., evolving tastes or economic trends). The use clause will impact several other clauses in the leases, including trade name, radius, signage, assignment, and exclusives, some of which will be discussed in more detail in later portions of this book.

Some restaurants derive a substantial portion of their revenues from the sale of liquor. Usually the lease will allow the sale of liquor provided the tenant obtains and maintains all necessary permits. In most cases, the sale of liquor will be limited to on-premises consumption. That is, carryout sale of liquor will not be permitted unless it is expressly stated in the lease. Will the license be a two-way license, meaning that it is limited to the sale of beer and wine, or will it be a so-called three-way permit permitting the sale of spirits or hard liquor? Some jurisdictions limit the number of bars within a particular zoning district. In this case, it may be necessary to ensure that the food menu will be available during all hours of operation so that the restaurant remains a "restaurant" as opposed to being classified as a bar or a nightclub. Some state laws prohibit the collection of percentage rent on sales of liquor, so the parties should be cognizant of this fact when determining the minimum rent charged for the premises.

The parties should also address whether a restaurant will be permitted to operate incidental uses from its premises. Some restaurant chains offer their own branded merchandise, such as apparel, mugs, and glasses. Others operate general gift stores from a part of their premises. Often these merchandise sales are limited to a specified square footage of the premises (e.g., 500 square feet or 5% of the floor space, or 50 lineal feet). The parties should consider whether the same percentage rent rate should be applied toward these sales as for food and beverages because the margins will vary. In an era where entertainment is merged with retail, restaurants may also want to operate arcades, game machines, or interactive video and computer games. A restaurant may want to operate a catering service from its premises. Will these catering sales be included in the gross sales of the premises for purposes of calculating percentage rent? Although the potential list of incidental uses is limitless, it is important that the landlord and tenant focus on the complete offering of uses from the premises as opposed to generalized language (e.g., "as is typical in an XYZ restaurant") so that future misunderstandings can be avoided.

Hours of Operation

For a fast-food restaurant located in an enclosed mall food court, there will be limited flexibility to adjust its operating hours. The mall owner will want the food court restaurant to be open the same mall hours as the retail shops are required to be open. With the emphasis on the combination of retail, food, and entertainment uses to lure shoppers away from their computers at home and into the mall, the landlord will want food service available at all standard hours the mall is open for shopping. Most enclosed mall hours are 10 a.m. to 9 p.m., with shorter hours on Sunday (e.g., noon to 6 p.m). Although at most food courts, food service often does not begin until 11 a.m., the landlord is unlikely to be sympathetic to the food court tenant's inability to draw customers before 11 a.m. The landlord has a vital interest in presenting a mall that looks vibrant the moment the doors unlock for shoppers each day. Retail tenants must be open the standard mall hours even though some hours may be slower than others; food court tenants are expected to do the same. For some enterprising food court operators, they may find an opportunity to make breakfast sales to mall employees, delivery personnel, or the proverbial mall walkers. If that is a possibility, the lease should clearly grant the food court operator the right to open early at no additional expense. Additionally, the food court tenant may want language stating that even if they must be staffed by 10 a.m. with the lights on, they are not required to offer food service until the mall is open to the public.

One area with which the food court operator should be concerned is additional mall hours (e.g., at Christmas). To get an edge on the competition, some mall owners may open at midnight or open early on Thanksgiving Day evening. For most food court tenants, it would not be economically feasible to open at midnight on Thanksgiving Eve or another holiday, but the lease may require it. The food court tenant should specifically negotiate in the lease that it is not required to be open those special hours. If the landlord is obstinate and will not concede this point, the food court tenant could request that it will be open these additional hours only if some percentage of the remainder of the food court and the retail tenants in the mall are also open or required to be open. Even if the food court operator is not required to be open for these "midnight madness" or similar type sales, the lease may require the exterior signage to be lit so that it gives an inviting appearance to shoppers who are walking by or simply resting in the food court after an exhausting shopping expedition. Also, the lease could specify which holidays the food court operator is not required to be open (e.g., Memorial Day, July 4, Labor Day, Thanksgiving Day, Christmas Day, or other recognized holidays). Some malls that rely heavily on tourists may be open on these holidays, so the food court tenant should address in the lease on which holidays they must be open. Some tenants may want to reserve a limited number of days per year they are not required to open at all or may open later for providing training or taking inventory. Other tenants may want an extended period of time (e.g., 60–90 days) to close for a major remodel or renovation. These exceptions to the standard operating hours should be clearly set forth in the lease so that the tenant does not run afoul of the continuous operations clause that requires the restaurant to be fully staffed and open during the hours required by the lease.

Depending on the type of cuisine, the table-service restaurant will have some unique concerns. If it is steakhouse or other fine dining establishment, it may resist opening prior to the lunch hours. If it does not have interior access to the mall, this may not be an issue. Even if the restaurant does have interior access or is located in a strip center, it may find that it is unprofitable to be open prior to the traditional lunch hours. Some fine restaurants refuse to open for lunch or want the decision to be optional for them. If this becomes a deal breaker, then the landlord's initial position should be that the tenant should open for lunch for a trial period and if sales do not reach a predetermined amount, then lunch hours will be optional. For these finer restaurants where the hours of operation are critical, at the very least, the landlord should insist that the restaurant be open a minimum number of hours per day. That way, the restaurateur can best determine which hours maximize sales. Alternatively, the parties could agree that the tenant would initially open each day by 4:30 p.m. so as to attract those shoppers who want to beat the crowds or didn't have the foresight to make a reservation. Similarly, they could agree that only the bar portion of the restaurant would open early, with some limited food service.

Unlike the food court tenants, who will be required by the landlord to close at the standard mall closing time, the table-service restaurant will want the right to remain open beyond that time. Aside from security and lighting concerns, which will be addressed later, this should not be a problem for the landlord, especially where the table-service restaurant does not have interior mall access or is located in a strip center. If the restaurant has interior mall access, the restaurant should be required to lock any doors that provide direct access to the interior of the mall. Neither the landlord nor the retailers want people strolling through the mall long after it has closed. Also, mall personnel would be actively cleaning the common areas at that time, which could lead to liability concerns (e.g., slip and fall cases). In most instances, earlier or later hours will not be of concern for a restaurant with a drive-through service in a strip center because the customers would not have access to any other interior portions of the shopping center. Still, a prudent tenant should reserve the right to open earlier or later in the lease. The landlord wants to maximize sales and percentage rent, so the additional hours of operation should not be an issue. However, as with the table-service restaurant, the parties may need to address parking lot lighting or security concerns and any additional charges for these services that are provided beyond the standard shopping center hours.

Some restaurants may want to tie their hours of operation to a specific anchor or to a specific number of anchors or other retailers. For example, if a restaurant is located adjacent to or near a theatre, it may not want to open prior to the theatre opening hours. A food court tenant may want to limit its operating hours to a certain percentage of other food court operators being open or required to be open during the same hours. For example, if a majority of the food court is not required to be open until 11 a.m., then the tenant could open at 11 a.m. notwithstanding that its lease required it to open at 10 a.m. Certain fast-casual restaurants in strip centers may offer only breakfast and lunch, so the lease should reflect their ability to close earlier in the day than the rest of the shopping center.

The lease form will often address the remedies for failure of the tenant to maintain the standard operating hours. Unless the tenant repeatedly and egregiously violates the hours of operation mandate, the landlord is not likely to terminate the lease. However, it is common for leases to provide for the payment of liquidated damages if the tenant opens late, closes early, or does not open at all on a particular day it was required to be open. Usually the liquidated damage amount is based on some percentage of the daily rent (e.g., 50% of the minimum rent, although 25% is more common). Another option is to deem the gross sales for the day the tenant did not open during a required period to be the average of the gross sales for a comparable period of time [e.g., same days over the prior month(s) or prior season]. The parties will often negotiate a "goldilocks" amount so that it is neither too harsh nor too permissive. The tenant may be able to negotiate a so-called habitual offender exception that permits it to violate the standard mall hours not more than a relatively few number of times during the lease year before the liquidated damages can be invoked for future violations. From a drafting perspective, it is vital that the lease defines each daily infraction as a separate violation. Otherwise, the tenant could argue that opening late for 7 consecutive days constituted but one violation. If a cumulative number of violations occur during the lease term, the habitual offender exception may become null and void for the balance of the lease term. The restaurant tenants will often ask for notice of any violation because the home office may be unaware of these infractions. The restaurant may want to negotiate some permissible excuses for casualty, condemnation, or force majeure. However, the tenant should be required to notify the landlord promptly of the occurrence of any such reasons.

Go Dark Provisions

Closely related to the hours of operation clause is the continuous operations clause. Most landlords require that the restaurant must initially open for business either by a fixed date (e.g., a specific calendar date) or by a determinable date (e.g., a certain number of days after which possession of the premises has been tendered to the tenant or other conditions have been met) and operate during the entire lease term fully stocked and staffed for the permitted use during all hours of operation mandated by the lease. This is the essence of the continuous operations clause. The landlord wants to present a vibrant atmosphere for its shopping center, and dark storefronts undermine this objective. Although most restaurants will accept this clause, a table-service restaurant operated by a national chain may insist on a wider degree of latitude. Many of these national chains are located on outparcels where they are not physically connected to the mall or the strip center. As a result, they may have virtually unlimited discretion as to whether they must continue to operate their business at all, even though they would still be required to pay the rental charges despite such closure. In some instances, the table-service or occasionally fast-casual restaurants will attempt to integrate this right to go dark into their leases where the restaurant is physically connected to the mall or strip center. Sometimes this right to go dark is simply used to modify hours of operation, but in most cases, it is used to close the restaurant permanently without such closure causing a lease default. The tendered rationale is that restaurants have much higher fixed labor and inventory costs, and it can be economically disastrous for the restaurateur to operate where sales do not meet expectations. The tenant will argue that as long as the rent is being paid, the landlord is not harmed, and this hiatus enables the parties to formulate an exit strategy and to find an acceptable replacement tenant. From the tenant's perspective, this is a far preferable outcome to expensive and protracted litigation or bankruptcy. This concept is always a source of vigorous negotiations between the parties. In the authors' experience, the restaurant must possess significant leverage to extract this concession from the landlord.

If a landlord agrees to this right to go dark, several considerations must be taken into account. The parties must agree as to the duration of the initial operating covenant. It would be a rare circumstance for the landlord to agree that the tenant never had to initially open for business or could close after only one day of operation, to cite some extreme cases. In all likelihood, the landlord will insist that the tenant operate for a period of years before it could invoke a go dark right. The time period could be tied to the date the tenant had the right to terminate the lease due to insufficient sales volume (i.e., a sales kickout). For example, if the tenant had the right to terminate the lease if its sales for the fourth lease year were less than $1 million, then the operating covenant would be tethered to this same period. In this instance, the tenant would have to operate its restaurant through the last day of the fourth lease year. Clearly, the landlord would not want to grant the tenant the right to go dark after one year but then give the tenant the right to terminate the lease under a sales kickout in the fourth lease year. From the landlord's perspective, this would have the deleterious effect of permitting the tenant to terminate the lease simply by closing the restaurant early enough in the lease term that its sales for the fourth lease year never hit the sales threshold figure.

Even if there is not a separate sales kickout clause in the lease, it still may be useful to tie the ability of the tenant to go dark to some specific dollar figure. By way of illustration, if the tenant's average gross sales for a specified number of years are less than a predetermined amount, then the tenant could go dark. The restaurant undoubtedly knows what its breakeven point is, and this would provide an objective basis on which the tenant could demonstrate that it is no longer viable to operate. Sometimes this figure is based on gross sales for a "trailing twelve period" prior to the exercise of the right to go dark, and sometimes it is based on a profit and loss statement for some trailing period of time. If the landlord agrees to the latter, a useful concept is to base the "loss" on what is referred to as "four-walls EBIDTA." In other words, the tenant would have to demonstrate that its earnings for that period, as determined in accordance with generally accepted accounting principles, was less than zero or less than some defined amount before interest, depreciation, taxes, and amortization were deducted, along with other noncash charges or payments made to affiliates.

Some landlords insist that the operating covenant extend until the tenant has paid base rent equal to the amount of any tenant improvement allowance given to the tenant. Although the tenant has an obligation to continue to pay rent during any go dark period, the odds of recovering this amount are less if the tenant has closed up shop because the tenant has one less source of cash flow from which to pay the rent. If a tenant has options to renew, sometimes the operating covenant expires at the end of the initial term of the lease. That way, the landlord gets the full benefit of an operating tenant through the initial term while giving the tenant some flexibility during the option period to explore a different use for the premises or find a buyer for the lease and the business. Whatever operating covenant is agreed upon, the landlord will often insert a provision in the lease that once the tenant goes dark, the tenant loses the benefit of any "exclusive" in the lease (i.e., the sole right to operate a specific type of restaurant or to offer a particular cuisine or food products at the shopping center). In addition, the tenant may be required to forfeit the benefit of any co-tenancy clauses that permit it to pay reduced rent if certain occupancy levels at the shopping center are not met, as well as lose any option to renew the lease or extend the term of the lease. Furthermore, the tenant could be required to relinquish its right to go dark if it exercises an option to renew the lease. Once the restaurant has shuttered its doors, the landlord may insist that the tenant no longer has the right to these special privileges. Of course, tenants with leverage do not agree that any of these rights should be conditioned upon continued operation. They argue that they negotiated a rental amount that contemplates all of these rights and they should be entitled to the benefit of their bargain so long as they continue to pay rent.

The lease should also stipulate the amount of advance written notice the tenant must provide before it goes dark. This can be a tricky issue. As soon as word gets out that the tenant is closing, it will be difficult to retain good employees, which can lead to a further decline in sales. Typically, this prior written notice can range from a minimum of thirty days to a maximum of 180 days. Ideally, the landlord would have sufficient notice so that it could announce a replacement tenant before the original tenant actually closes. In most cases, the tenant would have communicated to the landlord informally about its plans well in advance of the actual cessation of business so that re-leasing activity would have already begun and a longer notice period may not be necessary. There may be instances where the tenant wants more than thirty days and the landlord wants less than 180 days. Besides the tenant wanting to terminate the lease and thus its obligation to pay rent as soon as possible, the tenant often has a significant investment in its trade fixtures and equipment that it would like to sell to the replacement operator, in which case the tenant will be actively marketing for a replacement. Conversely, the landlord may have already found a replacement tenant or may have plans to repurpose the area where the restaurant is located, so it wants the tenant out sooner rather than later. The determination of the actual notice period will often be guided by the ease with which the space can be re-leased.

Of course, if the tenant fails to give the required advance written notice, that failure would be a default under the lease. In that case, the landlord would be required to give any applicable notice under the default clause, and the tenant would have the lease required or statutorily mandated cure period before the landlord could terminate the lease. If the failure to operate is treated as a lease default, some states might require an expedited judicial proceeding such as an unlawful detainer action before a physical eviction would be allowed. To avoid the time and expense of a default remedy, the landlord should add language to the go dark provision that would trigger the landlord's right to recapture the premises and terminate the lease immediately if the tenant closed up without the requisite notice being given. After all, the advance notice was for the landlord's benefit. Nonetheless, the tenant may require that such right of recapture be the landlord's sole remedy for the tenant's failure to operate in order to limit the landlord's right to recoup damages for such failure or seek specific performance.

Once the tenant has been dark for the requisite time period, the landlord has the right to recapture the premises and terminate the lease. The same considerations that applied to the number of advance days of written notice required of the tenant would apply in the situation where the landlord is giving the notice of termination. The rent no longer accrues as of the effective date of the termination, so the landlord needs to be mindful of that fact. If the space can be easily leased, the landlord may want a shorter period of time before the lease is terminated. Conversely, a longer period of time might be in order if the landlord expects some difficulty in re-leasing the space. Of course, no one has a crystal ball at lease execution as to the appropriate length of time, but prior experience at that property or with similar restaurants may be the best gauge.

Some tenants may negotiate a redemption clause where if they reopen or a permitted assignee or subtenant opens prior to the expiration of the recapture date, then the right to terminate for that closure is nullified. If the landlord agrees to such a provision, the lease should address, at a minimum, the date by which tenant will reopen or complete its remodel for another use or its permitted assignee will open, failing which the termination date will be reinstated.

Sometimes the tenant will negotiate a window period within which the landlord must exercise its right to recapture or be deemed to have waived it. By forcing the landlord's hand, the tenant seeks a quick decision. Otherwise, an air of uncertainty hangs over the lease because the tenant does not know when, if ever, the landlord will terminate the lease. If the landlord declines to recapture by the specified date, then the tenant will have more flexibility in terms of negotiating a better price for a sale of the business, lease and trade fixtures, and equipment. As discussed above, the marketability of the space should dictate the duration of the window period.

There may be circumstances where the tenant has ceased operations for reasons beyond its control or for other legitimate reasons, and it should specifically exclude these occurrences from the definition of what constitutes going dark. A grease fire may have destroyed the restaurant. A tornado or 100-year flood may have ravaged the building. To widen a road or install traffic signals, governmental authorities may have temporarily taken critical parking or access points. The tenant may want or be required by the lease to remodel the premises during the lease term. Whatever the reason, the tenant might not be able to operate for a period of time but would not want to risk losing its lease over an involuntary closure. As a result, it is common to create exceptions to the go dark definition for casualty, condemnation, force majeure, and specified periods of time for remodeling.

Another issue that frequently arises in connection with the landlord's termination of the lease through a recapture right is the obligation of either party to pay a termination fee. The tenant may have spent a substantial amount of money on leasehold improvements for the restaurant and would want to be reimbursed for its unamortized costs. The landlord may not be sympathetic because it is losing an operating tenant and may have to invest more money in a new restaurant operator. In addition, the landlord may have paid a significant improvement allowance to the tenant, so the landlord would want to be reimbursed for those unamortized costs or have that amount deducted from the tenant's investment. Also, the landlord may insist on a liquidated sum equal to the lost rent following the termination of the lease, as it will take some time before the replacement tenant will open. As with most monetary issues in a lease, leverage is the key.

Definition of Premises

For most inline leases, the definition of the premises is not problematic. Usually a lease outline drawing is attached to the lease showing the room number, location, size, and dimensions of the space that is being leased. If the space was previously occupied by another tenant, the square footage is usually carried over into the next tenant's lease. However, there may be instances where the existing square footage should be questioned. First, the space may have been measured incorrectly. It is important to review the method of measurement contained in the lease. Often this leads to confusion. Many retail leases measure to the middle of common walls and to the lease line of front and back walls. Many tenants measure only to the interior finished wall or stud wall, and these differing methods may result in a discrepancy. In most landlord lease forms, the landlord's determination of the size of the premises is final, binding, and conclusive. A savvy tenant may want to insert language that gives it a certain period of time within which to remeasure and, in the event of a dispute, have a third party (e.g., an architect) measure; that measurement would then be determinative. If a third party will determine the actual size, then the lease should address the allocation of costs for these services. The fees could be split equally, or the loser could be required to pay (i.e., the party whose measurement was furthest from the binding measurement).

The actual square footage is important because the rental charges are often computed on a per-square-foot basis and because the architect, store planner, or contractor will use that square footage to draw its plans. Also, there may be unusable areas that the tenant will attempt to exclude, such as columns or an inaccessible corridor. The tenant should be aware of any legends contained on the lease outline drawing because they may show column lines or utility stubs. Whenever feasible, the tenant and landlord representatives should conduct a walk-through of the premises prior to lease execution so that an accurate measurement can be reached. If an existing tenant continues to operate in the premises, the survey may have to occur during nonpeak hours so that the existing business is not disrupted. Additionally, discretion may be in order if the existing tenant or its employees are unaware that the space may be leased to someone else. Some tenants will negotiate a clause where the square footage upon which their rental charges are based cannot be more or less than a specific number or percentage. Some leases may arbitrarily set out a pre-determined square footage on which the tenant will pay rent, irrespective of the actual size of the space. If the space is new construction, usually the landlord will have installed the demising studs. In that case, the measurement is easier to accomplish, but many of the aforementioned concerns may remain.

A tenant leasing a pad may pose a few additional wrinkles. A pad can be bare ground, or it can be poured with concrete or asphalt. The leased premises could be the pad and the building to be constructed on it or just the building. In most cases, the building will not be physically connected to the main buildings of the shopping center. These are often referred to as outlots or outparcels. The lease should address whether the rental charges are based on the square footage of the pad or the square footage of the building. Even the definition of the pad can be thorny. Will the pad be measured by a staked survey, or will it be measured from the curbline in? The definition of the outlot will also affect construction, repair, and maintenance obligations under the lease, which will be covered later in this book.

Patios, Sampling, and Food Courts

The tenant may conduct activities in the operation of its restaurant that are beyond the four walls of the interior of the premises. For example, many restaurants offer outside patio areas where customers can eat and drink. If this is to be permitted, then an exhibit defining the location and dimensions of the patio should be attached to the lease. Generally, the tenant will be obligated to maintain, clean, and insure these areas even though they are technically part of the common areas of the shopping center. If liquor is served on the patio area, then local requirements may mandate that a barrier be placed around the patio area, such as ornamental fencing or large planters. Although it can be a point of negotiations, the tenant usually does not pay any rental charges for use of the patio except for percentage rent on sales generated from the patio. If not covered elsewhere in the lease, the use of audio and video media on the patio should be restricted to reasonable volume levels so that it does not disturb other tenants or customers. Reasonableness could be determined by a decibel level or the distance beyond the patio the sound is audible. The lease should specify who is responsible for obtaining all necessary governmental approvals and third-party approvals (e.g., anchor stores) to operate the patio. If the operation of a patio is crucial to the tenant's business, then it may want language that allows it to terminate the lease within a specified period of time after lease execution if the approvals for the patio cannot be obtained. Often the patio will be for the tenant's exclusive use, especially if liquor is served. However, there may be instances where due to zoning or anchor store agreements, the landlord must reserve the right for other customers to pass through the patio area. In this case, the tenant should not be permitted to install a permanent barrier. Many patios are simply a collection of tables and chairs that are removed on a daily basis, so this is a common solution to the non-exclusivity issue. Finally, approval of the design of the patio is usually subject to the prior written approval of the landlord. The landlord needs to ensure that the appearance of the patio blends with the décor of the remainder of the shopping center.

Some food court tenants want the right to offer samples or give away coupons in the common areas. If the landlord is amenable to sampling, then it will be subject to certain parameters. Generally, there will be a defined area where the employee will be permitted to offer samples. A common boundary is extending an imaginary line between the side lease lines of the premises outward five feet. The landlord does not want one tenant encroaching on the area of an adjacent tenant, so this clearly shows where the boundary is. It also does not want tenants roaming through the common areas offering samples to uninterested customers. Usually only one tenant employee will be permitted to offer samples at a time, and the employee must be stationed at least five feet away from the lease line of any other tenant. Sampling may be limited to certain hours of the day so that it does not interfere with the queues in front of other food court counters. The sampling tenant will not be permitted to conduct its sampling in a manner that interferes with the flow of customer traffic through the shopping center. The sampling employee may be required to wear the standard company uniform so that a customer can readily identify who is approaching and why. If the tenant does not conduct the sampling in a clean and orderly manner, the landlord may reserve the right to revoke the right to offer samples.

Food court tenants have some unique issues in that, by definition, they share tables and chairs with other tenants located within the same food court. In many cases, the food court tenants will be assessed a surcharge for the landlord's operation and maintenance of the food court above and beyond the customary common area expense charge. This surcharge can be a separate charge, or it can be rolled into the regular common area expense charge. If it is billed separately, the food court tenant should identify what the initial surcharge will be and how it is determined. Some landlords allocate these food court expenses among the food court tenants based on their square footage in relation to the total square footage of the food court spaces or to the square footage of food court spaces then leased or occupied. The former computation is favorable to the tenant because the actual occupancy of the food court spaces is irrelevant. The latter computation is favorable to the landlord because the landlord can pass through its expenses that would otherwise be billed for a vacant space to the food court tenants that are open and operating. To illustrate this concept, in an extreme case if only one food court tenant was open in the food court, it would be responsible for 100% of the expenses of operating the food court. Although this extreme example is unlikely to occur or to result in the hapless food court tenant paying all of the expenses, it does underscore the reality that the operating tenants' food court charges could be higher if the food court is not fully leased. In this case, it would be prudent for the food court tenant to ask for a "floor" on this denominator so that the square footage on which the food court tenant's share is based would never be less than a certain percentage of the total food court square footage premises (e.g., "the leased or occupied square footage of the food court spaces will never be less than 80% of the total square footage of the food court spaces." That way, the landlord bears some of the burden for these unrecoverable expenses. Some landlords establish a fixed initial charge that increases yearly by a specific percentage whereas other landlords increase the fixed charge by changes in the CPI or by the percentage of its increase in costs over the prior year. However it is determined, the food court charge can be a significant ongoing expense, so the tenant must factor this amount into its pro forma as well as have a clear understanding as to how this charge can increase over time.

The landlord will generally be responsible for supplying the tables and chairs for the food court, the bussing of tables and the removal of trays and general cleaning of the food court. The tenant may want some assurance in the lease as to the minimum number of tables and chairs that will be available on an ongoing basis. In most cases, the food court tenants will provide their own trays and be responsible for cleaning them. Removal of trash from the food court seating area is often the obligation of the landlord. Of course, all of these expenses incurred by the landlord are included as part of the food court costs, which are reimbursed by the food court tenants. The food court tenants may be subject to a unique set of rules and regulations. The employees may be required to post their menus, and as discussed above, the landlord may attempt to obtain approval rights over changes to the menu. The employees are often required to wear uniforms that are customary for that tenant's business. Like any other tenant cooking on the premises, the food court tenant will be obligated to clean its grease trap on a regular basis and provide proof of such cleaning to landlord. Sometimes the landlord will clean the traps itself and charge the tenants so that it is assured that the task has been done correctly. The food court tenant will also be obligated to dispose of grease and other food waste so that it does not clog sewer or water lines. The most common cause of flooding in a multilevel mall is the failure of a food tenant to clean these traps and dispose of its grease and waste properly, so this is a significant concern to landlords. Landlords may require food court tenants to carry higher limits of insurance so that damaged third parties can be compensated. Landlords may also require special waterproofing of the floors within the food court spaces to contain these spills.

The landlord may require the tenant to use a preferred vendor for removal of trash from the dumpster, or the landlord may contract directly with the vendor and charge the amount back to the tenant on a monthly basis. The tenant should determine the contract rate and the method of increases. A tenant may ask to set out the maximum first-year charge in the lease and to specify that such charge cannot increase by more than a particular amount (e.g., a certain percentage or the rate of increase based on the CPI). If the landlord will not agree to such caps, then the tenant might ask that rates be competitive with like providers offering comparable service in the metropolitan area where the shopping center is located. In some instances, the tenant may want to contract directly with its own vendor, but this may not be possible if the landlord has negotiated a mallwide or nationwide contract. Sometimes the trash cost will be billed separately, but sometimes it may be included as part of the tenant's obligation to reimburse for its share of common area expenses. In addition, the tenant may be required to obtain or pay for periodic pest control services. The same concerns would be applicable to trash removal charges. It is essential that the tenant address these issues before lease execution so that there are no unpleasant surprises later on.

Radius Clauses

In its simplest form, a radius clause restricts the tenant from operating a competing business within a particular geographical area. The area is often stated in terms of miles from the boundary of the shopping center, but it can be defined in other ways as well, such as a metropolitan area or an intersection, along a particular street, or within a specific project (e.g., a competing mall down the road). The clause generally restricts the operation of a business that directly or indirectly competes with the business operated on the landlord's project. This net cuts a wide swath and can ensnare the unwitting tenant. The landlord will justify the radius on various grounds. The landlord may have invested a great deal of money in the tenant's construction whether through a construction allowance or substantial landlord work. The tenant may have been given a below-market rent or other rental concessions to induce the tenant to lease space at the subject shopping center. The landlord may want to preserve the exclusivity of its tenant mix by prohibiting the tenant from competing with the landlord's shopping center. In addition, the landlord expects to collect percentage rent from the tenant's sales at the shopping center, and this could be impacted by a nearby competing location.

Of course, the tenant will resist the imposition of any radius, reasoning that it is the best judge of how many restaurants it can open within a given market without cannibalizing sales. The tenant is basing its total occupancy costs at the shopping center (e.g., base rent, taxes, insurance, common area costs, and utilities) on the assumption of estimated sales per square foot, and it would be disastrous for it to dilute sales by opening a competing restaurant in close proximity. In the highly competitive world of restaurants, the tenant does not want to be caught flat-footed if a new market emerges for its brand but, due to the imposition of a radius, it must cede expansion to another chain.

For a food court tenant, a radius could be very problematic. Food court operators concentrate on fast-food delivery, so convenience is at a premium. Most customers will not drive a long distance simply to buy fast food. Fast-food restaurants are on almost every commercial street corner in the urban and suburban areas where most shopping centers are located. Opening a competing hamburger joint down the street may have no impact on the mall traffic because the food court is not a destination in and of itself. Moreover, the landlord rarely has a big financial investment in a food court tenant. If a radius is agreed upon, it will generally be limited to other food courts or to food courts in enclosed malls or to food courts that are a much shorter distance than the distance contained in the landlord's boilerplate lease form. It may specifically exclude freestanding buildings that are stand-alone uses (e.g., a hamburger chain with a separate building and drive-through that is not connected to or contained within a shopping center).

For the fast-casual and table-service restaurants, the landlord may have a more significant stake in the restaurant, such as a large investment in the construction of the restaurant or in the granting of rent concessions, so it will resist elimination or dilution of the radius. Typically neither of these types of restaurants will have as many locations within a particular geographical area as fast-food operators, so customers may drive farther to patronize them. These restaurants will have more of the characteristics of a destination tenant. The radius is often hotly contested between landlords and fast-casual and table-service restaurants. If the restaurant operator has been granted an exclusive to operate within the shopping center for its particular use, then a landlord may insist on a radius in return. Furthermore, if the tenant has the ability to terminate the lease early due to low sales volume, the landlord may insist on a radius at least through the measuring period for determining the volume of sales.

Assuming that a radius is agreed to in a lease, the restaurant operator must determine what precise use will be restricted. As noted above, the landlord will often define competition in the broadest terms possible. If a tenant owns separate franchises for a hamburger outlet and a sub shop, it would argue that one does not compete with the other. However, depending on how broadly the definition of competition is written in the lease, the landlord could argue that both are fast-food restaurants and thus do compete. A restaurant operator who owns both a steakhouse and a fine dining Italian restaurant could be in a similar predicament. In fact, many national chains own multiple concept restaurants. In such cases, the radius might be limited to "other fine dining Italian restaurants" so that the operation of a steakhouse would not be restricted. Even two steakhouses might not compete depending on price points, so the radius might be worded such that if the average ticket price is less than a certain dollar figure, it would not be deemed a competitor for the white tablecloth steakhouse. If the tenant contemplates or has various restaurant concepts, it must exclude these possibilities from falling within the purview of the radius. The more precisely the definition of a competing use is phrased, the less likelihood of a dispute later on. Obviously, any existing restaurants in operation as of the date the lease was signed must be excluded from the scope of the radius but in appropriate circumstances the landlord may insist that the leases of such existing operations not be renewed nor their terms extended. A savvy tenant will also insist that if its parent company acquires an existing chain, the restaurants in that chain will also be excluded from the scope of the radius. Sometimes the radius is limited to restaurants operating under the same trade name because this often differentiates brands of a restaurant chain. The landlord may insist on the radius also covering similar trade names so that the tenant cannot wriggle out of a radius simply by calling a restaurant "Joe's" rather than "Joe's Place."

The lease will also set forth the remedies for a radius violation. Usually it is not treated as a lease default due to the potential liability for restraint of trade or antitrust claims. However, in special circumstances, it could be a lease default or give rise to a landlord right to terminate the lease. If, for example, the landlord paid for the entire cost of building the restaurant or gave generous rent concessions or relinquished other leasing opportunities, it might prevail in court in an action to terminate the lease for a radius violation, especially if the lease recited that this radius was bargained for consideration for the leasing inducements. Barring some unusual circumstances, though, most courts will adhere to the legal maxim that "the law abhors a forfeiture" and will be reluctant to terminate the lease. It is also extremely difficult to prove damages from a radius violation, which is why specified remedies are often set out in the lease. Most of these remedies are set forth to deter the tenant from opening a competitor rather than to establish a measure of damages.

The most common remedy for a radius violation is the inclusion of sales of the competing store in the gross sales for the violating store. If the violating store is obligated to pay percentage rent, then increasing its overall percentage rent by treating the violating store's sales as its own can have an inhibiting effect. In essence, the restaurant could be paying percentage rent on the competing store's sales twice, once to the aggrieved landlord and once to the landlord of the competing location. However, if the sales breakpoint is set too high, the combination of sales from the two restaurants may never be enough to obligate the tenant to pay percentage rent. Thus, this remedy is wholly ineffective for the landlord. The landlord will need to reserve audit rights for these competing locations; otherwise, it will never know what the sales were. Tenants may also attempt to limit the inclusion of gross sales of the competing restaurant by including only a portion of those sales (e.g., "50% of the competing store sales").

An additional or alternative remedy for a radius violation is to increase the base rent by a certain percentage for the period of the radius violation. The lease could provide that the base rent increases by 50%, which the tenant will try to negotiate downward. The parties will often agree to 25%. The challenge for the landlord is for any remedy to be reasonable so that it can be viewed by the courts as liquidated damages as opposed to a penalty because the courts will generally not enforce a penalty. The base rent could also be increased by the amount of average percentage rent payable by the tenant over the prior lease years of the term or some variation thereof. However, as noted above, this remedy will not work for the landlord unless the tenant was paying percentage rent in the prior years.

Other potential remedies include loss of a termination right due to low sales, loss of an exclusive, or nullification of a right to pay reduced rent in the event of a co-tenancy violation. In turn, the tenant may insist that the radius is unenforceable if the landlord violates an exclusive granted to the tenant. Generally, the landlord will attempt to retain as many remedies as possible, including a catch-all provision that it reserves all rights available to it at law or in equity.

Exclusives

As part of the lease negotiations, a tenant may request an exclusive, which is a provision that limits the rights of other tenants in offering competing goods and services within the shopping center or some portion thereof. As with other major issues, the decision of whether to grant an exclusive will rest to a large degree on the leverage of the parties. If the tenant offers a new or trendy dining concept, it may have several suitors and the landlord may be compelled to grant an exclusive to that restaurant operator or lose the deal to another landlord. A signature restaurant or celebrity chef may be enticed to operate in the shopping center only if the landlord offers an exclusive. The tenant may be making a substantial investment in the restaurant and needs to protect that investment against other restaurants that may undercut its price points. The landlord may be desperate to fill vacant space as part of a new development or to replace a departing tenant. The landlord may have offered other tenants a co-tenancy based in part on a certain number of restaurants at the shopping center. In a world where customers increasingly demand food and entertainment options in order to shop at malls populated by brick-and-mortar stores, demand may outstrip supply and landlords may find themselves outbidding each other for restaurant uses.

The motivations for granting an exclusive are limitless. However, it is essential that both sides recognize the relative leverage they may have with respect to each other. Landlords are reluctant to grant exclusives because it limits their ability to lease to other restaurants and imposes on the landlord the burden of policing other tenants' menus and business operations. In general, landlords want the ownership of commercial real estate to be a passive investment. They are concerned with sweeping the floors, mowing the grass, plowing the snow, and otherwise maintaining the common areas of the shopping center, to name but a few of the landlord responsibilities. They do not want to engage in monitoring the day-to-day operations of their tenants' businesses.

If business necessity requires the landlord to grant an exclusive to a restaurant, it will want to draft the scope of the exclusive as narrowly as possible so that it does not impinge on other restaurants uses. The landlord wants to provide the customer with the broadest choices available at its shopping center. It cannot predict changes in customer preferences and does not want to be restricted in adapting to these changes over time. Moreover, the landlord does not want to be embroiled in expensive litigation with either the tenant who has the exclusive or the tenant who has presumably violated the exclusive. In addition to legal costs, the landlord may be subject to an abatement of rent for the violation, which reduces the landlord's operating income.

By contrast, the tenant wants the scope of its exclusive to be as encompassing as possible. Operating a restaurant is an expensive endeavor compared with retail uses, and the tenant does not want to see its success undercut by imitators. Imitation, as the saying goes, is the sincerest form of flattery, and that axiom certainly applies to restaurants. If the restaurant is successful, then it is likely that other restaurant operators at the shopping center will try to cash in. If there is a long line for chicken sandwiches at the food court, then it won't be long until other food court operators offer their version as well. This is especially true where use clauses are loosely drafted. The landlord must be especially vigilant so that it does not inadvertently violate another tenant's exclusive by drafting an overly broad use clause. For example, does an exclusive for "an Italian restaurant" prohibit the operation of a fast-food pizza use in the food court? Does an exclusive for "pizza" for an Italian fast-food operator prohibit the sale of Mexican pizza by a Mexican fast-food restaurant?

For various reasons, food court mall tenants are least likely to be granted exclusives. First, fast-food restaurants are more prevalent, so the landlord may have heightened flexibility in choosing the right operator. The food court tenant relies on traffic generated by other uses and may not be able to replicate that traffic in a strip center, so it may not have sufficient bargaining power if it needs to be in the mall. Also, many fast-food operators are part of national chains that offer a variety of menu items, so competition is to be expected. Food court leases tend to be shorter in duration than other types of restaurant leases, and turnover is more prevalent. Finally, the financial investment in a fast-food stall is substantially less than a fast-casual or table-service restaurant.

The fast-casual restaurants will often have more leverage than the fast-food operators. They often fill end space or space with separate entrances directly onto the parking lot that is not ideally suited for retail sales. For economic reasons, health concerns, and convenience, there is an increasing consumer demand for fast-casual restaurants. The industry has not yet reached a saturation point, so more landlords are chasing the fast-casual chains than the other way around. The fast-casual restaurant fills a niche that is not served by fast food, although that gap is narrowing as fast-food operators attempt to mimic the success of the fast-casual chains in terms of food quality and customer preferences. Additionally, many of these fast-casual restaurants are part of a national chain where the tenant may exact an exclusive in return for multiple deals with the landlord.

The table-service restaurant sits at the top of the pyramid in terms of obtaining exclusives from landlords. There are fewer of them than the other types, so the competition between landlords is intensified. This is especially true when the restaurant will be operated by a local or national celebrity chef or is a signature restaurant in terms of service, quality of food, and overall dining experience. It is not unusual for building costs to be in the millions of dollars with or without a construction allowance from the landlord. Moreover, a signature restaurant can set the tone or establish an upscale image for a shopping center. With the emphasis on entertainment in shopping centers by adding theatres, comedy clubs, and music venues, the right table-service restaurant can attract more customers who will stay longer at the shopping center. In many ways, a table-service restaurant can be a mini-anchor in terms of driving traffic.

As noted earlier, a loosely drafted use clause can accidentally open the door to competing uses. Aside from drafting a tightly written use clause, there are a few tips the landlord can follow to avoid stepping on this land mine. Many restaurant leases limit the operator to selling specific items on a menu attached to the lease. Any deviations from that menu require the landlord's consent. The tenant may want to qualify that the consent not be unreasonably withheld, conditioned, or delayed. The tenant may seek to add a provision that it could add items consistent with the menu or as required by its franchisor, but this might open the door too far unless limited in some way. For example, a pizza operator might be allowed to add "Italian pasta" plates but not simply "pasta" dishes as that might be too broad considering other ethnic cuisines.

The exclusive could be limited to restricting other restaurants whose primary use is the sale of specific food items or a particular ethnic concept. In the absence of a definition, primary would mean that 50% or more of its business is derived from a particular category of food. However, the landlord does not want the primary use to be defined in terms of sales because that is too difficult to monitor. It simply isn't practical to tell another tenant that it must quit selling a successful menu item because it has exceeded a specific quota. A more practical approach would define the exclusive in terms of entrée menu items. For example, an exclusive for a Mexican restaurant could be written so that no other tenant could have more than a specific number of entrée items or a specified percentage that were burritos, tacos, or enchiladas. This entire distinction is key because restaurant menus often include multiple beverages and sides that dilute the total percentage of a certain type of food offered and can make a restaurant that is clearly a Mexican restaurant not qualify as one for purposes of the exclusive provision. Alternatively, the exclusive could be worded so that no other restaurant could have a menu that is substantially similar to the menu of the holder of the exclusive. A broad exception could be granted for incidental sales. A list of specific competitors could be named as illustrative of the types of businesses encompassed by the exclusive or prohibited outright. That way, arguably a fast-food Mexican restaurant would not be prohibited by an exclusive for a white table cloth Mexican restaurant.

Often the landlord will specify that anchor tenants are not subject to the exclusive. This is rationalized on the basis that anchor tenants have very broad uses clauses such as "any lawful use." The landlord will also want to exempt existing tenants from being subject to the exclusive. The use clauses of existing tenants may be unduly broad with tags such as "and other related uses or food" added to the end of the clause. However, the tenant may want to modify this exemption so that if the landlord has any approval rights over a change of use, it will not exercise it in a manner that would violate the tenant's exclusive. The landlord may want an exception for rogue tenants, which are tenants who are intentionally violating their use clauses. In this situation, the landlord would be given a period of time within which to rectify the matter, such as evicting the rogue tenant or suing it in court before the holder of the exclusive could exercise any remedies under the lease or place the landlord in default.

The landlord may insist that the exclusive is not assignable. In other words, it does not "run with the lease" so that in the event the tenant assigns the lease or sublets the premises, the exclusive is not enforceable by the assignee or sublessee. From the landlord's perspective, the exclusive was specifically bargained for in order to induce a particular tenant or use to the shopping center. For example, if the original tenant was an expensive table-service steakhouse but assigned its lease to a steakhouse operator with much lower price points, then the rationale for granting the exclusive vanishes. Obviously, the existence of the exclusive may add value to the lease, so the tenant may want it to "run with the lease" because it can extract more value in the event of a sale of the business or transfer of the lease. Under some circumstances, the landlord may permit intra-corporate transfers such as to a parent, an affiliate, or a subsidiary of the tenant but only so long as the use remains the same. If the steakhouse converts to a pizza parlor, then there is no need for the exclusive to continue because the tenant no longer needs to be protected from competing steakhouses. Of course, the tenant may argue that it agreed to a certain level of rental charges in return for granting the exclusive and food competes with food. It also gives the tenant a bargaining chip if the landlord wants to put in another steakhouse later. In that case, the tenant may be able to negotiate a lower rent or longer term of the lease in return for relinquishing the exclusive.

The prudent landlord will not permit the exclusive to be enforceable in the event the tenant is in monetary or material nonmonetary default under the lease beyond any applicable cure period. This prohibition is based on the equitable principle that a wrongdoer who does not have "clean hands" should not be allowed to profit from its own wrongdoing. If this concept is introduced to the exclusive, then the lease should make clear whether the exclusive will be reinstated once the default is cured or disappears forever. Related thereto is a prohibition against the exclusive being enforceable once the tenant has ceased operating after its operating covenant has expired. The tenant is not in default because the closure, in and of itself, is permitted but the tenant may argue that the exclusive was a material part of the consideration for the rent in the lease and it should not matter that it has closed. Some landlords will insist that the exclusive become unenforceable during any renewal term of the lease. The thought is that the tenant should not be renewing the lease if it still needs the protection of an exclusive to operate its business. On the flip side, the tenant may argue that it always needs the protection of an exclusive because the margins for operating a restaurant are so low.

The remedies for an exclusive violation are similar to those for a co-tenancy violation. They usually turn on rent abatement and termination rights. If the lease does not specify a specific remedy, then the tenant presumably has all rights at law or in equity or can resort to other general remedies under the lease. These could include the right to sue for damages, to sue for specific performance or injunctive relief, or to file an action to terminate the lease. The determination of whether to limit the tenant to specific remedies for violation of an exclusive is a difficult one for the landlord. Without sole and exclusive remedies, the landlord could be subject to expensive litigation, loss of lease, and even punitive damages. On the other hand, leases often say that there is no right to offset against rent unless expressly permitted, so the tenant puts its lease in jeopardy if it unilaterally withholds rent. If the tenant takes the landlord to court, it may have a difficult time proving damages, especially if its sales did not decline. Moreover, it may be difficult to demonstrate that sales would have been even better had the competitor not opened because that gets in the realm of speculation. Most importantly, even if the tenant prevails in the litigation, it may be a Pyrrhic victory because the tenant may be out of business by the time the judgment is entered.

In most cases, the parties will agree upon certain remedies for violation of an exclusive, whether they are sole remedies or supplemental remedies. The initial remedy is often an abatement of rent. The tenant will be required to notify the landlord of the violation, and the landlord will have a specific, usually limited (e.g., 30 days), period of time within which to cure the violation. The rent abates upon expiration of the cure period or abates retroactive to the date the violation commenced or the date the tenant notified the landlord of the violation.

The landlord may insist on a demonstration of a sales decline during the cure period. Often the sales during the cure period or other measuring period are compared to sales for a comparable period of time immediately prior to commencement of the violation. The comparable period may be a significant factor in measuring the decline. If the competitor opens during the restaurant's slow season but this period is compared with sales for the tenant's high season, then there may not be a sales decline. For this reason, it is often best to use an "apples to apples" comparison so that if the measuring period is the first six months of a calendar year, then this measuring period would be compared against the same six months in the prior year. To minimize the possibility that the sales decline may have been due to circumstances unrelated to the opening of the competitor, such as bad weather, poor management, or an aggressive price hike in food input costs, the parties may compare the restaurant's sales against sales for its other restaurants during the same time period. Correlation is not causation. No measure can demonstrate causation with mathematical certainty, but it at least gives the parties a benchmark to assess harm. The amount of sales decline can be a significant factor as to whether there has been a showing of harm. Restaurants often operate on a lower profit margin than do retailers of soft goods. A 10% or 15% sales decline may be an acceptable approximation that a shoe retailer has been damaged. For a restaurant, a 5% decline in sales may be all it can bear before the loss of business is catastrophic, especially for a table-service restaurant with high labor costs and high food input costs.

The amount of the abatement usually centers on a reduction in the base rent or a complete abatement of the base rent and possibly other rental charges and the substitution thereof of a percentage of gross sales during the abatement period. There is a myriad of possibilities for structuring the rent abatement. For example, the base rent could be reduced by the percentage decline in the tenant's gross sales for the measuring period. However, this is often unsatisfactory to the tenant for the reason cited above, which is that the margins may be so thin that a 5% abatement in rent may be wholly inadequate to compensate the tenant for the actual loss to its business. Alternatively, the parties could agree that the base rent would be reduced by 50% or more so that it is more reflective of the harm suffered by the tenant. The larger abatement also serves as a deterrent should the landlord be tempted to violate the exclusive. The most frequent form of remedy is the complete abatement of base rent, and in lieu thereof, the tenant pays a percentage of gross sales until the landlord has cured the violation. This percentage is often based on the percentage rent rate, but that is simply a rule of thumb. If the additional rental charges are also abated, then the landlord may want a larger percentage rent rate for the alternate rent period.

With respect to abatement of additional rental charges such as taxes, common area expenses, insurance, and the like, the lease should be clear whether all additional charges are waived or only certain charges are waived. There are certain consumable charges that the landlord may insist the tenant continue to pay, such as utilities, trash removal, and HVAC. From the tenant's perspective, it is advisable for the lease to state that the tenant "may" rather than "shall" pay alternate rent during the period of the violation. It is conceivable that the competitor may draw more traffic to the shopping center and that after the period of initial decline, the sales of the restaurant with the exclusive may actually increase, in which case it could be paying more in rental charges than the original contract rent. The tenant wants the rent abatement to be permissive. Another way to address this issue is for the lease to state that the tenant will pay the lesser of the contract rent or the alternate rent.

Landlords usually insist on a sunset clause where after a period of time, the tenant must either terminate the lease or revert to full rent. The landlord wants the abatement to stop as soon as possible, so it might require that the decision be made within 6–12 months after the alternate rent period began. The tenant may be amenable as well because it may need to cut its losses, but in some instances, the tenant may want a longer period of time to assess whether it can recover the lost sales. Another variation could be to allow the tenant to stay on alternate rent indefinitely, while the violation continues, but give the landlord the ongoing right to require the tenant to "put up or shut up" by either terminating the lease or reverting to full rent. It is not unusual for a new restaurant to initially draw customers away from other restaurants at the shopping center, but after a time, the degree of attraction levels off and the customers return to the original restaurant. Moreover, the tenant has a significant investment in its construction of the restaurant that it does not want to lose. Some tenants with substantial leverage will require the landlord to reimburse the tenant for the unamortized cost of its leasehold improvements if the tenant terminates the lease due to the sunset clause. Although this reimbursement will be resisted vigorously by the landlord, if it does agree to reimburse, then the reimbursement should be offset by the amount of the construction allowance given the tenant. Most leases provide that these amounts will be amortized on a straight-line basis and assume a useful life equal to the initial lease term, but the parties are certainly free to negotiate the actual amounts. In a rare case, a demonstrated loss of profits may be part of the reimbursement.

A final wrinkle to this discussion of exclusives is whether the tenant should be required to earn the right to enforce the exclusive by demonstrating that its sales reached a specified threshold prior to the violation of the exclusive. If the parties projected that the tenant's annual sales would be $3 million and the actual sales were only $1 million prior to the exclusive violation, then this underperformance undermines the tenant's claim that it has been harmed by the presence of the competitor. Furthermore, the landlord may insist that if the tenant's sales before or during the exclusive violation exceed a certain amount, then the exclusive can no longer be enforced because the tenant is performing at or above projections. Of course, the tenant's counterargument is that but for the competitor, its sales would have been even better. Who needs the other the most will often dictate the outcome of these negotiations.

Chapter 3

Construction Issues for Restaurants

Condition of Premises

Every restaurant tenant should perform some degree of due diligence prior to lease execution. The scope of this due diligence will depend on the condition of the premises being leased, the extent of work necessary for the operation of the restaurant, and the amount of financial investment in the construction of the premises. For a food court tenant leasing an existing food court space, the due diligence could be limited to a site inspection of the premises and a determination of what existing equipment will remain and whether it can be reused or must be replaced. For a tenant leasing raw space that exists only on paper or space that will entail significant construction, the time and effort devoted to due diligence could be substantial. Before delving into the numerous items of due diligence that must be considered, it is first necessary to determine the condition of the leased premises. Various terms are loosely used in letters of intent and deal proposal letters. It is impossible to define each of these terms because it can vary within the construction industry, but a few general guidelines can be identified.

An "as-is" space is one where the tenant accepts possession of the premises in its current condition. Usually this is space that was previously occupied or previously built out. The lease will generally disclaim any representations or warranties regarding the habitability or functionality of the premises or its compliance with code. The burden is on the tenant to retrofit the space for its permitted use. In this case, the tenant should attempt to visit the site and walk through the space with a landlord representative. If the space is currently occupied, this may require coordination with the existing tenant so that no inspection disrupts operations. Most leases also require some advance notice of any inspection or showing of the premises. The prospective tenant and the landlord may have to be prudent as to what they tell the existing tenant's employees. If the employees are unaware that their employer's lease is not being renewed, they may bolt and leave the existing tenant in a difficult position where it is unable to retain qualified employees. Even an "as-is" space can have some qualifications. The tenant may be able to obtain a commitment by the landlord to remove any existing hazardous materials from the premises. For example, some older centers used certain glues to affix floors to the slab or certain types of insulation that are no longer permitted. For bigger landlords, environmental surveys may have been performed so that these issues have been rectified, but for others, the degree of adherence to law may be spotty. If available, the tenant should review the as-built drawings of the prior tenant because that may show locations of ducts, conduits, and shafts. The tenant may also want to hire a consultant to inspect the premises. If the tenant has sufficient leverage, it may extract a lease commitment from the landlord to repair any latent, structural, or hidden defects in the premises. Although most landlords are reluctant to accept any responsibility because they do not know exactly what the prior tenant did in the space, they may accept some liability for structural components because the obligation to repair structural components of the premises is often imposed elsewhere in the lease on the landlord. Whatever obligation the landlord assumes is usually limited by the requirement that the tenant notify the landlord of the defect within a certain period of time (e.g., 30 days after actual discovery or one year after taking possession). Still, with regard to leasing existing space, caveat emptor usually applies. Let the buyer beware.

A space in "shell condition" is where some basic level of construction has or will be performed at the premises prior to its delivery to the tenant for commencement of the tenant's work. A shell space is often the condition of the premises where a new shopping center is being built or a new wing of an existing shopping center is being added. Generally, it consists of a roof, metal or wood stud walls installed around the perimeter of the premises, a dirt or gravel floor, a sprinkler grid connected to the main sprinkler line for the building containing the premises, and utility conduits stubbed to the premises. A construction exhibit will be attached to the lease, defining the parameters of the shell space, and the tenant should examine this exhibit carefully. Sometimes this shell work is done by the landlord at the landlord's expense, but sometimes the landlord does the work and charges the cost thereof to the tenant. The parties will often negotiate this allocation of costs. The cost to the tenant for these construction chargebacks could be waived in whole or in part, or certain charges could be capped. If the tenant wants some concession in this regard, it would be advisable to negotiate the waiver or capped amount at the deal proposal stage so that the tenant can get an early grasp on what its overall construction budget will be. The landlord often performs this shell work so that it can control the actual size of the various premises being leased or because of governmental requirements. The tenants may be unable to obtain building permits in some jurisdictions unless some minimal code required amount of work is already performed (e.g., installation of sprinkler grids or fire alarm systems). Also, the landlord may want to control the quality of this shell work because it is the "bones" of the space and may impact future usage or have structural implications.

The tenant's architect or general contractor should review the criteria for each of these shell obligations. If the landlord installs the roof, does it also install the thermal insulation for the roof or is that the tenant's obligation? What is the insulation rating for the roof, and will that be sufficient for the tenant's purposes or insurance carrier? Even though the landlord may install the stud walls for the premises, it is typically the tenant's obligation to install the insulation behind those stud walls, so the tenant must understand what insulation material can be used. Typically the tenant would be responsible for installing the drywall on the premises. The tenant must determine what type of ceiling it will require. Some restaurants want an open ceiling concept whereas others want a dropped ceiling. Based on where the landlord has installed the sprinkler grid, will the ceiling heights be adequate for the tenant's design or will retrofitting of the sprinkler grid be required? For sprinklers, the landlord will provide a main grid, but the tenant must install the individual sprinkler heads in the premises. Where will the utility conduits be installed? Some work letters say that the location will be as determined by the landlord or as set forth on the base building drawings. The tenant needs to know this location as soon as possible because the cost of relocation would generally be borne by the tenant. What utility services will be provided other than sanitary sewer, water and electrical? Many restaurants will require gas service for cooking, and this can be a significant expense if not already stubbed to the premises. For electricity, phone, and data, the landlord may provide only an empty conduit with a pull string, meaning that the tenant must run the actual wire from the premises to the electrical panel or communications panel. It can be costly to run these lines if the distance is considerable. The work letter should specify the size of the various conduits to be supplied so that the tenant can verify that these capacities will be adequate for their usage. Sometimes the term *cold dark shell* is used. In general, this refers to the shell work referenced above without live electrical service or any HVAC system installed. A "warm shell" would be one where the landlord has or will provide the dedicated HVAC system for the premises. These are subtle differences that can cost tenants tens of thousands of dollars if they have not defined these terms in the lease.

A "vanilla" or "white-box" space is a shell space with some upgrades. These upgrades may include any or all of the following: installation of drywall on the tenant's side of the premises sanded, spackled, and ready for paint; installation of a bulkhead upon which tenant can install its exterior storefront signs; installation of rear service door; installation of HVAC system for the premises; installation of ADA-compliant restrooms; installation of acoustical ceiling and tiles; installation of electrical outlets and all wiring from the electrical panel to the premises; and pouring of a floor slab on grade. If a tenant gets a space in vanilla box condition as outlined above, then the only work that remains to be done by the tenant is installation of wall coverings, floor coverings, storefront sign, and installation of the tenant's furnishings, furniture, and equipment. Obviously, the cost of design and construction to the tenant is significantly lower if the landlord agrees to build the vanilla box at the landlord's expense and the tenant would be able to open for business sooner after delivery of possession. Vanilla box spaces are more prevalent in strip centers, but if the tenant has sufficient leverage, they can be used in the mall setting as well.

The next type of space condition is the "turnkey," which is a fully finished space. In addition to the shell work and vanilla box work described above, the turnkey space would include painting, floor and wall coverings, HVAC systems, and all trade fixtures, furnishings, and equipment needed for the operation of the restaurant. The theory behind the turnkey space is that the landlord hands over the keys to the premises and the tenant turns the key in the lock, opens the door, and begins operating for business almost immediately. All that would be left for the tenant to do would be to bring its menus, tableware, cooking and eating utensils, and food and beverage. In other words, the entire burden of constructing the restaurant is borne by the landlord. Of course, the parties may allocate the cost of the turnkey. For example, the landlord could pay for the shell space work or vanilla box work and the tenant would be obligated to pay the remainder of the cost. In some situations, one party may be obligated for the entire cost. It is essential that the lease address the design of the restaurant and the scope of the turnkey work in order to avoid disputes during the construction phase. The parties may attach a preapproved set of plans to the lease, or they may reference a prototypical set of drawings that the tenant has used for other locations. Alternatively, the lease could set forth a procedure for preparation of the plans and review by the other party, the review continuing until both parties had approved the plans. In this latter case, the parties may want to include a provision that if they cannot agree on plans within a certain period of time after lease execution, then either party may terminate the lease. Also, the lease may contain an "upset price" clause where if the bids for the job exceed a certain dollar amount, then the party obligated to pay for such excess may require rebidding or terminate the lease unless the other side agrees to contribute all or a specified portion of the excess. The turnkey space is most often used for marquee restaurants where there is serious competition for that restaurant among shopping center developers or where the tenant does not have the financial wherewithal or expertise to build a restaurant. Timing may be an issue as well. The landlord may be able to mobilize more quickly, especially if the tenant is not familiar with the permitting process and construction trades in that area.

Finally, there are "pad" deals where the landlord's only obligation is preparation of the pad. This obligation usually centers on two issues: making the pad ready for construction of tenant's building and the location of utilities. The pad is often defined as the area where the footprint of the building will be constructed along with an area surrounding the perimeter of the pad (e.g., 10 feet). If the tenant is obligated to install a dumpster pad, sidewalks, drive-through lanes, or parking, this perimeter will be expanded accordingly.

Putting the ground in pad-ready condition will often require that a certain type of suitable soil and fill material be utilized to a specific grade so that the pad will provide adequate support for the building and excavation work for foundations, sewers, utilities, or grease traps. Suitability would generally exclude construction debris, landfill materials, and hazardous materials. The pad specifications may also include the degree to which the soil must be compacted. Often the geotechnical engineer will supervise and test each level of fill material used. Many of these technical standards are governed by ASTM, which sets forth a comprehensive guide for construction industry standards. The tenant may require a report from a geotechnical engineer classifying the soil and fill suitability. The report should set out the method used or to be used to achieve the particular pad specifications. The lease may require the landlord to provide this report if it is the landlord's obligation to deliver the pad to a certain degree of suitability. Upon completion of the pad, the geotechnical engineer will often be required to certify compliance with the site specifications. Even if the landlord provides this report and certification, some tenants will hire their own expert to conduct soil testing. Whatever the scope, it is essential that the lease set out the pad specifications that landlord must satisfy.

The landlord may also be obligated to install certain utility lines to a point at the perimeter of the pad or within 5 feet of its perimeter. Often these utility lines cross over common areas or even areas owned by anchor tenants. The landlord will usually want to control construction that occurs in its common areas, especially when these lines tie into other lines already maintained by landlord. Also, if the utility lines must cross an anchor tenant parcel, the landlord is in a better position to obtain approval for installation, or the landlord may already have easement rights pursuant to a reciprocal easement agreement with the other anchor tenants. If the landlord installs the lines, then the tenant may be required to submit a point of connection plan showing where the utilities should be stubbed so that neither party would have to redo the work later to accommodate the tenant's layout of its building. The lease should specify who is responsible for the payment of any imposition charged by applicable governmental jurisdictions or utility providers, which are commonly referred to under one of the following names (list is included for illustrative purposes only and is not intended to be exhaustive): connection charges, availability fees, tie-in fees, meter fees or charges, "tap-in" or tap fees, transportation fees, or impact charges and any similar imposition charged by applicable governmental authorities or utility providers.

The lease should also specify the capacity of utility service that will be made available to the premises. Restaurants generally require greater electrical capacity than do retail tenants, so the typical 100 amp service for a shoe store may be wholly inadequate for a restaurant. Depending on its mechanical drawings and load calculations, a restaurant could require up to 800 amp service. The lease or work letter should address the electrical voltage to be provided and state whether a transformer to transform voltage from one level to another will be necessary in order to provide the requisite amperage. If a transformer is required, the lease should address whether it will be mounted at the pad or located in the common areas, in which case additional conduit and wiring will be required. The size of the water line could be significant because a pad restaurant can be a heavy user of water for cooking and cleaning. It should be determined whether the landlord or tenant or utility company will install a consumption meter and at whose expense. The size of the sewer line and its depth should be addressed as well because the tenant would like to avoid the use of sump pumps to discharge sewage. The tenant will need to know the location of the fire main for installation of its sprinkler system and where the irrigation line will be stubbed to the pad. The size, capacity, and pressure of natural gas service will need to be stipulated. The location of telephone and data transmission cables will need to be identified. The number, size, and depth of grease traps serving the premises should also be addressed.

If the landlord is performing work in the premises, the tenant may want a right to submit a punch list of incomplete or defective landlord work in the premises. After all, the tenant will ultimately be liable for most maintenance and repair of the premises during the lease term. Generally, the landlord will want this punch list submitted within a specified period of time after the landlord delivers possession of the premises to the tenant for commencement of the tenant's work. From the landlord's perspective, it wants to correct any deficiencies before the tenant undertakes a significant amount of work to minimize economic waste and cost. For example, if the landlord installs a plumbing line that is defective, it wants to know of that deficiency before the tenant pours the concrete floor slab that will cover up the plumbing line. Otherwise, there will be the added cost of drilling into the concrete and repouring the concrete slab. Most leases with punch list clauses give the tenant 30-60 days after delivery of possession to notify the landlord of defective construction; otherwise, the claim is waived. The parties may also negotiate a walk-through where the landlord and tenant representatives inspect the premises within a reasonable period of time after receipt of the punch list to verify what must be done and then a final inspection to confirm that the punch list items have been completed.

Most punch list items deal with "patent defects" (i.e., those that are visible to the naked eye). However, the premises may also contain "latent defects" (i.e., those that could not have been reasonably discoverable during any inspection of the premises). Usually the landlord lease form will disclaim any responsibility for latent defects. Often the landlord may not know exactly what a prior tenant installed, so it does not want to assume liability for matters that were not within its knowledge or control. However, the tenant may be subjected to significant hidden costs as it undertakes its demolition and construction work and discovers problem that did not appear on the as-built drawings or could not have been discovered until demolition began. If the parties agree that there will be some responsibility on the part of the landlord for latent defects, then it will limit its responsibility for those claims brought to its attention within one year after delivery of possession. At some point, there must be a right of repose where the landlord no longer has to worry about latent defects.

Some tenants will also request a warranty from the landlord that the landlord's work in the premises will be free of defective workmanship and materials for a period of one year from delivery of possession with landlord's work substantially complete. This warranty must dovetail with the warranty the landlord obtains from its general contractor or subcontractors. Otherwise, the landlord may incur out-of-pocket expense to rectify the work. Sometimes these warranties may be assigned directly to the tenant, but in other cases, the landlord may be obligated to directly enforce them on tenant's behalf.

The lease should clearly establish who is responsible for compliance with federal, state, and local accessibility requirements so that there is no misunderstanding when the punch list is submitted. In many cases, the landlord will be responsible for compliance with common areas and the tenant will be responsible for compliance with respect to the premises. Another approach is that laws of application to real estate in general will be the landlord's obligation whereas compliance with laws as a result of tenant's specific use of the premises or as a result of tenant's design or work in the premises will be tenant's obligation. In any event, most landlords will want to limit their responsibility for accessibility requirements to the scope of the landlord's work as opposed to the entire premises. For example, if the landlord is obligated to install a restroom in the premises but the tenant is responsible for all of the hardware, the landlord does not want to be liable for moving, raising, or lowering the level of toilet roll holders or faucets because the tenant did not install them at the code required heights.

Due Diligence

The condition of the premises the landlord is required to meet at delivery of possession to the tenant will dictate to a large degree the scope of the due diligence the tenant must perform either prior to or after lease execution. Obviously, a turnkey space will require less due diligence because the burden of construction will be borne solely by the landlord. A food court space generally will not require extensive due diligence either except for obtaining building and health permits or business licenses. For discussion purposes, we will assume that the tenant is taking the premises as either a pad or a shell space because this is where more extensive due diligence may be required.

In the restaurant leasing context, due diligence generally revolves around permit and licensing requirements, liquor licenses, title and survey, utility verification, soil testing, and zoning verification. Ideally, this due diligence would occur prior to lease execution, but circumstances often dictate that some or all of it will be performed after lease execution.

If the landlord is constructing a new shopping center or an additional wing or is delivering a dirt pad, then some of this information may not be available at the time of lease execution. For financing purposes or simply for establishing the tenant mix for the shopping center, the lease may be finalized far in advance of the actual delivery date. Additionally, some national restaurant chains will not expend any significant funds on a project until the lease is signed. Often this due diligence is framed in terms of an overall contingency period that enables the tenant to terminate the lease within a specified period of time after lease execution. The duration of the contingency period is hotly contested. Because the landlord will not usually spend much money on the landlord's work until it is comfortable the tenant has waived or satisfied all contingencies, a lengthy due diligence period effectively takes the space off the market until the tenant is ready to proceed. In turn, that delays the eventual opening of the restaurant or, in a worst-case scenario, compels the landlord to find a replacement tenant. For these reasons, the landlord wants the tenant to decide as soon as possible whether it is ready to move forward without conditions.

The most important contingency will be the permit contingency clause. In many landlord-oriented leases, rent commences the earlier of (a) the date tenant initially opens for business or (b) a specified number of days after landlord delivers possession of the premises to tenant, which latter date will be referred to herein as "Completion Date." The tenant does not want to be in a position where it must begin paying rent before it opens for business because that drains operating capital from the business. For that reason, the tenant must investigate how long it takes to obtain a building permit in the applicable jurisdiction. For our purposes, the term *building permit* includes all types of permits required to perform the tenant's work, including but not limited to demolition permits, zoning approvals, environmental permits, utility permits, structural permits, building permits, and certificates of occupancy but in most cases specifically excluding liquor licenses. The length of time to obtain the building permit can vary widely. In some states, it may take six months or more even with the use of a permit expediter. If the tenant cannot get its building permit prior to lease execution and the completion date is tied solely to the delivery of possession, then the tenant may have insufficient time to complete its work before rent starts. The tenant will also need to verify with its contractor the length of time it will take to perform the tenant's work once the building permit is obtained. By way of example, if the completion date in the lease is 180 days following possession but the time for obtaining permit after lease execution is 60 days and the time for performing work is 150 days, then the tenant will be obligated to pay rent 30 days before it can reasonably expect to open. This is a situation the tenant would like to avoid. If the tenant is new to the municipality, it may need this permit contingency to establish that it can obtain the permit without undue expense and in a timely manner. If it cannot, it may need to exercise its right to terminate the lease under the permit contingency clause or else renegotiate the completion date under threat of exercising its termination right.

Sometimes the permit contingency language is framed in terms of the tenant having a specified period of time (e.g., 30 days after lease execution to investigate how long it will take and what cost it will incur to obtain its building permit). In other cases, it will be structured in terms of the length of time it actually takes to obtain such permit, which is usually longer than 30 days. If the landlord agrees to permit contingency language, it prefers the former rather than the latter, but leverage and circumstances may dictate otherwise. If structured as the number of days to obtain the permit, then the tenant may negotiate a certain number of 30 day extensions to obtain the permit so long as it is diligently pursuing the same. Alternatively, the landlord may reserve the right to obtain the permit if the tenant is unsuccessful in doing so before the tenant will be permitted to terminate the lease. In many cases, the landlord will retain a comparable right to terminate the lease after a period of time unless the tenant waives the contingency because the landlord does not want the premises to be off the market indefinitely.

In some instances, the landlord may not agree to a permit contingency clause. Instead, it simply adds the expected number of days for the tenant to obtain permits to the normal period for completing the tenant's work, and that becomes the completion date. For example, if the tenant's standard time to perform the tenant's work in its premises is 120 days and the expected time to obtain permits is 60 days, then the completion date would 180 days following delivery of possession of the premises to the tenant. If the tenant agrees to this concept, it needs to confirm that the sum of the two time periods is adequate.

Another alternative to the permit contingency clauses referenced above is to tie the tenant's completion date to the later of (a) a specified number of days after delivery of possession of the premises to the tenant or (b) a specified number of days after the tenant has applied for the tenant's building permit. If the landlord agrees to tie the completion date in whole or in part to the actual receipt of the permit, then, at a bare minimum, language should be added requiring the tenant to promptly apply and diligently pursue such permits. However, diligence can be in the eye of the beholder, so to prevent misunderstandings, it might be useful to set forth specific benchmarks so that the degree of diligence can be measured to some extent. For example, the lease could set out a specific time period by which the tenant must apply for its permits after either lease execution or approval of the tenant's plans by the landlord and then resubmit based on the applicable jurisdictional authority's comments, as well as a date by which the tenant must notify the landlord that it has either obtained or been unable to obtain such permits. If the tenant fails to achieve these benchmarks, then it would forfeit the right to tie its completion date to receipt of permits. In addition, at some point, the landlord must have the right to terminate the lease or require the tenant to waive the receipt of permit as a condition of the completion date.

For a pad deal, the tenant may require an inspection period (e.g., 30–60 days) to conduct a site inspection of the premises in order to determine the suitability of the soil, to verify zoning, to perform environmental testing, or to obtain a metes and bound survey of the property or in some cases a topographical survey. This period is also used by some tenants to perform traffic studies and to evaluate the availability of utilities to the premises. The tenant may also want to obtain a new Phase I environmental report, which is a report obtained from reviewing documents on file with various federal, state, and local regulatory agencies regarding the environmental condition of the premises. In certain cases, a review of the Phase I report may lead the tenant to perform actual soil borings in order to test for potential contamination of the land. Ideally, the inspection of the pad would occur prior to lease execution, but this may not always be possible. The landlord may be filling in dirt as part of its landlord's work, but that work may not be done until after lease execution. Usually upon expiration of the inspection period, the tenant must waive the contingency or terminate the lease. If the tenant has the right to terminate, the landlord should either have the right to cure the objection or it should keep the inspection period as short as possible so that it knows when it has a firm deal.

Many restaurants derive a substantial portion of their revenues from the sale of liquor, so it is critical that the tenant understand the requirements for obtaining a liquor license within the applicable jurisdictional area. This procedure can vary widely from state to state and even between communities within a particular state. Often the tenant will need to retain a local lawyer who is familiar with the procedures for the obtainment or transfer of a liquor license. Two-way licenses (i.e., for the sale of beer and wine) are usually more readily available than the three-way license, which also includes spirits. As with the building permit contingency, the tenant should commence its due diligence well in advance of lease execution. Some authorities will not allow an application for a liquor license to be filed until the lease is fully executed, so in certain instances, the landlord and tenant may agree to a liquor license contingency clause in the lease.

The clause should set forth the general type of liquor license to be obtained (e.g., two-way or three-way). All costs and expenses of obtaining the liquor license are typically borne by the tenant, and the lease should reflect that fact. If liquor licenses are expensive in the applicable jurisdiction, the tenant may require the lease to provide that the tenant is not obligated to spend more than a designated sum for purchase of the liquor license. The lease should set forth the time period within which the tenant must apply for its liquor license after lease execution, and there should be language that the tenant must diligently pursue the same. If a diligence standard is too elastic, the landlord may insist on specific dates by which the tenant must satisfy or waive certain benchmarks of the application process. In any event, there should be a "drop dead" date by which either party may terminate the lease if the liquor license has not been obtained or cannot be obtained at a designated cost. Sometimes the lease will permit either party to extend the termination date by a specific number of 30 day periods as long as the application has been diligently pursued. Alternatively, the tenant could have the right to waive the liquor license contingency if the landlord has exercised its right to terminate. Similar to the building permit contingency, the parties could instead agree that the tenant need only investigate whether it can obtain a liquor license as opposed to actually obtaining one. This course of action would be most appropriate when the application process is not unduly burdensome. In this case, the parties could agree to a 30-45 days after lease execution in which the tenant will investigate the time period for obtaining the liquor license and would either waive or terminate the lease within that period of time. Failure to notify the landlord of its election within that time period would be deemed a waiver of the contingency and the right to terminate.

For liability reasons, the insurance coverage required by the lease to be maintained by the tenant will often be greater than for a retail merchant. The tenant should verify that it can obtain such coverage. Also, certain states may have so-called "dramshop" or liquor liability laws that impose strict liability on an owner or operator dispensing liquor to a customer who later causes death or personal injury to a third party while under the influence of alcohol. Such judgments may be a lien against the real estate itself encumbering the landlord's title to the property. Although the landlord will be insistent on adequate insurance requirements to protect itself against any such liability, including being named as an additional insured on the tenant's policy, the landlord may permit the tenant to form a special purpose entity whose only assets are the lease and the liquor license. This protects the tenant's other operations from being subject to an adverse judgment. However, if the landlord agrees to this arrangement, it will undoubtedly require a strong personal or corporate guaranty to ensure that all lease obligations are met.

Occasionally, the tenant will acquire a liquor license directly from the landlord, especially where liquor licenses are scarce or expensive. Sometimes this transaction is documented in a separate purchase and sale agreement, and at other times, it is addressed in the lease itself. Although it is beyond the purview of this discussion to cover the intricacies of this type of transaction, it is important to note that the landlord will often want a reversionary right to obtain the liquor license once the lease has expired or terminated. In most states, the grant of a liquor license is a privilege rather than a property right, so the landlord will be unable to perfect a security interest in the liquor license itself. To give the landlord some assurance that it will get the license back, a variety of strategies can be employed.

The lease can provide a right of first offer or right of first refusal for the landlord to purchase the liquor license upon expiration or earlier termination of the lease. Under the right of first offer, the tenant would have to offer to sell the license back to the landlord before it could offer the license for sale to a third party. Under the right of first refusal, the tenant could market the license and then present its best offer for the landlord to match. If the right of first offer is utilized, then the purchase price would need to be stipulated in the document. Depending on state law, it could be the fair market value at the time of the exercise or it could be the price the tenant originally paid the landlord for the liquor license, to cite two common but not exclusive methods. If the tenant is unwilling or unable to pay the entire purchase price at the time the liquor license is transferred to it from the landlord, then the landlord may require the tenant to sign a promissory note for the purchase price, which will be canceled upon transfer of the liquor license back to the landlord. Alternatively, a portion of the rent could be allocated to the purchase price of the liquor license that is amortized over some or all of the lease term.

Title and Survey

The next topic to be discussed is whether a restaurant tenant should obtain title insurance and order a survey of the premises. Generally, the tenant will order title insurance and a survey when its building is located on an outparcel, when it constitutes a freestanding premises, or where the tenant has a substantial investment in the construction of the restaurant. If the tenant will obtain a leasehold mortgage on the premises, title insurance and an ALTA survey will often be required by its mortgagee. The title commitment or a preliminary title report, which lists all recorded documents affecting title to the property, can be useful in identifying any easements that affect the restaurant parcel, as well as disclosing any restrictions or covenants that might impact the use or operation of the restaurant. The title commitment can then assist the surveyor in mapping the items shown on the commitment, such as finding utility easements, building setback lines, and establishing a legal description for the premises. Most restaurant leases provide that if the tenant desires to obtain a title commitment or a survey, it must do so during the course of its due diligence period. The survey will often contain a metes and bounds legal description or, if the parcel is part of a platted subdivision, a lot number referenced from the plat. Surveys, especially ALTA surveys, require substantial lead time, so the tenant should ensure that the time for obtaining the survey and the due diligence period are consistent. Usually the cost of the title commitment, the title policy, any endorsement to the title policy, and the survey is borne by the tenant.

It is beyond the scope of this presentation to delve into the various title exceptions to which the tenant should object or endorsements it could request. However, it is common for the tenant to request that the title insurance company delete or insure over the standard exceptions that can be addressed by an ALTA survey or an owner's affidavit. Common endorsements would include access to a public street, contiguity if the restaurant premises occupied more than one parcel, zoning to ensure that the restaurant use is permitted under the applicable zoning code, and a restrictions endorsement to provide that any access easements or reciprocal easement agreements would not be terminated as a result of a violation or default under such agreements. The latter could be very important if the premises are part of a larger shopping center that is subject to a reciprocal easement agreement that governs access to the shopping center, parking rights, and building restrictions.

To jump-start the title search, the tenant should ask the landlord to provide any existing title work or survey on the shopping center in its possession. The lease may grant the tenant the right to object to title exceptions disclosed by the title commitment. Whether the landlord is obligated to remove these exceptions is a matter of leverage during the lease negotiations. If the same can be done at minimal cost to the landlord, it may be amenable to curing such title exceptions because it does not want the tenant to terminate the lease. In most cases, however, it is optional with the landlord as to whether to cure any title exceptions and, as a result, with regard to the state of title, the tenant must "take it or leave it." The lease may provide that the tenant can terminate the lease within its sole discretion if it finds any objectionable title exceptions, or the landlord may impose a reasonableness standard or require the exception to be material in terms of costs before the tenant could terminate. Failure to object to or terminate the lease within the due diligence period for objectionable title matters will be deemed a waiver of the tenant's right with respect thereto.

Food court tenants and many tenants located within an enclosed mall or within the building of a strip center usually do not have any due diligence rights under their leases. In these cases, the tenant may ask for a representation or warranty under the lease that the landlord is the fee owner of the property or has a leasehold interest in the property that extends beyond the tenant's lease term. In addition, these tenants may require a representation or warranty from the landlord that the shopping center is zoned for the tenant's restaurant use and that there are no agreements affecting the shopping center that would impair or prohibit the use of the premises for the contemplated restaurant. The landlord may be required to indemnify the tenant against any breach of such representations or warranties. Although these representations or warranties do not give the full protection of a title policy, they would give the tenant some assurances that its occupancy will not be disturbed by title matters.

Plan Approval by Landlord

For food court tenants and local restaurants without a signature look, the plan approval process will be straightforward. The lease will require these tenants to prepare preliminary plans of the tenant's work for the landlord's review. If the space was previously occupied and only minimal construction will occur, then the preliminary plans may be combined with the working drawings. The working drawings are what the contractors will use to perform their work and are used by the restaurants to obtain bids for the cost of the tenant's work. For our purposes, the preliminary plans and working drawings will be referred to as the "tenant's plans" unless a specific distinction is noted. The lease will provide a deadline by which the tenant's plans must be submitted. It could be tied to a date after lease execution, receipt of a space layout drawing of the premises, receipt of the landlord design criteria, or some combination of the foregoing.

Before signing the lease, the tenant should confirm with its architect or space planner that the time period for preparation of plans is sufficient. Prior to lease execution, the tenant and its architect or contractor should endeavor to perform a site inspection of the premises with a landlord representative. Sometimes this is difficult to arrange if a going concern is operating from the space. The site inspection may have to occur after hours or at least during nonpeak hours. Occasionally, some degree of subterfuge is necessary so that existing employees of the current occupant are not alerted to the fact that their employer will be vacating the premises in the near future. If the space was previously occupied, the tenant should request copies of the as-built drawings of the former occupant. However, many landlords do not retain working drawings of the prior tenant because they are bulky and require a great deal of storage space. Even if it is newly constructed space, the tenant may want to review the landlord base building drawings, which are the plans the landlord used to construct the new building or addition where the premises are located. These base building drawings can assist in identifying hidden conditions that are not readily apparent from a visual inspection of the premises. With the advent of digital technology, many leases require the tenant to submit plans in a PDF or CAD format rather than paper drawings so that they can be transmitted via e-mail. This not only saves postage and delivery charges but also can expedite the entire plan review process. If the plan reviewer is on the road, that person can still access the plans on a computer or tablet. This digitization of the plan preparation will enable landlords to archive these plans for use by future space occupants.

If the as-built drawings or the base building drawings are not available, then the tenant should require that the space outline drawing in the lease show column lines, utility locations, and other conditions important to construction or retrofitting of the space. The tenant may request language in the lease that if the space outline drawing is inaccurate or there are hidden conditions in the space, then the landlord will reimburse the tenant for the additional cost of modifying its plans as needed. If the landlord agrees to this concept, then it will usually limit that reimbursement to actual out-of-pocket expenses not to exceed a specified dollar amount.

National fast-casual or sit-down restaurants may have a signature look that is reflected in their prototypical design drawings. This design is the common look that customers would see from city to city. Sometimes this prototype is attached as an exhibit to the LOI and then the lease, and at other times, it is reviewed by the landlord during the course of lease negotiations. Occasionally, there is a conflict between the prototype and the design criteria for the shopping center, and this must resolved prior to lease execution. Most landlords give substantial leeway to the tenant in terms of its interior décor. The landlord is usually most concerned about the elevation drawings and exterior appearance of the restaurant and its consistency with the remainder of the shopping center. Attaching an approved elevation drawing to the lease will often resolve the landlord's main concerns regarding a tenant prototype. Alternatively, the parties could reference a different location and specify that the space will be built in a manner substantially similar to that other location. Attaching a prototype or an elevation drawing to the lease or referencing another location's design does not obviate the need for the tenant to submit its plans for landlord review. If the landlord is performing work in advance of delivery to the tenant, it will want to see the tenant's plans so that it can incorporate its work in a manner that is consistent with the tenant prototype or elevation drawing and costs a reasonable amount. In addition, if the landlord is responsible for building the space per the prototype, it will need the working drawings so that it can obtain bids on the cost of the work and then ultimately perform the work in a manner consistent with the prototype.

The lease should clearly set forth the standard of review the landlord must apply in approving the tenant's plans. If the lease is silent, then common law or statutory standards may apply. In states where a reasonableness or good faith standard is prevailing, that would be the implied standard. Some states may not have this standard, in which case the tenant could be subject to the whim and caprice of the landlord. The best practice from the tenant's standpoint is to provide that the approval of the landlord will not be unreasonably withheld, conditioned, or delayed. If the landlord has unique design criteria for the shopping center, it may modify that standard so that it will act reasonably as long as the tenant's design is consistent with the design criteria specified or referenced in the lease. Most leases will specify the period of time during which the landlord will provide comments to the tenant on the tenant's plans and during which the tenant must respond. Restaurant drawings may require longer review periods than those for the standard retail tenant, such as a shoe store. Many landlords and restaurant operators use outside consultants to review utility loads, structural drawings, and HVAC requirements, so additional time must be built into the review time. Some tenants attempt to incorporate an alarm clock provision where if the landlord has not responded to the tenant's plans within a specified period of time, they are deemed approved. Most landlords resist this clause because that gives the tenant a blank check if, through inadvertence, a formal response is not sent within the requisite time period. If a preapproved prototype drawing and work letter are attached to the lease, the tenant is a national chain with a signature look, and the construction of the restaurant is wholly the tenant's responsibility, it may not be problematic to grant this alarm clock provision. However, even in this rare instance of granting an alarm clock provision, the tenant should be required to provide the landlord with a "second chance" notice in bold and conspicuous type that if the landlord does not respond with comments to the tenant's plans within a shortened period, then they will be deemed approved.

In certain cases, the parties may negotiate a termination right if the landlord and the tenant cannot reach agreement on the tenant's plans within a certain period of time or if the cost of construction per the landlord's requirements exceeds a certain dollar amount ("upset price"). If an upset price provision is used, the landlord may want the opportunity to bid the job itself in an effort to cut costs or to nullify the tenant's termination by agreeing to pay the excess over the upset price.

An adjunct to the plans for tenant's work is approval of its signage. Signage can take many forms. First, there will be exterior signage on the premises, and many chains have a national look they will want to use. This must be balanced against the landlord sign criteria, code requirements, and recorded restrictions contained in reciprocal easement agreements and memoranda of lease of other tenants, including but not limited to department stores, big-box users, and other restaurants. There may be size and height restrictions on this exterior signage and type of illumination. The tenant should investigate these restrictions prior to lease execution and then memorialize the resolution in the lease itself. Some sit-down restaurants may require directional signage in a large mall. The number and location of these directional signs must be determined. Often these signs are placed by the landlord and shared with other tenants. If the restaurant is located on an outlot, it may want rights to install its own monument or pylon sign. If this is permitted, the monument or pylon will generally be located on the pad the tenant occupies. Usually the tenant will be required to construct and maintain these monument or pylon signs at its expense.

A select number of restaurants may negotiate the right to place a panel on the shopping center pylon or monument sign. Often this signage is reserved for identification of the shopping center name as well as panels for the anchor tenants. Most tenants want either the top or bottom panel to improve visibility of their name. Priority is often a matter of leverage and timing. Anchor tenants who commit early to a project often get preferred location on these signs. If a restaurant is fortunate enough to locate a panel on the shopping center pylon, then the size, location, and design of the panel must be addressed along with who manufactures, installs, and maintains the tenant's panel. Sometimes an exhibit is attached to the lease showing the location and dimensions of the various panels on the pylon. The lease should also specify who maintains the pylon irrespective of the individual panels and who pays for the electricity to illuminate the pylon at night. Often this is included in the common area maintenance charge, but it can be a separate charge based on the pro rata share of each occupant of a panel on the pylon. This pro rata share is generally determined by dividing the size of the tenant's panel by the size of all panels on the pylon or monument sign.

Completion Date for Tenant's Work

Unlike traditional retail space, which can generally be constructed or renovated within 60–90 days after possession of the space is delivered to the tenant, the typical sit-down restaurant space will take between 180 and 270 days to construct depending on the condition of the premises at delivery and the type of restaurant that will operate from the premises. If the space is in a food court and is delivered in shell condition or was previously occupied and the new tenant is performing a minor renovation, then the 60- to 90-day time period may be appropriate. In many cases, a fast-casual or table-service restaurant that is remodeling an existing space may be able to perform its work in less than 180 days. Spaces that are delivered in shell condition or circumstances where the tenant is constructing its own building on a pad may require between 180 and 270 days for construction. If the landlord is building a turnkey space, then the tenant may need only 60–90 days to install its interior décor and open for business. It is not just the actual number of days to construct the premises that must be considered. If the tenant does not have a permit contingency in the lease, then it must also factor in the number of days that will be required to obtain its building permit. For example, if the time for construction is typically 60 days and it takes 30 days to obtain a permit, then the parties may agree that the tenant's date for completion of tenant's work will be 90 days. In the absence of a permit contingency, the risk of obtaining the building permit rests solely on the tenant, so it is essential that the tenant focus on the permitting period prior to lease execution. Many municipalities will not grant a building permit in the absence of a fully executed lease. The key point for the restaurant operator is to account for all of these factors when it agrees to a specific date for completion of its work. The landlord lease form will typically start rent the earlier of the date tenant opens for business or the date for completion of the tenant's work. The tenant does not want to be in the position of being obligated to pay rent prior to opening for business. Irrespective of which of the above conditions are negotiated in the lease, the provision generally states that it is the latest to occur of the conditions before the completion start date is triggered.

Many savvy tenants negotiate certain conditions that must be met before the clock starts ticking on their completion date. To some extent, these may overlap the contingencies discussed above that enable one or both parties to terminate the lease if the events described in the contingencies do not occur. The most obvious condition is the delivery of the premises. If landlord work is required, then the lease should specify that the delivery of possession will occur with the landlord's work substantially complete or complete subject to punch list items. Certain landlord work may not be able to be performed until the tenant has submitted certain plans or completed a portion of its work, so this work should be excluded from the landlord delivery obligation; otherwise, a separate delivery date should be established for that work. Another condition could be lease execution. Due to company policies and other business reasons, some tenants cannot begin preparation of plans or begin tenant work prior to a fully executed lease. This also gives the tenant some assurance that the deal will not get retraded after the tenant signs the lease but before the landlord signs it. Once the tenant has spent substantial money or signed contracts for the tenant's work, it would be difficult to back out of a deal if the landlord attempted to change a material term.

Receipt of a building permit is another common condition in restaurant deals. This was discussed extensively above. The upshot is that the tenant should be required to diligently apply for and pursue such permits. Specific dates or timetables may be necessary to refine the extent of the due diligence required. At some point, the landlord may insist on the right to terminate the lease or otherwise reduce the tenant's construction period by the number of days the tenant has not received its permit beyond a specified date. Approval of the tenant's plans by the landlord can also be a condition. The landlord will insist that this condition of plan approval be tied to the tenant's strict adherence to the dates required for submission and resubmission of plans in the lease.

Occasionally, a tenant with substantial clout may be able to negotiate a condition that the landlord must have obtained a subordination, non-disturbance, and attornment agreement (SNDA) with the holder of the first mortgage or deed of trust on the shopping center. On an order of magnitude, the capital investment in a restaurant is significantly greater than that of a typical apparel merchant. If the landlord defaults on its mortgage, the lender could foreclose on the shopping center and eradicate the restaurant operator's right to possession. The tenant's entire investment could be at risk, or it could be required to renegotiate its lease on less favorable terms. To avoid this result, a national tenant may require this SNDA, which essentially says that as long as the tenant performs under the lease, the lender or future landlord will abide by the terms of the lease. If the landlord is compelled to tie the opening date or completion date to the tenant's receipt of an SNDA, a request to the lender should be made early in the lease negotiations so that the SNDA can be finalized contemporaneously with lease execution. Otherwise, the landlord is at the mercy of the tenant and the lender to negotiate a document over which the landlord has little or no control.

Sometimes tenants will request that their completion date be subject to "force majeure" delays or other delays beyond their reasonable control. If the landlord agrees to such an exception, then the tenant should be required to notify the landlord within a specified number of days of the occurrence of the delay, the reason for the delay, and the expected period of delay in order to invoke a force majeure delay. The reason for this notice is two-fold. First, the landlord would like to assist the tenant in overcoming the delay. The sooner the tenant is open, the sooner the rent begins. Second, it is difficult to assemble a record of delays long after the fact. If the tenant opens 30 days after it was required to do so and the landlord bills the tenant rent from the original completion date, then the tenant may dispute why it is being billed for that 30 days if it thinks its late opening was due a force majeure delay. Memories fade, employees change, contractors move on to other jobs, and paperwork may be lost or destroyed, so it becomes a war of e-mails. That is not a good way to start a long-term relationship.

The tenant may also consider adding a blackout period to the lease during which it is not required to accept possession or to initially open for business. In a cold weather climate, the tenant who is obligated to construct a building on a pad would not want to begin its work when there is snow, ice, and frozen ground. In a coastal operation, such a tenant might not want to begin during the height of tornado or hurricane season. Irrespective of the weather, some tenants may not want to undertake construction during their peak season because the emphasis then is on turning tables as quickly as possible. Devoting time and energy to new construction may divert personnel from maximizing profits at existing locations. There may be budgetary constraints where a set amount of capital expenditures are approved by a board of directors or senior management for a particular calendar or fiscal year.

Similarly, the blackout period may apply to periods when the tenant is not required to initially open for business. For example, the post-Christmas season in January and February is often a soft period for sales at shopping malls, with customer traffic often reduced during this time. A restaurant may not want to have its initial or grand opening during this period of time because first impressions can be critical to customer perceptions. A restaurant may want to time its initial opening to a particular holiday (e.g., Thanksgiving Day, Christmas Day, or Mother's Day) when families are more likely to shop or eat out together. A restaurant near a football stadium or basketball arena may want its initial opening to occur around the start of the football or basketball season, respectively. The factors that may influence opening are too numerous to count. The important point is that the tenant must determine when its ideal opening time would be and then verify that the plan submission dates, permit dates, and completion dates in the lease will coincide with that projected opening. Otherwise, the tenant could be opening at a time when demand is low and sales are poor.

Construction Allowances

Some tenants are provided a construction allowance as an inducement to enter into a lease. This allowance generally takes the form of either a cash payment or a rent credit. The allowance is used to defray a portion of the costs of completing the tenant's work. Some leases limit the allowance to the cost of permanent leasehold improvements and soft costs related thereto whereas others allow it also to be used to defray the cost of the tenant's fixtures, furnishings, and equipment package (FF&E). If the tenant is relying on this allowance to pay for its FF&E, it needs to specify that in the lease; otherwise, the landlord may reject that portion of the allowance request when it comes time to pay. Many leases cap the cash allowance at the lesser of the actual cost of completing tenant's work or a fixed dollar amount, so it is vital that the tenant understand what the construction allowance can be used for.

Because restaurants typically require substantial cash outlays for construction, the restaurant tenant may need to negotiate for progress payments of the cash allowance. From the landlord's perspective, the landlord wants to pay the cash allowance when the tenant's work is complete, when the tenant has opened for business, when the tenant has paid the first month's rent, and when the tenant has submitted all lien waivers for the tenant's work. However, the tenant may not have adequate liquidity to fund the cost up front and then wait for reimbursement from the landlord. Progress payments can take a variety of forms. The most common approach is a draw based on percentage of completion. For example, a payment of 33% of the cash allowance when 33% of the tenant's work is complete, a second payment of 33% of the cash allowance when 66% of the tenant's work is complete, and the remaining 34% of the cash allowance when 100% of the tenant's work is complete and the tenant is open for business. A slight modification of this approach would be for the third payment to be 24% of the cash allowance with a final payment of 10% of the cash allowance upon receipt of final lien waivers. A variation of this approach is that the draws be based on a specified amount of expenditures (e.g., the tenant would apply for payment when it had incurred expenses in increments of $100,000 or more).

It is important that the tenant understand what paperwork it must submit to receive a payment. Otherwise, the tenant may not get reimbursed on time and then mechanic's liens get filed by anxious contractors, which can create a domino effect, where future applications for payment are not paid because of existing liens. These requirements may be dictated by the landlord's lender, or they may be based on internal audit policies of the landlord. For progress payments, the landlord may require an initial schedule of values that gets updated with each payment request. The schedule of values will set forth the overall cost of the tenant's work (permanent leasehold improvements and tenant's FF&E package) and then allocate percentages to each line item of tenant's work. This schedule of values not only gives the landlord a general idea of the total cost of the tenant's work but also shows what proportion of the tenant's work is being paid for by the landlord and what proportion is used for permanent leasehold improvements. It can assist the landlord in avoiding a situation where the general contractor gets upside down, meaning that he has been paid for more than he has completed or to alert the landlord that the tenant will likely have insufficient funds to complete the tenant's work.

Lien waivers from the general contractor, subcontractors, and suppliers are generally required before the landlord will issue a check for progress payments. Because mechanic's liens attach to the real estate, the landlord does not want to be in the position of paying for the same work twice, which could occur if the tenant does not pay the general contractor or if the general contractor does not pay the subcontractors and then the tenant or the general contractor files for bankruptcy or is otherwise judgment-proof. Additionally, any mechanic's liens against the mortgaged shopping center could trigger defaults under the landlord's mortgage or other loan documents. If a tenant has a substantial net worth, there is a creditworthy guaranty on the lease, or the general contractor has provided an adequate payment and performance bond, the landlord may be flexible in terms of what lien waivers are required. It may agree that the lien waiver of the general contractor only is required, or it may require lien waivers only from contractors and subcontractors over a specified dollar amount (e.g., $5,000) because for some jobs, it may be difficult to get a lien waiver from a subcontractor who did a minimal amount of work.

If the tenant is in dispute with a contractor, then bonding over the claim will suffice as a substitute for the lien waiver. This procedure entails obtaining a bond from an approved surety company in an amount equal to at least 150% of the amount of the claim so that any mechanic's lien will be removed as an encumbrance on the landlord's title to the shopping center. The bond becomes the security to assure the contractor that it will get paid if it prevails on its claim. If the period for filing a mechanic's lien has expired or if the contractor failed to comply with some statutory requirement for perfecting its mechanic's lien, then from an attorney authorized to practice in that state, the landlord may accept an opinion letter stating that the claim does not give rise to a mechanic's lien.

Some landlords may require invoices from the individual contractors rather than an overall invoice from the general contractor. Some landlords may require the tenant to provide proof of payment of such invoices before it makes the progress payment. This gets to the heart of the matter. The landlord prefers that the allowance be used as reimbursement rather than as the primary source of payment. Some tenant may not have the liquidity; therefore, they view the landlord as a construction lender of sorts. Before the lease is signed, both the landlord and the tenant need to determine which arrangement will be implemented; otherwise, problems may surface. Some landlords may require proof of sufficient funding by the tenant from the tenant's bank or require a letter of credit line so that the landlord has some assurance that the tenant's work can be completed lien free. The landlord may require financial statements of the tenant or general contractor so that it can assess whether there is adequate liquidity to finish the tenant's work. The landlord may require the tenant to deposit its fund for the tenant's work into an escrow account, which will be dispersed by a third-party escrow agent such as a title company in draws as outlined in the lease. In some cases, the construction allowance may be deposited into the same escrow account and paid out proportionately with withdrawals from the tenant's funds.

The landlord may require certificates or affidavits from the general contractor or the supervising architect that a certain percentage or dollar amount of the tenant work shown on the invoices is complete. The landlord may require a formal AIA application for payment, or it may have its own form. Prior to final payment, the landlord may require a copy of the tenant's certificate of occupancy and a copy of the as-built drawings of the premises.

It is the authors' experience that most unsophisticated tenants do not understand the amount of paperwork that will be required to pay the tenant allowance either in a lump sum or through progress payments. Even if the tenant cannot negotiate any changes to the landlord's requirements, the tenant must at least be prepared to obtain the necessary paperwork. Failure to do so will imperil the tenant's ability to get paid on time with the unfortunate result that the tenant may find itself embroiled in lawsuits.

If the allowance is a rent credit, then the lease must delineate when the rent credit begins, what it is a credit against, and what percentage of the rent can be taken as a credit. Often the rent credit begins when the tenant initially opens for business, but any trigger date can be negotiated. If the landlord has adequate cash flow on the shopping center, it may permit a 100% credit against all rental charges or at least against the minimum rent until the credit is exhausted. If there is a pledge of the rents to a lender as security for a loan, the rent credit may be limited to a certain percentage of the rent to be paid by the tenant (e.g., 50%). This limitation might be necessary to satisfy the debt service coverage ratio on the loan. Sometimes the credit is permitted only against the percentage rent. This would shift the risk of the rent credit to the tenant because it might not ever achieve sufficient sales to benefit from the credit.

Repairs and Maintenance of the Premises

An often overlooked but critical component of a restaurant lease is the delineation of who is responsible for repairs and maintenance to the premises during the lease term. There is little to worry about when everything is shiny and new and covered by warranties, but with the passage of time, pipes break, wires fray, equipment quits working, roofs leak, and other problems arise. Most leases take one of two approaches. The first approach is that the landlord will maintain its work during the lease term and the tenant will maintain its work during the lease term. However, this approach will not work in many situations. For example, the tenant could be taking an existing space in an as-is condition. If the roof leaks but it was waterproof at the time the tenant took possession, then the roof was not part of either party's description of work, so the potential for finger-pointing increases. Also, the landlord does not want to assume this ongoing obligation because it is not actively engaged in the tenant's business. This dichotomy between landlord's work and tenant's work may work best where the construction was a build-to-suit or otherwise involved construction of a new space where construction is starting from scratch. In those cases, it is usually clear who built what.

The more common approach in restaurant leases is that once any applicable warranty period expires, all repair and maintenance obligations in the premises are the tenant's responsibility except for specifically defined items. To avoid any gap between what the landlord maintains and the tenant maintains, it is not uncommon for the landlord lease to add a catch-all phrase that the tenant is responsible for all items that are not specifically the landlord's obligation under the lease. This makes sense because most of the wear and tear in the premises will be a result of the tenant's operation in the premises. Often the landlord will maintain responsibility for repairs or replacements to the roof, foundation, and structural components of the premises. Work on these items can affect other portions of the building in which the premises are located and could affect the structural integrity of the building itself. The restaurant tenant has a short-term interest in getting the work done as cheaply as possible whereas the landlord wants the work done so that problems may not resurface. If the tenant does a shoddy job of repairing the roof or waterproofing the floor, it may cause damage to other tenant spaces; then the landlord has insurance claims confronting it.

Many tenants will attempt to expand the scope of the landlord's maintenance and repair obligations. Generally, the tenant will not have access to areas beyond the four corners of its space, so it will want the landlord to maintain all utility lines, pipes, ducts, and conduits to the point of connection to the premises and to maintain all such items that pass through but do not exclusively serve the premises. The restaurant tenant might also request that the landlord maintain gutters, downspouts, and the like. If the restaurant premises have an exterior façade, then the parties should address who maintains this exterior. The landlord may want that exterior to harmonize with the rest of the exterior of the remainder of the shopping center, so even if it is the tenant's obligation, the design and any changes to the façade would be subject to the landlord's prior approval. If this exterior was part of the base building that the landlord constructed, then it might assume responsibility for repairs and maintenance to the exterior façade. Often the tenant will be required to maintain the doors, vestibules, courtyards, and windows that face outside.

For a pad tenant who constructed its own building, the lease generally provides that the tenant will be responsible for all maintenance of the building and its improvements, including any exterior patios or outside seating areas. The lease should address who is responsible for maintenance of landscaping around the building and hardscaping (e.g., sidewalks). If the tenant has its own dedicated parking, it may also have the obligation for cleaning, paving, and resurfacing the parking lot. If the tenant is simply leasing the pad on which its building sits, then the obligation for the parking lot and other common areas generally rests with the landlord.

The most problematic maintenance issue revolves around maintenance of the HVAC system serving the premises. If the premises are served by a central plant system that services other tenants within the shopping center or a zone within a shopping center, then the lease will likely require the tenant to pay a charge for the generation of heating and cooling to the premises. This is most often found in an enclosed mall setting. The charge covers both the supply of heating and cooling to the premises and maintenance of the central plant system. There are a variety of names for this charge (e.g., Central Plant Charge, HVAC Charge, Energy Charge, and Environmental Charge). The good news for the tenant that is served by a central plant system is that the tenant will have no responsibility for maintaining, repairing, or replacing the central plant system as that will be the landlord's obligation and such costs are generally already factored into the charge. The tenant's primary obligation would be maintenance of the thermostat and distribution ductwork within the premises.

However, there may be instances where tying into the central plant system is not practical. For example, a 2,500-square-foot restaurant will require more cooling than a 2,500-square-foot shoe store because the restaurant will generate more heat due to cooking and the mass of people within the restaurant. The load demands for a restaurant may be too great for the central system to handle. The landlord does not want other tenants complaining about how hot their stores are, especially when the primary reason is that the restaurant is draining so much of the capacity. Also, restaurants have different peak hours and are generally open longer in the evenings than are the retail tenants. This adds to the cost charged to the restaurant and may become cost prohibitive. In addition, many shopping centers, especially strip centers, do not have central plants. Each space is served by an individual rooftop HVAC unit.

Whatever the reason, if the premises are to be served by an individual unit, then the parties must address several issues. Who will be responsible for initial installation of the unit? If the landlord is responsible for installation of a new unit, then the tenant should require at least a one-year warranty on the unit, with a five-year warranty on the compressor. The lease should also provide that the warranties will be assignable to the tenant or at least that the landlord will enforce them on the tenant's behalf. If the tenant is taking over a space with an existing HVAC unit, then the tenant should examine its condition as part of its field study prior to lease execution and get an estimate from a third-party vendor as to its remaining useful life. Many landlord-oriented leases provide that the tenant takes possession of the premises in an as-is condition. The tenant may insist that the landlord represent the HVAC to be in good working condition at the time the premises are delivered. It may ask for an increase in its construction allowance to defray any immediate repair or upgrade costs. The parties should specifically negotiate the maintenance obligations once any warranty or representation expires. In most cases, the burden will fall on the tenant. Cleaning filters and getting general tune-ups on a periodic basis will often be required of the tenants. The most nettlesome dispute is between repairs and replacement. The parties could negotiate that individual repairs not exceeding a certain dollar amount are always the tenant's obligation; then there could be some allocation of the cost above that threshold. If the tenant is responsible for replacing its individual HVAC unit, then that can be an expensive proposition, especially if it occurs late in the lease term. The tenant does not want to spend a huge amount of money to replace a unit only to give the benefit of the new unit to a future occupant. In some cases, the parties will prorate the cost of the new system based on the remaining lease term, including any options. That way, the tenant is paying only for that portion of the capital cost that occurred while its lease term was still in effect. If the tenant is responsible for installation, maintenance, or replacement of the individual unit, it should verify that the lease gives it access or easement rights to the roof as well as any other portions of the shopping center that are necessary to perform its obligations.

In virtually all cases, these maintenance and repair obligations are subject to the release and waiver of subrogation clauses in the lease. The release and waiver of subrogation clauses essentially provide that if damage to the property of either party is covered or required to be covered by insurance, then it waives any claim against the other party to the extent of such required coverage and agrees to include in its insurance policy a clause that the insurer who pays the claim will not sue the party that caused the damage. For example, if the landlord repaired the roof but it leaked and rain damaged merchandise in the premises, the tenant would waive any claim against the landlord for that damage and instead seek reimbursement from its insurance company. Ordinarily, if an insurance company pays a claim, it is subrogated or "stands in the shoes" of the insured party and can sue the wrongdoer to recover its payment on the claim. Under waiver of subrogation, the insurer relinquishes the right to recover the amounts it paid to its insured. The waiver of subrogation is customarily included in insurance policies insuring commercial property. Two important considerations should be addressed in the boilerplate release and subrogation clauses. First, the lease should specify whether the waiver applies to all of the damage or just the portion for which the insured is reimbursed. Generally, the party who allegedly caused the damage will want the release to apply even if the insured party does not submit a claim to its insurance company. In other cases, the parties may limit the release to the extent of insurance reimbursement and reserve the right to sue for the unreimbursed portion. The second consideration is whether the damaged party insured the premises sufficiently. If a party has a huge deductible or self-insures, then these factors must be taken into account in terms of the release and waiver. The release and waiver language should be written so that the deductibles or self-insured retentions are deemed insurance for purposes of the release and waiver. Otherwise, the damaged party could skirt the release and waiver simply by under insuring or self-insuring.

Complicating matters is the indemnification clause. The standard landlord-oriented lease will provide that the tenant indemnifies, defends, and holds the landlord harmless from any and all liabilities, expenses, and claims for damage arising out of or in any way connected with the tenant's use of the premises. For example, if the ceiling was the landlord's responsibility and a leak from a restaurant above the premises caused damage to the tenant's carpeting, then absent any clause to the contrary, the tenant might be barred from making a claim against the landlord for that damage. Often the parties will negotiate exceptions to this indemnity for the landlord's negligence, willful misconduct, or breach of the lease. In addition, a reciprocal indemnity may be negotiated in which the landlord indemnifies the tenant from the landlord's negligence or from willful misconduct or breach of the lease. How does this impact the release and waiver clause discussed above? The tenant will cite the landlord indemnification to recover for the damage, and the landlord will cite the release and waiver of subrogation and tenant indemnification clauses. Ideally, the lease should contain a supremacy clause. Logically, the release and waiver of subrogation clause should prevail because that is why the lease requires the tenant to carry insurance, but it is an open question unless the lease specifies the primacy of the clauses. The purpose of this discussion is not to delve into matters of insurance law, but rather to put the parties on notice that insurance, waiver, and indemnification provisions may have some impact on the repair obligations under the lease. The parties must make certain that the clauses are consistent with each other and that there is a clear pecking order should damage to the premises occur.

Surrender of the Premises

Virtually all commercial leases contain a surrender clause specifying the condition in which the tenant must leave the premises at the expiration or earlier termination of the lease term. Usually the premises will be required to be in the same condition as when the tenant opened for business subject to reasonable wear and tear. The tenant may need to negotiate additional exceptions so that it does not incur added expenses when it vacates the premises. Most importantly, the tenant will want the right to remove all of its proprietary, trademarked, or logoed fixtures, furnishings, and equipment. Some restaurant chains have a specific prototype or look that customers can easily identify. The tenant does not want another user to copy this look. In fact, the tenant may need to remove these items in order to protect any trademark it has in those logos or that prototype. The landlord should be amenable to this removal so long as the tenant repairs any damage to the premises resulting from such removal.

Some leases require the tenant to remove all of the tenant's trade fixtures, furnishings, and removable equipment at the end of the lease term. Otherwise, the landlord has to pay to haul it away if it is old or obsolete and unlikely to be used by a future occupant. Generally, the tenant will be required to remove its storefront sign because it would not be of use to any future occupant of the space. Some leases say that if the tenant does not remove its trade fixtures, furnishings, and removable equipment by the end of the term or within a specified number of days thereafter, then the landlord can dispose of it in any manner it so chooses at the tenant's expense. The lease should clarify whether the tenant is required to remove its property or if it is optional. It should also specify whether specific items will remain. For example, if the landlord built a turnkey space for the tenant, then the landlord may not want the tenant to remove anything except the tenant's personal property. In virtually all cases, the landlord will want permanent leasehold improvements and permanent fixtures to remain. If the tenant has financed or leased restaurant equipment, then the lease should address the rights of the tenant or its third-party lender or equipment lessor to remove the financed or leased equipment. Other common exceptions to the condition of the premises on surrender date would be damage caused by casualty that is the landlord's obligation to restore under the lease and alterations to the premises that are permitted by the lease or otherwise approved by the landlord.

Often what stays or goes hinges on what constitutes a "fixture." Without delving into common law principles or case law, the prevailing view is that anything that is bolted down, screwed down, glued down, or nailed down is a fixture and must stay unless the lease specifically provides otherwise. For example, walls, flooring, doors, recessed or pendant lighting, HVAC equipment, ceilings, cabinets, sinks, faucets, toilets, stoves, ovens, freezers, and counters would ordinarily be considered fixtures. Tables, chairs, lamps, wall decorations, computer equipment, and cash registers would not be considered fixtures.

Some leases may set forth a specific de-branding procedure of what must be done before the tenant vacates. For example, the tenant could be required to remove storefront signs, repair sign bands, and patch bolt holes. It could be required to apply black visqueen on interior storefront windows so that no one can see inside. It could be required to patch nail holes and paint the walls a neutral color as designated by the landlord. It could be required to remove all cash wrap and point-of-sale equipment. It could be required to sweep or vacuum the floors and remove all debris so that the premises are in broom-clean condition for the next occupant. These are among the most common but by no means exhaustive requirements. The key point is that the parties should address the surrender condition during the lease negotiations so as to minimize misunderstandings, costs, and even defaults when the term has ended.

Chapter 4

Exhibits for Restaurants Leases

Access and Visibility

An important but sometimes overlooked aspect of the lease is the list of exhibits that are often appended to the leases. In many instances, these exhibits are prepared by engineers and architects, so the attorneys do not spend much time reviewing them. However, it is essential that the attorney ensure that these exhibits are consistent with the so-called legalese in the lease. The landlord usually reserves a broad right to expand, renovate, or modify the shopping center. It will have the right to add to or subtract from the size and dimensions of the shopping center, parking spaces, and entrances and exits to the shopping center. An exhibit to the lease showing the current layout of the shopping center may be attached, but typically there is no representation or warranty that this layout will remain the same throughout the lease term. In fact, the exhibit may contain language in small print disclaiming any such representations or warranties.

The first level of concern for the restaurant tenant should be to preserve its expected access and visibility. Depending on the type of restaurant use, this can take a variety of forms. For a food court tenant, leverage and practicality may dictate that the only concession the landlord will grant, if any, is that it will not affect access to or visibility of the premises in a materially adverse manner. Although this is an elastic concept, it may offer some protection so that its storefront sign and menu board can be viewed by customers passing by the food court. After all, the food court tenant does not want a large plant or tree blocking its visibility, nor does it want an escalator installed so that the tenant is underneath the escalator and cannot be easily seen by the mall patrons. On the other hand, the food court tenant may ask for some representation in the lease that any existing escalators or elevators remain because a great deal of traffic may feed from these access points. In addition, if an anchor tenant is located near the food court or a mall entrance is nearby, the tenant may ask for some protection in terms of a co-tenancy for the anchor or a representation that either the mall access will remain during the lease term or comparable substitute access will be provided. The food court tenant may also request that the food court contain a minimum number of seats so that customers are not jockeying for a limited number of tables. Although this issue does not directly impact access, if people have nowhere to sit, then access becomes a secondary concern unless the food court is strictly "grab-and-go." The food court tenant should carefully examine the rights of the landlord to remodel or renovate the shopping center. The landlord may have reserved the right to close off certain parts of the shopping center to perform construction or to add scaffolding. Either of these circumstances could impact the food court tenant's business in a significant way. In anticipation of either of these or similar events occurring, the food court tenant may ask for lease language granting rent abatement if the impairment to access or visibility occurs. If a landlord grants this rent abatement, it will usually condition the abatement upon proof by the tenant in terms of a sales decline over a specified period of time (e.g., 90 days) and a sunset clause that the rent abatement ceases upon elimination of the impairment or expiration of a particular period of time, whichever first occurs. The food court tenant should also carefully review the rules and regulation applicable to food court tenants. Typically, this is included in the body of the lease or is attached as an exhibit. The landlord always reserves the right to modify these rules and regulations, which could have some impact on access or visibility. The sophisticated food court tenant will request language that all rules and regulations will be uniformly applied against similarly situated tenants and will not materially increase the tenant's obligations or decrease its rights under the lease.

Protected Zones

The fast-casual or sit-down restaurant may have to go beyond general lease language. Access, parking, and visibility are critical for these businesses. If located in an enclosed mall, many of them have exterior entrances that lead from the parking lot and prominent storefront signs that identify the restaurant. They may have paid premium rents for their locations. They may be adjacent to a mall entrance or next to an anchor tenant. Even in the strip mall setting, the axiom, "location, location, location" is germane. Certain restaurant tenants may need to negotiate an exhibit to the lease to protect these rights. Although many terms are used to describe this exhibit (e.g., *protected zone*, *critical zone*, or *no-build zone*), they all address the same concern. The exhibit would define an area where no additional buildings or structures could be constructed without the tenant's consent. Depending on the leverage of the parties, any changes to the exhibit might be subject to the tenant's reasonable consent or the tenant's sole discretion.

If the landlord intends to reserve certain parcels for future development, these areas should be reflected on the exhibit as well. For future development parcels, the exhibit or the lease may establish limitations on the elevations of the buildings or a maximum footprint because both of these can impact visibility and parking. An elevation limitation should address whether that limit is inclusive or exclusive of any parapets, signs, or other architectural features that extend above the roof line of the building. Of course, both the landlord and tenant should verify that the protected zone does not violate any document affecting the shopping center, such as a reciprocal easement agreement or anchor tenant lease. The landlord certainly cannot commit to protect an area that is owned by another party, such as an anchor tenant, or where another party has already reserved the right to expand into this protected zone. Although the tenant may rely to some extent on the representations of the landlord, it is essential that as part of its due diligence the tenant verify these commitments through its title examination.

This exhibit or a separate exhibit may also show the parking field that cannot be altered. Usually the landlord will reserve the right to change the striping or angle of the parking spaces but may agree to a minimum number of parking spaces in the protected zone or parking field. This minimum amount could be a numerical figure (e.g., 100 spaces or one space per seat), or it could be couched in terms of code requirements or as modified by variance or other governmental approval. Most customers do not want to walk long distances to get to the restaurant entrance, so ample parking in the vicinity of the restaurant is critical. Some restaurant leases may prohibit high-traffic but nonretail uses such as health clubs from being located nearby because they consume so much parking but are destinations in and of themselves.

In addition, the protected zone exhibit may identify an access corridor that the tenant wants preserved during its lease term. For example, a main entrance to the shopping center or a ring road surrounding the parking lot with an access way that leads directly to the restaurant or to the parking spaces near the restaurant is very advantageous to the restaurant. This "easy-in, easy-out" ingress and egress is an ideal scenario. There may be multiple access points that lead to this area of the shopping center. In any event, the tenant does not want these existing access points disturbed because that could have a significant impact on traffic to its restaurant. However, the landlord does not want to restrict its future development opportunities. Relocating one or more of these access points could be critical to attracting a new anchor or renovating the property. This issue will often be subject to heated discussions. If the tenant has the leverage, the landlord may agree to identify a key access point that will not be disturbed or to identify a substitute area, if known, where that key access point could be relocated.

Even if a tenant is unable to extract any concessions in terms of a protected zone or an access point, it should nonetheless clearly understand the impact that material changes to its access, visibility, or parking could have on its business. It may want to consider a right to terminate the lease or to abate rent if sales decline significantly after a material change is made. Or it may want to consider a shorter lease term with more options to renew the lease in order to monitor the landlord's redevelopment activities. In a worst-case scenario, the tenant may need to invoke its right to "go dark" or cease operations if it negotiated such a clause in its lease.

Parking

For some fast-casual or table-service restaurants, a measurable portion of their sales may derive from take-out or carryout purchases. A customer who ordered ahead does not want to park a long distance from the restaurant entrance simply to conduct a brief transaction. If convenient parking is not available, the customer is unlikely to order from that location again. For this reason, some fast-casual or table-service restaurants will request a limited number of parking spaces (usually two or three) that will be designated for parking by customers who made carryout orders. Before granting this request, the landlord must first determine whether code or some third-party agreement allows this reservation of spots. An anchor lease or a reciprocal easement agreement may limit or prohibit these reserved spaces, especially if they are near an anchor or a mall entrance or are located on parking owned by the anchor tenant. The lease should specify who is required to obtain any necessary governmental or third-party approvals for such designated spaces. If these spaces are permitted, the lease will usually require the tenant to post and maintain the signs indicating that these designated spaces are reserved for carryout and to remove such signs at the expiration or earlier termination of the lease. The tenant is often given the responsibility of enforcing the restriction, and the lease should clearly state that any acts taken by the tenant to enforce this obligation are expressly covered by the indemnity clause of the lease. The landlord may need to reserve the right to relocate such spaces should there be a major redevelopment or renovation of the shopping center or if required by governmental authority.

If a tenant is permitted a certain number of "to-go" parking spaces, those spaces are often shown on a lease exhibit as well. These carryout spaces are more common with respect to the fast-casual restaurants where time is of the essence for customers. Not surprisingly, the tenant will want these spaces as close to the restaurant entrance as possible. As noted above, due diligence is in order. Anchor leases, reciprocal easement agreements, and parking code requirements will need to be reviewed to ensure that there is no violation if a right to these spaces are granted. The lease should address whether the spaces are exclusive or non-exclusive to the tenant and whether they apply to all hours of operation of the restaurant or just peak hours. Generally, the tenant will be obligated to install and maintain signage indicating that the reservation of these spaces is for their customers and the landlord may reserve the right to relocate them if required by code or anchor lease or if the tenant ceases offering a carryout service. Policing of these spaces is occasionally addressed in the lease. Although the landlord does not want a lease obligation to monitor who is using these spaces on an hourly basis, at the same time, it has control over the common areas and does not want tenants having other customers' cars towed. Usually this will be handled informally with a note left by security on the violator's car that in the future, the violator may be towed if he or she is not a carryout customer of the tenant.

Employee parking occasionally can be a nettlesome issue. The landlord wants the customers of the shopping center to have the most convenient parking spaces, which will usually be the ones closest to the mall or store entrances. The landlord does not want the employees monopolizing these spaces for their own use during working hours. The lease may reserve broad rights for the landlord to establish employee parking areas. The tenant and its employees should clearly understand where employees are permitted to park. As with valet parking, it will often be in areas toward the back of the parking lot or in other areas that are not customarily used by customers. For some centers, the employee parking may be off site. The lease may require the tenant to provide license numbers for its employees. The lease may also authorize the landlord to tow violating vehicles or assess fines and for the tenant to indemnify against all such costs. Usually the tenant will ask for some prior notice (e.g., an hour) or for the fine or towing to apply only for a repeated violation. If parking is very tight at a shopping center, an exhibit may set forth the parking areas where employees must park.

The most significant concern for the restaurant tenant will be the safety of its employees leaving work after the standard shopping center hours. For restaurants that provide bar service, it is very likely that its employees on the last shift will be leaving work when it is dark. If the lease does not provide that mall security will routinely patrol the employee parking area after hours, then the restaurant operator may be compelled to hire its own security. The tenant may be required to implement procedures such as the buddy system or a security guard available to escort employees to their vehicles so that its employees do not walk to their cars alone. The tenant may want assurance in the lease that the employee parking areas will be well lit and policed for at least an hour after the restaurant's closing time. The lease may require the landlord to provide late-night lighting in areas where the patrons and employees have parked. These hours should be specified in the lease. The landlord may assess a surcharge for the cost of this late-night lighting, which is prorated among those tenants staying open beyond the standard shopping center hours. An exhibit may define this late-night lighting area. In addition, a store manager may be carrying large sums of cash for deposit in a local bank. The tenant may ask for one or two dedicated spots near the store or mall entrance for use by the night manager. If this is granted, it too could be shown on an exhibit so that there is no confusion years later when the management of the restaurant or the shopping center changes. Nothing can hurt customer traffic at a mall quicker than the commission of crimes against person or property, so the tenant should ensure that either the shopping center owner or the tenant's internal policy provides adequate security.

Valet parking is almost exclusively a concern of upscale table-service restaurants. Because this customer typically spends more time and money at the restaurant, the customer expects an enhanced dining experience and valet parking is often considered an integral part of it. Very few restaurants require valet parking, but for those that do, several factors must be considered. First, it must be determined whether code, other leases, or reciprocal easements agreements affecting the shopping center impose any restrictions or prohibitions on valet parking. If permitted, the precise location of the valet spaces must be identified. Many anchors own their own parcels, and the landlord needs to verify that the valet parking spaces are located on parking owned by the landlord or that it can obtain the approval of the affected owner to use a certain area of its land for valet parking. Anchors and other tenants do not want prime parking spaces in front of an anchor entrance or a mall entrance to be used for valet parking, so valet spaces are generally located in areas that are not likely to fill up quickly. At the same time, restaurant customers do not want to wait an inordinate amount of time for their vehicles to be retrieved. The general rule of thumb is that the valet should be able to retrieve the vehicle within three to five minutes of the customer request. The landlord may need the right to relocate the valet spaces due to traffic concerns or to accommodate a renovation or redevelopment of the shopping center.

A determination must be made as to the number of valet parking spaces to be reserved and whether the valet spaces are exclusive to a particular restaurant or will be shared with other restaurants. The spots may be reserved only for dinner hours if that is when the highest demand occurs. The landlord may be required to mark or rope off these areas so that other shopping center customers do not use them during these dedicated hours. The lease should also identify the valet drop-off and pick-up stand. This stand should not interfere with an anchor or mall entrance or adversely affect pedestrian access along sidewalks. It also should not be located in an area that is likely to cause traffic congestion. Conversely, if the restaurant will not be offering valet service as part of its operation, it may seek in the lease to prohibit any valet stand within a certain distance of its entrance because it could interfere with access to the restaurant.

The lease must specify who will provide the valet service and the hours it will operate. Sometimes the landlord will have a specific vendor it is contractually bound to use. The landlord may initially provide the valet service but then reserve the right to discontinue the operation if it is unprofitable, at which point the tenant could operate its own service. The lease should also specify whether there will be a charge for the valet parking or if it is gratuitous. Generally, the landlord will assess a charge because the benefit is for the sole convenience of the restaurant's customers and because it may have contracted with a third-party to perform the valet service.

For a table-service restaurant, the tenant should verify the number of parking spaces that are available throughout the shopping center as well as the number of spaces within a field where its customers are most likely to park. Where parking is tight, the lease may designate a certain minimum number of spaces within this field or within the shopping center as a whole. The tenant should investigate whether the parking ratio for the shopping center complies with applicable code or if the shopping center has been granted a variance to provide fewer parking spaces than would be required. In dense urban areas, parking may be provided in whole or in part by parking garages. Under these circumstances, the tenant should verify the parking rates and confirm whether the landlord will provide a form of validated parking. Some garages will provide a few hours of free parking upon validation by the restaurant whereas others will provide a reduced rate. Some garages may not provide any free parking. As this can be a significant expense to the tenant and its customers, the lease should be clear on this point. The lease should also specify whether the landlord can impose parking charges in the future. If the landlord reserves this right, the tenant may want to address whether its customers or employees will be exempt from payment or at the very least to have the benefit of a reduced rate.

With the emergence of ride-sharing services, restaurants that would not need valet parking may still want to address stacking lanes or pick-up/drop-off points for restaurant customers. Whether for convenience or public safety purposes, the popularity of these services has exploded, especially in dense metropolitan areas. Rather than getting behind the wheel after several rounds of cocktails, the responsible drinker will have a designated driver, which increasingly is a ride-sharing service. However, having these vehicles stacked up in front of a mall entrance or an anchor tenant store or another restaurant may create parking circulation problems and lease violations. Code requirements, anchor leases, and reciprocal easement agreements, among other things, would need to be reviewed to determine whether these stacking lanes or pick-up/drop-off spots are permitted or available. In some cases, these ride-sharing services can alleviate parking congestion at the shopping center because not as many customers need to drive to the restaurant and park their cars. Some reasonable restrictions might include designated points for the pick-up/drop-off with adequate identifying signage; window periods when the pick-up/drop-off would be permitted or even designated areas of the parking lot similar in nature to the cell phone lots at airports or the "kiss and drive" lanes at public transportation centers where the ride-sharing service driver could wait until the client was ready to leave the restaurant.

Staging, Loading, Trash, Storage, and Temporary Areas

A tenant with substantial construction work in the premises may require a staging area to store equipment and materials. Obviously, the tenant wants the staging area to be located in close proximity to the premises. It may be an interior space or an exterior area. If only interior improvements to the premises are contemplated, an available vacant leasable space may be utilized. The tenant or its contractor would be required to construct or pay for the construction of a barricade shielding the front of the vacant space from the outside for safety and as a deterrent to theft. The parties should confirm, especially in the lease, that the tenant's insurance or the contractor's insurance covers any damage or liability arising out of the occupancy of this staging area and that the landlord will be indemnified against any such damage or liability. If the staging area will be an exterior area, then the parties will often define a specific location outlined on a lease exhibit. If language is used that the staging area will be "as determined by Landlord" or "as mutually agreed upon," then the tenant is forewarned that this is essentially a veto on the landlord's part because the landlord controls the shopping center and its common areas. The better approach is to outline the size and the location of this staging area on an exhibit. The landlord will not want this staging area to encroach on valuable parking spaces, so it may be at the rear of the parking lot or behind a building. The tenant may be required to construct a temporary security fence to shield and protect its equipment and materials. If excavation or grading will be done, as in a ground lease or dirt pad situation, the tenant must ensure that the area is large enough to park construction vehicles when they are not in service.

If the staging area is part of the parking lot for the shopping center, then the landlord may impose certain blackout dates when it cannot be used for staging. It would not be uncommon for a landlord to prohibit use of such a staging area during the Christmas season. The tenant would need to confirm that the staging area would not be necessary during this period of time. The parties should verify that any construction obligations in the lease (e.g., starting or completing tenant's work) are consistent with these restrictions. The landlord may require the tenant to downsize its staging area as construction progresses because large earth-moving vehicles would be necessary only for preparation of the building pad. The tenant will be required to keep the staging area in good repair and condition and to repair any damage resulting from its use once tenant's construction work is complete. The landlord may require a bond or security deposit to ensure compliance with these repair obligations. As is the case with the other exhibits, the parties must confirm that such staging areas do not violate other tenant leases or agreements applicable to the shopping center, such as reciprocal easement agreements, or that the required consents have been obtained.

Some tenants may need a loading dock or delivery area. For an enclosed mall, the landlord generally does not want to allow delivery of food items through the interior mall concourses. For that reason, there is usually a shared loading dock or receiving area where deliveries are permitted. The food is then transported through a hallway or corridor directly to the rear of the restaurant. The tenant should confirm the location of these shared receiving areas and verify that they are reasonably convenient to its premises. It may be prudent to identify these areas on a lease exhibit so that they cannot be changed at a later date to a location that is not feasible. The shopping center's rules and regulations may limit the hours that any shared receiving areas are used, so these restrictions would need to be coordinated with the tenant's vendors. The tenant should confirm that access to any loading dock has adequate turning radius and parking for its delivery trucks. Some tenants may have a rear service door that abuts directly onto the parking lot, so no separate delivery area is required. For a freestanding building that is not connected to the mall, the deliveries will generally be made through the rear of the building and no separate dock will be required.

Some restaurants may have their own dedicated trash storage areas outside the premises. This should be clearly identified in an exhibit attached to the lease. The tenant does not want to discover after the fact that it must carry its trash a long distance to dispose of it in a dumpster. It wants the dumpster to be located in close proximity to the premises. The parties should also establish the path of travel for trash removal. The landlord does not want the tenant to carry bags of wet garbage through the mall concourse where pedestrian traffic is present. If the premises are located within an enclosed mall, there will generally be a corridor behind the restaurant that they will be required to use to transport the trash outside to the dumpster. Some restaurants have a rear door that opens directly outside. In most cases, these dedicated trash areas will not be included as part of the premises for purposes of computing rental charges, but the lease should clearly state the intent of the parties in this regard. The lease should specify the minimum number of times per day the tenant must dispose of trash from its premises because wet garbage can produce unpleasant odors and result in vermin. Some shopping centers may obligate tenants to participate in recycling programs, which can be an added cost to the tenants. The restaurant operator should determine in advance whether it will have its own dedicated trash dumpster area or will share a dumpster with other tenants. If shared, the landlord may allocate the cost of removing trash from the dumpster among those using it. Because it would be difficult to monitor who disposed of the most trash on a daily basis, usually this pro rata computation will be determined on a per-square-foot basis. In other words, the larger spaces would be presumed to use the dumpster more often than the smaller spaces.

Some restaurants may require off-premises areas for storage of napkins, cooking utensils, silverware, and non-refrigerated food products. Often landlords have some otherwise unleaseable space in a basement or in a non-mall fronting space that they can lease for storage. Usually an exhibit is attached to the lease identifying such storage area and setting out its dimensions. In most cases, some rental charge is assessed for the use of the storage area, which is payable at the same time the minimum rent for the premises is paid. Although the storage space occupancy is generally coterminous with the lease term for the premises, occasionally either party may want a shorter term or the right to terminate the storage space occupancy on prior written notice. The landlord may want to recapture the space for purposes of a mall expansion or renovation or the tenant may determine that the storage space is no longer needed. Usually the only utility provided is electricity and the lease should specify who is paying that charge. The storage space is often either four walls of drywall with a door or a cube with chain link fencing all around. The lease should specify whether the tenant is taking the storage space in its "as-is, where-is" condition or if the space will be improved by either party prior to occupancy and at whose expense. The storage space agreement is often an ancillary document separate and apart from the lease of the premises but occasionally it is incorporated into the body of the lease for the restaurant premises. If the documents are separate, the landlord will certainly want cross-default language so that a default under one document constitutes a default under the other document.

Most restaurants hire key personnel well in advance of the actual opening of the business. For that reason, they may request space for a trailer or use of a vacant space in the shopping center to interview potential employees. If on-site interviewing and hiring is required, it should be addressed in the lease and the location or space number identified. Usually the trailer will be located within the staging area, if any, or at the back of the parking lot so that it does not interfere with customer parking. Also, the tenant would be required to arrange for its own temporary utilities so that the trailer would be functional. If the hiring will occur within a vacant space, the landlord may assess a monthly rental charge and require the tenant to pay for utilities consumed during its period of occupancy. In either case, a specific period would be designated for use of the trailer or the vacant space, after which time the tenant would be required to remove the trailer or vacate the temporary space.

Whatever notations are made on these exhibits should be clearly marked. Too often they are shown with a highlighter pen, which markings fade over time or cannot be easily reproduced by copy machine or a PDF. Nothing is more frustrating than to look at a twenty-year-old document where the markings are illegible. The better practice is to use various formatting options such as cross-hatching, bold lines, or shading in gray. Other color shadings may require use of a color printer. It may be necessary to prepare several pages of exhibits if the markings for all of these notations are too small to read unless they are enlarged significantly. Ideally, the reader should be able to see all of these markings clearly without needing to use the zoom feature on a computer.

Chapter 5

The Emergence of Grocerants

At the time of writing of this book, Amazon had acquired Whole Foods. To date, most of the emphasis has been on whether Amazon will be able to adapt its "click and deliver" model from retail products to groceries. However, this acquisition could also have a significant impact on restaurants within a shopping center. Many grocery stores have long had delis within their spaces so that customers could order a "grab and go" sandwich. Many also offer salad bars. However, Whole Foods and other gourmet groceries have taken these enhancements to a new level by installing tables and chairs where customers can dine inside the store or outside on a patio. Some even provide table service. The offering of food for immediate consumption has expanded from the simple delicatessen and salad bar to gourmet burger bars, pizzerias with wood-fired ovens, brewpubs, taquerias. and wine bars. In fact, the food possibilities are limitless because the items necessary to prepare a meal are already offered for sale in the grocery stores. The concept has become so prevalent that a new term has been coined for the combination grocery and eatery: "grocerants."

It is no wonder that grocery stores are adapting to this new reality. Although grocery stores often operate on thin margins, restaurants have the potential for much healthier profits. Steady and significant foot traffic, lower input costs for prepared meals, the use of fresh ingredients, and the opportunity for the customer to spend an hour or more at the grocerant can give it an advantage over the traditional restaurant. Studies have shown that the price of a meal at a grocerant can be 50% lower than a similar meal at a fast-casual or fast-food restaurant. For cash-strapped millennials and families, this can be a significant lure. Many of these grocery stores have or will have tablets and computers where customers can order their groceries and sip a glass of wine or munch on a taco while the order is being filled. Others offer "sip and stroll" programs where customers can quaff a glass of craft beer while they stroll down the aisles selecting groceries.

A fast-casual or fast-food restaurant may now have to view the grocery store not as a desirable anchor drawing customers to the shopping center and, with any luck, to the restaurants, but as a direct competitor who can undercut them in terms of price and service. For example, an ethnic restaurant such as a Japanese restaurant that thought it filled a niche at the shopping center that no one else did may find that its sales have dried up because of the sushi bar at the grocerant. When evaluating a site for a restaurant, the restaurateur will need to assess its ability to compete with the grocerant if one is located at the shopping center. Even if the restaurateur exacts an exclusive from its landlord as an inducement to sign a lease, most exclusives do not apply to anchor stores such as grocery stores. Moreover, many exclusives are written in terms of restricting other tenants whose "primary use" is the sale of the protected product, but a grocerant will still see a considerable increase in sales volume generated by groceries. Finally, landlords will be reluctant to restrict the use clauses of grocery stores to prevent them from becoming grocerants because they need that anchor in their shopping center. Department stores, large format bookstores, and other big-box users are disappearing from enclosed malls and shopping centers, so everyone is chasing the next flavor of the month, which at present is the grocerant. If customers of the grocerant are spending hours at the store, it may crowd out parking for the traditional restaurant. Drive-through lanes for the grocerant may affect traffic patterns to and within the shopping center.

Similar to the grocerant is the food hall, which is a large space under common ownership or control that offers a variety of restaurants, groceries, utensils, and other food preparation items. To the authors, it would not be surprising if the marriage between Amazon and Whole Foods results in a combination grocerant, showroom for Amazon products, and order fulfillment center. While their groceries are being bagged, customers can eat lunch or dinner and browse the Web for product offerings. Much like the big-box "fast fashion" retailers have siphoned sales from the traditional clothing retailers, the grocerant or food hall will pose some vexing challenges to the traditional restaurant. Only time will tell what impact the grocerant will have on the traditional restaurant, but the restaurateur needs to be aware of these challenges when developing its business model, undertaking site selection, and evaluating expansion opportunities. The creative destruction of capitalism in which old models are discarded and replaced with new concepts is very much apparent in the transformation of retailing and restaurants. Adaptability and creativity will be the hallmarks of the successful restaurant of the future.

Appendix

Restaurant Leasing Clauses

I.

Computation of Rental Charges and Rent Offsets

CPI Increases

A Minimum Annual Rent equal to the greatest of (a) eighty percent (80%) of the Minimum Annual Rent and Percentage Rent payable by Tenant during the immediately preceding Lease Year, or (b) the Minimum Annual Rent payable by Tenant during the immediately preceding Lease Year increased by the increase in the Consumer Price Index (as defined herein) during the immediately preceding Lease Year, or (c) payable in equal monthly installments, in advance upon the first day of each and every month during the Lease Term. The term "Consumer Price Index" as used in this Lease shall mean "United States City Average All Items for All Urban Consumers (CPI-U, 1982–84=100)" published by the Bureau of Labor Statistics of the U.S. Department of Labor. If the publication of the Consumer Price Index of the U.S. Bureau of Labor Statistics is discontinued, comparable statistics on the purchasing power of the consumer dollar published by a responsible financial periodical selected by Landlord shall be used for making such computations.

Rent Stabilization Clause

Commencing upon the sixth (6th) Lease Year and continuing through the end of the Lease Term, Minimum Annual Rent shall be the sum of eighty percent (80%) of the average of the Minimum Annual Rent paid by Tenant to Landlord for the previous five (5) Lease Years (hereinafter called "Minimum Rent") plus the positive difference, if any, between Minimum Rent and ten percent (10%) of Tenant's Adjusted Gross Sales, (hereinafter called "Overage Rent") for each Lease Year, payable to Landlord in monthly installments equal to the sum of one-twelfth (12th) of Minimum Rent plus the Overage Rent for each month. At the beginning of the eleventh (11th) Lease Year, the sixteenth (16th) Lease Year, if the Lease is renewed, and the twenty-first (21st) Lease Year, if the Lease is renewed, Minimum Rent shall be recalculated to be the average of the Minimum Annual Rent paid to Landlord for the previous five (5) Lease Years.

Fair Market Rental Value

If Tenant is not in default beyond any applicable cure period, is open for business in the Premises, and this Lease is in full force and effect (and subject to the conditions set forth below), Landlord hereby grants to Tenant the option to renew this Lease [,_____ times,] for an additional term of five (5) years [in each instance]; provided, however, that the [Minimum Monthly Rent] [Fixed Rent] payable by Tenant during the term of [an] [the] Extension Option shall be the "fair market rental value" for the Premises starting as of the commencement date of the renewal term [in each instance] (which fair market rental value shall be determined in the manner described below), but which in no event shall be less than the [Minimum Monthly Rent] [Fixed Rent] in effect immediately prior to the commencement of the renewal term (the "Extension Option").

(a) [An] [the] Extension Option, if exercised by Tenant, must be accomplished by written notice from Tenant to Landlord (the "Option Notice") at least one (1) year prior to the expiration of the term [in each instance] (the "Option Exercise Date"). Should Tenant fail to provide Landlord with the Option Notice on or before the Option Exercise Date, Tenant shall be deemed to have elected not to exercise the Extension Option and the term of this Lease shall expire in accordance with its terms. Time is of the essence with respect to the requirement that Tenant give timely notice of its election to exercise [an] [the] Extension Option. Tenant's failure timely to exercise [an] [the] Extension Option shall constitute a material, irredeemable and incurable failure to satisfy a condition precedent to the vesting of such right, and Tenant hereby expressly waives any right to claim relief from forfeiture, or any other equitable relief from the consequences of its untimely exercise of [an] [the] Extension Option. The mutual covenant of good faith and fair dealing, as may arise by implication or otherwise under this Lease, shall not be construed to impose an obligation upon Landlord: (i) to notify Tenant in advance of the impending deadline (i.e., the Option Exercise Date) for the exercise of [an] [the] Extension Option, (ii) to excuse a default by Tenant, however slight, that invalidated the effectiveness of Tenant's attempt to exercise [an] [the] Extension Option, or (iii) to give Tenant confirmation, in advance of said deadline, of the validity of any purported exercise of [an] [the] Extension Option. Moreover, Tenant shall not have the right to exercise [an] [the]

Extension Option: (i) during the time commencing from the date Landlord gives to Tenant a written notice that Tenant is in default (and Tenant, indeed, is in default) pursuant to this Lease, and continuing until the default described in said notice is cured, or (ii) during time commencing from the date Landlord gives to Tenant a written notice that Tenant is in default (and Tenant, indeed, is in default) pursuant to this Lease, and continuing until the default described in said notice is cured, or (ii) during the period of time commencing on the day after a monetary obligation to Landlord is due from Tenant and unpaid and continuing until the obligation is paid. The period of time within which [an] [the] Extension Option may be exercised shall not be extended or enlarged by reason of Tenant's inability to exercise the Extension Option prior to satisfaction of the foregoing conditions precedent.

(b) If Tenant elects to exercise [an] [the] Extension Option, within fifteen (15) days after receipt of the Option Notice, Landlord shall notify Tenant of Landlord's good faith option whether the fair market rental value for the Premises as of the commencement date of [that] [the] renewal term exceeds the [Minimum Monthly Rent] [Fixed Rent] in effect immediately prior to the commencement of [that] [the] renewal term, whereupon Landlord and Tenant shall attempt to agree upon such fair market rental value, using their best good faith efforts. The "fair market rental value" of the Premises shall mean the [Minimum Monthly Rent] [Fixed Rent] as of the commencement date of [that] [the] renewal term, taking into consideration all of the terms and conditions of this Lease.

(c) If, within thirty (30) days following Landlord's notice as provided above, Landlord and Tenant have been unable to reach an agreement regarding the fair market rental value of the Premises, the [Minimum Monthly Rent] [Fixed Rent] during [that] [the] renewal term shall remain unchanged unless Landlord elects to give notice of its desire that the fair market rental value be determined in accordance with the provisions below.

(d) Should Landlord make such election, Landlord shall identify in its notice, as provided above, a date not less than fifteen (15) days nor more than thirty (30) days following such notice on which Landlord and Tenant shall exchange written opinions, at the Shopping Center manager's office, of the fair market rental value of the Premises. Such exchange shall be accomplished by the concurrent delivery by Landlord and Tenant of each party's opinion of fair market rental value, which opinion shall be contained in a sealed envelope. Such envelope shall be opened, simultaneously, in the presence of a representative of each of the parties.

(e) If, upon exchange of opinions of fair market rental value as provided above, the higher of the two opinions of value is not more than five percent (5%) greater than the lower opinion of value, the two values shall be averaged, and the average shall be thereafter conclusively deemed to be the fair market rental value of the Premises;

but, which in no event shall be less than the [Minimum Monthly Rent] [Fixed Rent] in effect immediately prior to the commencement of [that] [the] renewal term.

(f) If the higher of the two opinions of value is more than five percent (5%) greater than the lower opinion of value, and the parties have not otherwise reached agreement on the fair market rental value of the Premises, the fair market rental value shall be determined by the so-called "baseball" arbitration procedure hereinafter set forth.

(g) Landlord and Tenant shall, within ten (10) business days after the exchange of the sealed envelopes containing their respective opinions of fair market rental value, agree upon the appointment of an arbitrator who shall: (i) be by profession a licensed commercial real estate broker or an MAI real estate appraiser, (ii) be familiar with the Shopping Center, and (iii) have been active (over the three (3) year period ending on the date of such appointment) in the brokering or appraisal of comparable premises within the Shopping Center or in comparable shopping centers in the ______________ metropolitan area. If the parties cannot agree upon such arbitrator, the arbitrator shall be selected in accordance with the Expedited Procedures in the Real Estate Valuation Arbitration Rules of the American Arbitration Association then in effect. The arbitration shall be conducted no more than thirty (30) days after the selection of the arbitrator, in ____________, ____________, in accordance with those Expedited Procedures. The determination of the arbitrator shall be limited solely to the issue of whether Landlord's or Tenant's opinion of the fair market rental value of the Premises (which shall take into account opinions, if any, proposed in writing subsequent to the aforesaid exchange of sealed envelopes, provided that they are delivered at least two (2) business days prior to the date of the arbitration) is closest to the arbitrator's opinion of the fair market rental value of the Premises as above defined.

In the event the arbitrator has not determined the fair market rental value of the Premises prior to the commencement of [that] [the] renewal term, Tenant shall pay as [Minimum Monthly Rent] [Fixed Rent], effective as of and subsequent to the commencement of [that] [the] renewal term until such time as the [Minimum Monthly Rent] [Fixed Rent] for [that][the] renewal term is determined, the same [Minimum Monthly Rent] [Fixed Rent] in effect immediately prior to the commencement of [that] [the] renewal term. If such [Minimum Monthly Rent] [Fixed Rent] is thereafter fixed at a higher amount, such new [Minimum Monthly Rent] [Fixed Rent] shall take effect retroactive to the commencement of [that] [the] renewal term, and Tenant shall pay to Landlord that sum which is accrued and unpaid as a result of such retroactive application, with interest thereon at the Lease Rate (as that term is defined in this Lease), together with the next monthly installment of [Minimum Monthly Rent] [Fixed Rent] payable by Tenant. The cost of the arbitration shall be paid by Landlord and Tenant equally.

Gross Sales Exclusions

(i) tips and gratuities payable to, or collected and retained directly by, employees, or collected by Tenant on behalf of its employees and then paid to such employees, (vi) discounted employee meals, not to exceed two percent (2%) of Tenant's Gross Sales per annum on a non-cumulative basis, (ii) charitable contributions, (iii) promotional discounts, *e.g.*, for example, and not in limitation of the foregoing, if a dinner which may normally cost $20.00 is sold at a special price of $15.00, or for which the customer has a $5.00 coupon, only the $15.00 paid shall be included in Gross Sales; (iv) complimentary meals not to exceed, in any calendar year, two percent (2%) of Gross Sales for such calendar year; (v) bad debts, bad checks and credit card charges on sales previously included in Gross Sales which are uncollectible accounts, not to exceed one percent (1%) of Gross Sales for such calendar year, subject however to inclusion in Gross Sales if such accounts are subsequently collected; (vi) bulk sales of obsolete, discounted or damaged merchandise to non-consumer purchasers, (vii) bulk sales or sales of Tenant's inventory incidental to the cessation of business at the Premises or otherwise occurring other than in the ordinary course of business, (viii) gift certificates or like vouchers, until such time as the same shall have been converted into a sale by redemption and net of any commissions or other fees paid to third parties in connection with the sale of such certificates, (ix) sales, excise or similar tax imposed by governmental authority and collected from customers and paid out by Tenant, (x) revenue from vending machines and pay telephones installed for the convenience of customers; (xi) insurance proceeds, (xii) costs incurred with respect to valet parking and/or validation, (xiii) fees charged by credit card servicers, not to exceed two percent (2%) of Gross Sales per annum on a non-cumulative basis.

Historical Tip Percentage

As of the date hereof, Tenant intends to allow the practice of customers tipping Tenant's service employees when customers pay their checks to Tenant. Pursuant to subsection (i) in the paragraph above, the amount of those tips are excluded from the definition of Gross Sales (the "Gratuities Exclusion"). In the event Tenant modifies this practice, such that Tenant discourages or prohibits its customers from paying tips to Tenant's employees by, for example, excluding a line item in a credit card receipt for a customer to include a tip to Tenant's service staff, and concurrently increases the salaries and/or wages paid to service staff ("All-Inclusive Model"), then, upon no less than 30 days' notice from Tenant to Landlord (the "All-Inclusive Model Notice"), which All-Inclusive Model Notice shall include evidence reasonably satisfactory to Landlord of the implementation of the All-Inclusive Model, the following exclusion from Gross Sales shall be effective in lieu of the Gratuities Exclusion (other than cash tips paid directly to employees of Tenant) for as long as Tenant continues to implement an All-Inclusive Model:

1. In the event Tenant has been open for business for 12 full calendar months or more, then along with the All-Inclusive Model Notice, Tenant shall deliver to Landlord monthly sales figures for the past 12 full calendar months providing documentation reasonably satisfactory to Landlord of (i) Gross Sales derived from the sale of food and beverages ("Food and Beverage Gross Sales") paid by credit card ("CC Sales") and (ii) the amount of tips paid by customers with respect to CC Sales ("CC Tips"). For so long as Tenant employs the All-Inclusive Model, an amount equal to Food and Beverage Gross Sales for the reporting period in question, times the Historical Tip Percentage (as hereinafter defined) shall be excluded from Gross Sales. "Historical Tip Percentage" is defined as a number, expressed as a percentage, calculated by dividing CC Tips by CC Sales.
2. In the event Tenant has not been open for business for 12 full calendar months, then for so long as Tenant employs the All-Inclusive Model, an amount equal to Food and Beverage Gross Sales for the reporting period in question, times eighteen percent (18%), shall be excluded from Gross Sales.

Sales Tax on Rents

Tenant acknowledges and agrees that the amounts set forth herein as rent or additional rent do not include any and all applicable sales tax. Tenant shall pay to Landlord any and all applicable sales tax due and payable to any governmental authority as a result of the rent or additional rent being paid hereunder.

Fixed CAM Charge

Tenant shall pay Landlord, in addition to all other amounts provided in this Lease, as Tenant's share of Landlord's Common Area Costs, at a fixed rate of ____________ and No/100 Dollars ($) per square foot of Store Floor Area per annum (subject to adjustment as provided herein below), payable in advance in equal monthly installments on the first day of each month during the Lease Term. If the Commencement Date is other than the first day of a calendar month, then Tenant shall pay a prorated partial payment of Tenant's share thereof for the period prior to the Commencement Date with Tenant's first Minimum Annual Rent payment, and in any Partial Lease Year, a prorated payment thereof. At the end of each Lease Year during the Lease Term, the rate due hereunder shall be increased by an amount equal to ____________ percent (______________%) of the rate then being charged at the end of the previous Lease Year (or Partial Lease Year) during the Lease Term until the expiration or earlier termination of this Lease.

Landlord Right to Redistribute Utilities

Tenant shall not install any equipment which can exceed the capacity of any utility facilities and if any equipment installed by Tenant requires additional utility facilities, the same shall be installed at Tenant's expense in compliance with all code requirements and plans and specifications approved in writing by Landlord, which approval shall not be unreasonably withheld. Tenant shall be solely responsible for and promptly pay all charges for its use or consumption of sewer, gas, electricity, water and all other utility services. Landlord may make electrical service available to the Premises, and so long as Landlord continues to provide such electrical service Tenant agrees to purchase the same from Landlord and pay Landlord for the electrical service (based upon Landlord's reasonable determination from time to time of Tenant's consumption of electricity), as additional rent, on the first day of each month in advance (and prorated for partial months), commencing on the Commencement Date at the same cost as would be charged to Tenant from time to time by the utility company and/or alternate provider as reasonably designated by Landlord which otherwise would furnish such services to the Premises if it provided such services and metered the same directly to the Premises, but in no event at a cost which is less than the cost Landlord must pay in providing such electrical service. Landlord may supply water or other utilities to the Premises, and so long as Landlord continues to provide water or such other utilities Tenant shall pay Landlord for same Tenant's actual use (based on a submeter or meter installed by Landlord, at Tenant's cost, if such submeter or meter installation, is requested by Tenant) at the same cost as would be charged to Tenant by the utility company and/or alternate provider as reasonably designated by Landlord which otherwise would furnish such service to the Premises if it provided such service and metered the same directly to the Premises, but in no event at a cost which is less than the cost Landlord must pay in providing such service, and in no event less than the minimum monthly charge which would have been charged by the utility company in providing such service. Subject to the applicable rules and regulations of the State Public Service Commission, Landlord may provide a shared tenant telephone service to the Premises and so long as Landlord continues to provide such telephone service Tenant agrees to purchase the same from Landlord and pay Landlord for the telephone service at the same cost as would be charged to Tenant by the utility company which otherwise would furnish such service to the Premises if it provided such service directly to the Premises, but in no event at a cost which is less than the cost Landlord must pay in providing such telephone service. Landlord, in its reasonable discretion, shall have the right to designate an alternate third-party utility company or provider to provide any such utility service to the Premises and/or the Shopping Center.

Check Meter

Upon Tenant's request, unless prohibited by law, Landlord shall install a Landlord-approved revenue-grade check meter to monitor Tenant's electrical usage at the Premises. Such installation shall be performed at Tenant's sole cost and expense and shall be completed within ninety (90) days after Landlord's receipt of Tenant's written approval of the check meter installation quote provided by Landlord to Tenant.

Following installation, Landlord shall, at Landlord's sole cost:

1. Read the meter on a monthly basis. Such meter readings shall be final, binding and conclusive.
2. Utilize such readings, when available, to retroactively adjust the electricity charges for the period from the date of the last adjustment through the date of the adjustment.
3. Utilize such readings to establish reasonable new escrows following the date of the adjustment.
4. Perform all repairs and maintenance of the check meter. Landlord shall retain sole ownership of the check meter equipment.

Landlord shall provide to Tenant (i) copies of the meter readings of Tenant's usage and (ii) access to the check meter for the Premises upon Tenant's reasonable request.

Direct Metering of Utilities

Tenant shall also pay all charges for sewer, water, gas, electricity, and other services furnished to the Premises during the Lease Term. Each service provider shall be directed to place service in Tenant's name.

Separate Tax Parcel

a. Tenant shall, during the Lease Term, as additional rent, pay and discharge punctually, as and when the same shall become due and payable, all taxes, assessments and other governmental impositions and charges of every kind and nature whatsoever, extraordinary as well as ordinary, which arise or accrue from and after the Commencement Date and which shall or may during the Lease Term be charged, levied, laid, assessed, imposed, become due and payable, or liens upon or for or with respect to the Land or any part thereof, or any buildings, appurtenances or equipment owned by Tenant thereon or therein or any part thereof, together with all interest and penalties thereon incurred as a result of Tenant's failure to timely pay any bill received by Tenant prior to its due date, under or by virtue of all present or future laws, ordinances, requirements, orders, directives, rules or regulations of the federal, state and county governments and of all other governmental authorities whatsoever (collectively, the "Taxes"). Tenant shall deliver to Landlord satisfactory evidence of such payment within thirty (30) days of Tenant's receipt of written request therefor from Landlord. Any Taxes attributable to any period prior to the Commencement Date shall be paid in full by Landlord. Tenant shall further be responsible for the payment of all impact fees, traffic fees or trip fees, development fees or other similar type fees or assessments imposed by any governmental authority with respect to the development of the Land.

b. Taxes for the calendar years in which the rent obligations of Tenant under this Lease commence and terminate shall be prorated in accordance with the respective portions of such years included within the Lease Term for which basic rent is payable. If any Taxes are payable in installments, then Tenant may pay the same in the maximum number of permitted installments. Landlord shall pay all Taxes assessed for the period prior to the Commencement Date.
c. Tenant, at its sole expense, may contest or seek review of Taxes by any lawful means (if necessary, in the name of and with the cooperation of Landlord, in which case Landlord shall execute all documents necessary to accomplish the foregoing). Notwithstanding the foregoing, Tenant shall promptly pay all such Taxes if at any time the Land or any part thereof shall otherwise be immediately subject to forfeiture, or if Landlord shall be subject to any criminal liability arising out of the non-payment thereof.
d. Any refund or rebate on account of Taxes paid by Tenant under the provisions of this Lease, less the reasonable costs, if any, incurred by the contesting party in obtaining such refund or rebate, shall belong to Tenant. Landlord will, upon the request of Tenant, sign any receipts which may be necessary to secure the payment of any such refund or rebate, and will pay over to Tenant such refund or rebate as and when received by Landlord.
e. Nothing contained in this Lease shall require or be construed to require Tenant to pay any inheritance, estate, succession, transfer, gift, franchise, income, gross receipts (whether imposed on Landlord or Tenant), excise or profit taxes that are or may be imposed upon or assessed against Landlord, its heirs, successors or assigns.

Ring Road Maintenance Fee

Tenant will pay Landlord, in addition to all other amounts provided in this Lease, as Tenant's share of Landlord's costs to maintain all roadways within the Shopping Center, all entrances and exits to the Shopping Center, traffic control signals serving the Shopping Center and all directional signage for the shopping center, a flat rate of _____ and no/100 Dollars ($_____) per Lease Year ("Ring Road Maintenance Fee"), in equal monthly installments, payable in advance beginning on the Rent Commencement Date and on the first day of every month thereafter during the Lease Term. Tenant's share shall be prorated for any partial month at the beginning or end of the Lease Term. The Ring Road Maintenance Fee due hereunder shall be increased by _____________ percent (_____%) at the beginning of each Lease Year until the expiration or earlier termination of this Lease.

Self-Help

If Landlord fails to make any required repairs or replacements and this adversely affects the Premises for more than thirty (30) days after Tenant's notice [except when the repairs require more than thirty (30) days for performance and Landlord commences the repair within thirty (30) days and diligently pursues the repair to completion], Tenant shall have the right, but not the obligation, to cure such action on behalf of Landlord and charge Landlord for such reasonable, out-of-pocket expenses that Tenant actually incurred. Landlord shall reimburse Tenant for such costs within thirty (30) days after receipt of a billing with reasonable backup enclosed. In the event Landlord fails to make such payment within thirty (30) days after receipt of a bill substantiating the cost so incurred by Tenant, Tenant may thereafter set off or deduct such cost from one-half (½) of the Minimum Rent next falling due until the total cost incurred by Tenant has been recovered; provided, however, that the right of set off or deduction shall not be binding upon Landlord's mortgagee's interest in the Premises nor anyone claiming title to the Premises by, through, or under such mortgagee. However, if Landlord reasonably disputes the necessity of the repair and provides Tenant with a written detailed explanation of the basis for such dispute, the obligation to make same or the cost thereof, then Tenant's remedy shall be an action at law and Tenant shall not be permitted any offsets or deductions from Rent.

Rent Abatement for Non-Payment of Construction Allowance

If Landlord fails to pay the Allowance within thirty (30) days after notice to Landlord that the same became due, then Tenant shall be entitled to deduct the unpaid and overdue portion of Allowance from the Rent otherwise becoming due hereunder.

Opening Co-Tenancy

Tenant shall be required to open for business on its Completion Date. However, if Tenant opens to the public for business to the general public prior to the time the Opening Co-Tenancy, as defined below, is initially satisfied, then Tenant shall pay, in lieu of Minimum Rent, Percentage Rent and additional rent (except consumable charges, for example, and not in limitation of the foregoing, utilities and services, and trash services), ____________ percent (____________%) of Adjusted Gross Sales in an amount up to fifty percent (50%) of Minimum Rent ("Alternate Rent"), monthly in arrears, within twenty (20) days after the end of each calendar month until such Opening Co-Tenancy has been initially satisfied; provided, however, that upon the occurrence of a monetary default by Tenant beyond any applicable notice and cure period at any time prior to the date the Opening Co-Tenancy has been satisfied, all such Minimum Rent, Percentage Rent and additional rent shall thereafter be payable for so long as the default continues. The "Opening Co-Tenancy" shall mean all of the following tenants being open for business in the Shopping Center ____________. If the Opening Co-Tenancy has not been initially satisfied within eighteen (18) months after Tenant initially opened for business then Tenant may, upon ninety (90) days' prior written notice to Landlord, terminate this Lease, provided such notice of termination is given within sixty (60) days after the expiration of such date. If Tenant's Adjusted Gross Sales for the twelve (12) month period prior to the exercise of Tenant's right of termination are in excess of $____________, then Tenant's exercise of its right of termination shall be nullified.

If Tenant has paid Alternate Rent for twenty-four (24) consecutive months and Tenant's Adjusted Gross Sales for the consecutive twelve (12) month period immediately preceding the end of the twenty-fourth (24th) month while Tenant is paying Alternate Rent are in excess of $____________ Landlord may, at any time thereafter during which Tenant is paying Alternate Rent, terminate this Lease upon sixty (60) days' prior written notice to Tenant ("Effective Date") and upon the Effective Date this Lease shall terminate with the same effect as if such date were the scheduled expiration date of this Lease, provided, however, that if Tenant notifies Landlord within thirty (30) days after receipt of such notice that it has elected to waive the Alternate Rent and immediately resume payment of full Rent, then Landlord's notice shall be deemed revoked and Landlord's exercise of its right of termination shall be nullified for that particular instance. As a condition precedent to the rights granted Tenant under the provisions of this Section, Tenant shall have continued to operate its business in the Premises during the hours specified in this Lease, notwithstanding Tenant's rights to close pursuant to the terms of this Lease.

Operating Co-Tenancy

If at any time following the satisfaction of Opening Co-Tenancy Requirement, Tenant is open and operating the Premises but all of the following co-tenants are not open and operating in the Shopping Center; (a) collectively, the "Key Tenants," and (b) the occupants of at least ____________ percent (%) of the remaining gross leaseable area of the Shopping Center, excluding the Premises and the Key Tenants, (the "On-Going Co-Tenancy Requirement") (the occurrence of any one or combination of (a) and (b) above shall be deemed to be an "OCT Failure") then, beginning twelve (12) months after the date the OCT Failure first occurred (i.e., the date the OCT Failure is determined to have actually occurred, not a later date when Tenant become aware that such OCT Failure had occurred), Tenant shall pay to Landlord, in lieu of the Rent (i.e., Minimum Annual Rent, Common Area Maintenance Charge, Property Tax Charge, other components of Additional Rent and Percentage Rent otherwise payable under this Lease, ____________ percent (____________%) of monthly Gross Sales ("Alternate Rent"), during such period of continuing OCT Failure, in arrears, within fifteen (15) days after the end of each calendar month. Once such OCT Failure has been cured, Landlord shall provide Tenant with written notice thereof and Tenant shall thereupon commence the payment of the Rent to Landlord as set forth in this Lease. For the purpose of this Section Tenant will be deemed to be open and operating even if the Premises are temporarily closed for remodeling (diligently pursued) or due to a casualty, condemnation or other force majeure event, so long as Tenant is otherwise in compliance with the terms and provisions of this Lease.

Should such OCT Failure continue for a period of twelve (12) additional consecutive months, then Tenant shall have the right, within thirty (30) days after the end of such twelve (12) month period, to terminate this Lease upon ninety (90) days prior written notice to Landlord. If such right to terminate is not exercised in the manner set forth herein, then Tenant's election to pay Alternate Rent shall cease and Tenant shall immediately resume full payment of Rent.

II.

Operational Issues for Restaurants

Sample Use Clause

The Premises shall be occupied and used by Tenant solely for the purpose of conducting therein the operation of a restaurant serving traditional Mexican and TexMex cuisine with service of alcoholic beverages for on-premises consumption, pursuant to Tenant's normal and customary menu and Tenant shall not use or permit or suffer the use of the Premises for any other business or purpose. Tenant may add or delete items from the menu from time to time without Landlord's consent provided the menu remains predominantly Mexican and TexMex cuisine.

National Chain Use Clause

Throughout the Lease Term, Tenant covenants and agrees that it shall have the right to occupy and use the Premises solely for the operation of a fine dining table-service Italian restaurant ("Permitted Use"), and for no other use or purpose whatsoever, without the express prior written consent of Landlord, which consent shall not be unreasonably withheld, condition or delayed. Notwithstanding the foregoing, Tenant may change the Permitted Use without Landlord's consent to (a) any other full service restaurant concept then owned and/or operated by Tenant (or a subsidiary thereof) having a check average of at least ____________ and No/100 Dollars ($_____) per person in [insert year] U.S. Dollars, provided Tenant gives prior written notice thereof to Landlord, so long as Tenant (or a subsidiary thereof) owns and operates such new use, and so long as such change in restaurant concept (i) does not violate any use which is prohibited by this Lease, any matter of public record shown on the Title Report or any applicable law or ordinance and (ii) does not violate any then effective exclusive use right provided to another restaurant at the Shopping Center (provided that Landlord discloses any and all such exclusive use rights, whether of public record or not, to Tenant within sixty (60) days after receiving Tenant's written request therefor); or (b) any full-service restaurant having a check average of at least ____________ and No/100 Dollars ($_____) per person in [insert year] U.S. Dollars that is commonly found in "first class" retail centers that (i) does not duplicate, and is not substantially similar to, the primary cuisine of another restaurant then in the Shopping Center, (ii) does not violate any use which is prohibited by this Lease, any matter of public record shown on the Title Report or any applicable law or ordinance, (iii) does not violate any then effective exclusive use right provided to another restaurant at the Shopping Center (provided that Landlord discloses any and all such exclusive use rights, whether of public record or not, to Tenant within sixty (60) days after receiving Tenant's written request therefor), (iv) is not a restaurant primarily marketed to an adult crowd with servers who are scantily dressed or wear revealing apparel and (v) has at least ten (10) open and operating units of its proposed use in other "first class" retail centers of a similar size and/or quality to the Shopping Center. Subject to (a) Landlord's performance of its obligations under this Lease, and (b) Tenant obtaining all necessary permits for the operation of its business in the Premises, Tenant shall initially open and operate for business to the public at the Premises as a typical "XYZ" restaurant within the first sixty (60) days after the Commencement Date. After opening for business in the Premises as aforesaid, Tenant shall continuously operate such business in the Premises for twenty-four (24) consecutive months but thereafter Tenant shall have no obligation to remain open and operating therein. Tenant would not enter into this Lease except for its rights contained in this Section ____________. Except as otherwise provided in this Section ____________, Tenant acknowledges that the Permitted Use shall be nonexclusive, and that other occupants in the Shopping Center may operate businesses which are similar to Tenant's. The Permitted Use is a material consideration to Landlord in entering into this Lease so as to permit Landlord to maintain an appropriate occupant mix within the Shopping Center.

Minimum Hours of Operation

After initially opening for business, Tenant agrees to remain open and operate its business during the hours and on the days and evenings of the week determined from time to time by Tenant in Tenant's reasonable discretion, but in no event less than eight (8) hours per day, six (6) days per week. Subject to applicable law, Tenant, at a minimum, may open as early as 6:00 a.m. daily (including to serve breakfast) and close as late as 2:00 a.m. daily.

Go Dark Provision

Subject to casualty, condemnation, force majeure, closure for permitted repairs to the extent required by any governmental directive or as otherwise expressly provided in this Lease, Tenant will occupy the Premises upon the Commencement Date and thereafter continuously operate and conduct in one hundred percent (100%) of the Premises during each hour through the last day of the _____ Lease Year of the Lease Term (the "Operating Period") when Tenant is required under this Lease to be open for business the business permitted, with a full staff and full stock of merchandise, using only such minor portions of the Premises for storage and office purposes as are reasonably required in accordance with Tenant's customary operating procedures. Thereafter, Tenant shall have the right to cease operations on a continuous basis from the Premises at any time after the last day of the _____ full Lease Year. The right to cease to operate its business as provided herein shall not affect Tenant's obligation to pay Rent and to perform all covenants and obligations hereunder. Tenant shall give Landlord sixty (60) days written notice of its intent to cease operations prior to ceasing business operations in the Premises. In the event that Tenant ceases business operations in the Premises for a period in excess of one hundred twenty (120) consecutive days pursuant to the provisions of this paragraph then Landlord shall have the right to terminate this Lease upon sixty (60) days' prior written notice to Tenant unless Tenant re-opens for business prior to such termination date. In the event Tenant ceases operation in the Premises for a period in excess of one hundred twenty (120) days pursuant to the provisions of this paragraph, Tenant's rights (a) to an exclusive, (b) to exercise a right to termination due to insufficient sales volume and (c) to invoke any co-tenancy right under the Lease shall immediately and thereafter be null and void.

Patio Area

a. License to Use Patio Area. So long as the federal, state and local laws, codes, zoning restrictions, ordinances, regulations and safety requirements permit, Landlord agrees that Tenant shall have, throughout the Lease Term, the exclusive right and license to establish and use, in accordance with the provisions of the Permitted Use Clause and this Section, an outdoor dining area with tables, chairs and other improvements in the location shown on the attached Patio Exhibit (the "Patio Area"), provided that:

i. Tenant's use of the Patio Area complies with all laws, codes, zoning restrictions, ordinances, regulations, safety requirements, approvals, permits and licenses relating thereto; and
ii. All necessary approvals, permits and licenses in connection with such use are obtained and paid for by Tenant (with copies furnished to Landlord) and remain in full force and effect during Tenant's use of the Patio Area.

b. Operation of Patio Area. Tenant shall open the Patio Area for business only during those hours when the Premises are open for business.
c. Furniture in Patio Area. Tenant shall install, at its sole cost and expense, all furniture, equipment, lighting, televisions, speakers and signage (collectively, the "Furniture") in the Patio Area. Tenant acknowledges and agrees that:
    i. The Furniture shall meet the highest standards of quality and appearance consistent with a first-class restaurant and the design and construction of the Shopping Center (and the Premises);
    ii. The Furniture shall not be used or placed in the Patio Area until its quantity, design, materials, size, color, position and method of attachment or installation are first approved by Landlord in writing; and
    iii. Tenant shall be solely responsible for any destruction, damage, theft or vandalism of, or to, the Furniture.
d. Restrictions on Tenant's Use. Tenant hereby covenants and agrees that it shall not:
    i. Restrict access to the Shopping Center or pedestrian flow through the Common Areas outside the Patio Area;
    ii. Erect or place any canopy or other enclosure or covering on the Patio Area without Landlord's prior written approval, provided that such approval is hereby given with respect to the Patio Area canopy shown on Tenant's Plans as approved by Landlord;
    iii. Permit any music or other similar sounds to be heard in the Patio Area without Landlord's prior written approval; provided that such approval is hereby given with respect to Tenant's right to place televisions and speakers within the Patio Area and to feature sporting event broadcasts and/or play recorded music at reasonable volumes therein; or
    iv. Permit loitering in the Patio Area by persons who are not customers of Tenant.

e. Cleanliness of Patio Area.
   i. Tenant shall, at its sole cost and expense, clean and keep in good repair the Patio Area and the Furniture. Tenant shall remove all trash generated therefrom on a daily basis or more frequently as needed.
   ii. If Tenant fails to maintain the Patio Area as required, then, in addition to and not in lieu of any other remedy to which Landlord may be entitled under this Lease, Landlord shall have the right, but not the obligation, upon twenty-four (24) hours' prior written notice to Tenant, to clean, repair or remove trash therefrom on Tenant's behalf; and Tenant shall pay the cost of such cleaning, repair or trash removal to Landlord within ten (10) days after receiving Landlord's written demand therefore.

f. Repairs to Common Areas. Tenant shall reimburse to Landlord, within ten (10) days after receiving Landlord's written demand therefor, the cost of any repairs or restoration of the Common Areas arising out of Tenant's use of the Patio Area or acts or negligence of Tenant, its customers, employees, agents, contractors, invitees or licensees.

g. Lease Provisions Apply to Patio Area. Notwithstanding anything in this Lease to the contrary, the Patio Area shall be deemed to be a part of the Premises pursuant to all of the terms, covenants and conditions of this Lease and, to the extent applicable, all provisions of this Lease shall apply to Tenant's use and occupancy of the Patio Area. The square footage of the Patio Area shall not, however, be used in the calculation of the Minimum Annual Rent or ancillary charges due hereunder.

h. Percentage Rent. Tenant hereby understands and agrees that all sales and revenues derived from services performed and sales made in the Patio Area shall be included in Gross Sales for the purpose of determining the Percentage Rent payable under this Lease.

i. Landlord Not Liable. Landlord shall have no liability to Tenant if Tenant is unable to use the Patio Area for any reason other than Landlord's negligence or willful misconduct.

j. Landlord's Approvals. Unless otherwise expressly provided for in this Section, Landlord's approvals relating to Tenant's use of the Patio Area must not be unreasonably withheld, conditioned or delayed.

Sampling

So long as the Tenant is operating as an XYZ franchisee, and is itself (or through a bona-fide franchisee of ABC Enterprises, Inc. or other permitted transferee under this Lease) in occupation of and conducting business in the whole of the Premises and is not in default under the terms of this Lease, Tenant shall, throughout the Lease Term, have the right to distribute within five feet (5') from directly in front of the lease line of the Premises and within the lease lines of the storefront width of the Premises (the "Area") or such area as may otherwise be agreed upon between Tenant and mall management free samples of the products which Tenant is permitted to sell pursuant to the Permitted Use to customers and passersby in connection with the promotion of Tenant's business from the Premises provided that:

1. Such distributions of free samples do not in any way interfere with the customers or interfere in any manner with the flow of pedestrian traffic in the Shopping Center (it being agreed that Tenant shall not set up any tables or any other type of structure for display purposes within the Area);
2. If, in Landlord's sole opinion, the distribution of free samples by Tenant is disturbing any customer of the Shopping Center, Tenant shall (upon request by Landlord) immediately cease the distribution of free samples until further notice by Landlord;
3. Tenant shall keep the Area where the distribution of free samples is permitted, clean and in good repair at all times throughout its possession thereof. If Tenant does not maintain a standard of cleanliness, maintenance and repair within the Area satisfactory to Landlord, Landlord shall have the right to clean, maintain or repair or cause to be cleaned, maintained or repaired the Area and the cost of such cleaning, maintaining or repairing of the Area, together with an administration fee of fifteen percent (15%) of such costs shall be paid by Tenant to Landlord forthwith upon demand as additional rent;
4. In connection with the Area, the Tenant hereby agrees to pay to the Landlord all out-of-pocket costs and expenses directly incurred by the Landlord for cleaning of the Shopping Center, including the Common Area, as a result of the Tenant's use of the Area;
5. The insurance requirements of Tenant as set out in this Lease shall also include the business operations of the Tenant with respect to the Area; and
6. Tenant's use of the Area is subject to all of the terms, covenants and conditions set out in this Lease.

Exclusive Use

In consideration of Tenant's agreement not to change the Permitted Use of the Premises to an operating format that duplicates a then existing operating format of another tenant at the Shopping Center, as set out in Section ____________ and only so long as the primary use at the Premises is the operation of a full-service fine Italian restaurant, Landlord shall not lease space in the portion of the Shopping Center shown on the attached exhibit ("Exclusive Zone") for, nor shall Landlord grant any consent so as to permit another tenant or other occupant within the Exclusive Zone to operate, as a full-service fine Italian restaurant, meaning a restaurant where the sale of Italian entrees constitute thirty percent (30%) or more of its entrée items (a "Competing Use"). A tenant or other occupant shall be considered to be operating for a Competing Use with Landlord's consent only if: (i) Landlord after the date of this Lease entered into a lease or other occupancy agreement with the tenant or other occupant in question permitting it to engage in the Competing Use, or (ii) Landlord's consent is required for a change to a tenant's or other occupant's permitted use, and Landlord consents, after the date of this Lease, to change such use to permit such tenant or other occupant to operate for a Competing Use. A tenant or other occupant shall not be considered to be operating for a Competing Use with Landlord's consent if such tenant or other occupant has been permitted to assume a lease or operate its business based upon or as a result of bankruptcy, insolvency, or similar action or if such tenant or other occupant has been permitted to operate as the result of an action or order by a court. The definition of Competing Use shall specifically exclude (i) Major Tenants; (ii) fast food restaurants under 2,500 square feet that offer counter service only; (iii) a parent, subsidiary or affiliate of Tenant; (iv) existing tenants and replacement thereof at the Shopping Center whose use clauses either allow or do not prohibit such tenants from operating for a Competing Use; (v) occupants of outlots; (vi) fast casual Italian restaurants having a check average of less than $____________in [Insert Year] Dollars. Landlord and Tenant agree that in the event Landlord violates the foregoing Competing Use restriction and such violation continues for at least one hundred eighty (180) days after receipt of written notice thereof from Tenant to Landlord and Tenant's Gross Sales during such one hundred eighty (180) day period decline by at least ten percent (10%) as compared with Tenant's Gross Sales for the immediately preceding comparable one hundred eighty (180) day period; then, in such event, retroactive to the date of such notice and continuing only until the earlier to occur of: (i) the date on which such violation is cured, or (ii) the date Tenant is in default under the terms of the Lease beyond any applicable cure period (herein the "Alternative Rent Period"), Tenant shall pay, in lieu of the Minimum Rent and Percentage Rent only, the lesser of (i) ____________ percent (____________%) of Tenant's monthly Adjusted Gross Sales and (ii) fifty percent (50%) of the monthly Minimum Rent otherwise paid hereunder (herein the "Alternative Rent"). Tenant shall continue to pay all additional rent and charges due under the Lease and the Percentage Rent sales breakpoint during the Alternative Rent Period shall be reduced to zero. All Adjusted Gross Sales made during the Alternate Rent Period shall be included in calculations of Alternate Rent. In the event Landlord fails to cure said violation of the Competing Use restriction within the period of twelve (12) consecutive calendar months commencing on the date of said violation (hereinafter "Termination Cure Period"), then Tenant may elect to terminate this Lease upon written notice given to Landlord. In the event that Tenant, for any reason, fails to exercise its right to terminate as provided herein within said thirty (30) days after the expiration of the Termination Cure Period, then Tenant's said right to terminate shall lapse and Tenant will immediately revert to full Minimum Rent and Percentage Rent.

Italian restaurant shall be defined as a restaurant primarily serving any of various Italian food preparations containing, flour, water and sometimes egg and/or rice primarily of Italian origin, which is formed into a variety of shapes that are hard when dry and soft when cooked, usually served with an Italian sauce and sometimes stuffed, including but not limited to, spaghetti, linguine, rigatoni, penne, ravioli, strozzapreti, malfatti, pici, lasagna, cannelloni, risotti, suppli, arancini, bigoli, bucatini, cappellini, fusilli, anelloni, maccheroni, perciatelli, vermicelli, ziti, bavette, fettuccine, mafalde, pappardelle, pizzoccheri, stringozzi, trenette, cavatappi, cellentani, garganelli, gemelli, manicotti, paccheri, rotini, farfalle, trenne, tortiglioni, tuffoli, cavatelli, conchiglie, gnocchi, campanelle, capunti, lumache, maltagliati, orecchiette, pipe, rotelle, trofie, anelli, ditali, orzo, pastina, quadrettini, risi, stelle, agnolotti, fagottini, mezzelune, tortellini, passatelli for use in preparing Italian pasta dishes.

III.

Construction

As-is Condition

Tenant agrees to accept the Premises in their present "as is" condition. Further alterations of the Premises will be at the Tenant's sole expense and deemed to be Tenant's Work, including, but not limited to, all work designated as Tenant's Work in this Lease, and Tenant shall do and perform all Tenant's Work diligently and promptly and in accordance with the following provisions. Tenant's taking possession of the Premises shall be conclusive evidence of Tenant's acceptance thereof in good order and satisfactory condition. Tenant shall acknowledge taking possession of the Premises in writing. Tenant agrees that Landlord has made no representations as to conformance with applicable laws respecting the condition of the Premises or the presence or absence of Hazardous Materials (hereinafter defined) in, at, under or abutting the Premises or the environment. Tenant also agrees that no representations respecting the condition of the Premises, no warranties or guarantees, expressed or implied, INCLUDING, WITHOUT LIMITATION, ANY IMPLIED WARRANTY OF MERCHANTABILITY OR FITNESS FOR A PARTICULAR PURPOSE, with respect to workmanship or any defects in material, and no promise to decorate, alter, repair or improve the Premises either before or after the execution hereof, have been made by Landlord or its agents to Tenant unless the same are contained herein.

Description of Shell Condition

I. WORK BY LANDLORD AT LANDLORD'S EXPENSE—The following work is to be performed exclusively by Landlord at Landlord's sole expense:

A. COMMON AREA. This may include, without limitation, the sidewalks, parking areas, parking decks, access roads, driveways, landscaped areas (interior and exterior), truck serviceways, pedestrian bridges, interior corridors, loading areas, any enclosed areas, all seating areas, courts, stairs, ramps, any elevators, any escalators, comfort and first-aid stations, public restrooms, bus stops, retaining walls, drainage systems, water and sewage systems, trash disposal facilities, and lighting facilities designated by Landlord as part of the Common Area. Such Common Area work shall also include, without limitation, all landscaping, irrigation and hardscape up to the footprint of the building in which the Premises are located.

B. STRUCTURE. The structural framing, columns, beams and roof deck shall be constructed of non-combustible framing in accordance with local and state building codes.

C. ROOF. The roof assembly shall consist of a weather-resistant layer, thermal insulation and structural components.

D. EXTERIOR WALLS. Exterior walls shall be of non-combustible construction and a finish of suitable nature and/or appropriate materials having a finished appearance and decorative quality designed by Landlord's architect.

E. CEILINGS. The Premises will be left open to the structural systems overhead. Enclosed public areas in the Shopping Center will be provided with acoustical lay-in ceiling, finished drywall or other surface as determined by Landlord. Enclosed service areas may be exposed structure.

F. UTILITIES. Subject to the provisions of Article _____ of the Lease to which this Exhibit is attached: (but the foregoing shall not limit Landlord's obligations under this Subsection F.):

1. HVAC Systems. A heating, ventilating air-conditioning (HVAC) system will be provided to any enclosed Common Areas.
2. Plumbing. A 4" sanitary sewer and 1 ¼" domestic water will be installed at a point to be determined by Landlord. A 4" sanitary sewer and 2" domestic water line (which domestic water line will consist of a copper line and shut off valve with a minimum pressure of 50psi) will be installed at a point determined by Landlord. Tenant shall install a separate meter(s) at a location as determined by Landlord. A 4" grease line will be stubbed within the Premises at locations determined by Landlord within the existing leave out location. Landlord shall also provide an external

grease interceptor sized to comply with local codes for Tenant's restaurant type and vented to comply with local codes. Landlord shall install sanitary sewer line from grease interceptor to common line, per code. Tenant shall provide Landlord with engineered calculations in order for Landlord to correctly size the grease interceptor.

3. Fire Protection. A fire protection system will be installed where required for the Common Areas with capacity to service tenant areas.
4. Electrical Service. An electrical distribution system will be installed at a building location as determined by Landlord with an available 800 amp service at 277/480 volts, empty conduit and pull string from the service location to the Premises. Tenant shall pull wire from Landlord distribution room to the premises and install transformer to step down as necessary within the premises. In the event the electrical service is distributed by Landlord, Tenant shall install a sub meter with remote readout per Landlord's requirements. Tenant shall provide Landlord with load calculations justifying the 800 amp requirement prior to delivery to Tenant. In the event Tenant's loads are less than 800 amps, Landlord will provide service at a size compatible with Tenant's design loads.
5. Communication Services. Communication and broadcast/data communication point will be provided to specified building locations as determined by Landlord.
6. Life Safety Systems. If required, a fire alarm initiation and notification system shall be provided for the enclosed Common Area with capacity to service tenant areas.
7. Natural Gas. Natural gas shall be made available to a point to be reasonably determined by Landlord for Tenant's HVAC equipment and other equipment, as necessary. Pressure regulated by utility company to meet Tenants design loads. Landlord shall provide a manifold tap behind ____________ which is approximately ____________ feet from the Premises; Tenant will be responsible for pipe from the manifold to the Premises.
8. Kitchen Exhaust. Existing fire rated shaft per code as shown on Landlord's base building drawings.

II. WORK BY LANDLORD AT TENANT'S EXPENSE—The following work, if performed or installed by the Landlord, shall be of a size, capacity and at a location as indicated in the Tenant Information Package, the cost for which shall be at Tenant's expense as indicated below. Notwithstanding, if Landlord does not elect to perform same, the same shall become Tenant's responsibility for the Premises.

A. FLOOR SLAB.

1. A reinforced concrete slab throughout the Premises, with a blockout or strip in the rear of the Premises (without concrete) to allow for Tenants sanitary connection: Blockout is for first floor Tenants only. Concrete slab shall be 4" per Landlord's base building plans and soils report recommendations. Landlord shall leave a portion of the slab out in accordance with Landlord's base building drawings and Tenant shall remove and replace all existing concrete that is required for Tenant utilities.
2. A structural or precast concrete slab for Tenants on the second level.

B. PARTITIONS. Partitions may be provided to separate Premises from Common Areas and other tenant spaces. Demising partitions shall extend from the finished floor to the underside of the overhead structure to separate the Premises from other tenant spaces and shall be of exposed studs unless otherwise required by code prior to Tenant's start of construction.

C. UTILITIES AND SERVICES. Subject to the provisions of Article ____________ of the Lease to which this Exhibit is attached:

1. HVAC Systems. A central outside air duct for first level Tenants use in a multiple level building. Landlord will not provide such system for one level buildings.
2. Central Toilet Exhaust. A central toilet exhaust system for first level Tenants use in a multiple level building. Landlord will not provide such system for one level buildings.
3. Plumbing Vent. A master sanitary vent system for first level tenants use in a multiple level building. Landlord will not provide such system for one level buildings.
4. Fire Protection. A bulk main shall be provided for Tenant's connection.
5. Life Safety Systems. A fire alarm initiation and notification circuit connection shall be provided.
6. Electrical Conduit and Breaker. Electrical conduit (without wire) for the Premises from Landlord's distribution point. Conduit size and breaker shall be solely as determined by Landlord. Any upgrades requested by Tenant shall be at Tenant's expense.
7. Communication Conduit. A 1" empty conduit with pull string for communication services for the Premises from a central distribution location.

Vanilla Box Condition

The following work is to be performed exclusively by Landlord at Landlord's sole expense to Landlord's standard drawings and specifications. All Landlord work is based on Landlord's plans dated ____________ and is being delivered as such. Any changes or upgrades shall be by Tenant at Tenant's expense:

A. Structure. The structural framing, columns, beams and roof deck shall be constructed of non-combustible framing in accordance with local and state building codes.
B. Roof. The roof assembly shall consist of a weather-resistant layer, thermal insulation and structural components.
C. Exterior Walls. Exterior walls shall be of non-combustible construction and a finish of suitable nature and/or appropriate materials having a finished appearance and decorative quality designed by Landlord's architect.
D. Concrete slab—A wire-mesh reinforced concrete slab.
E. Demising Wall. Metal studs with drywall—5/8" Type X fire-rated gypsum board, taped/sanded ready to receive primer and paint. Walls shall extend from floor slab to roof deck.
F. Storefront System with entry door(s).
G. Sanitary sewer, sprinkler and domestic water main lines—Will be installed to service all tenants. Size and location to be determined by Landlord.
H. HVAC Equipment—Standard 10-SEER HVAC rooftop unit(s) and controls will be sized for every_____________ square feet of sales area as required to maintain 75° F at 90° F outside temperature. HVAC units to be mounted on roof of the Premises and compressors shall have a manufacturer's five-year warranty. The heating system shall be designed as either electric or gas (at Landlord's option) to maintain 70° F at –8° F outside temperature. Rooftop installations shall utilize matching full perimeter curbs.
I. HVAC, controls and distribution—Landlord shall install a standard thermostat and all air distribution. At Landlord's option, ductwork shall consist of ductboard, rigid sheet metal or spiral duct with exterior insulation. All work shall conform to SMACNA standards.
J. Restroom—Restroom(s) (as required by Code) in conformance with ADA requirements. Minimum facilities shall include grab bars, lighting, a water heater, a water closet, sink and one exhaust fan, wired to light switch. All other toilet room accessories included, but not limited to toilet paper holders, soap dispensers, mirrors, shelves and towel dispensers.
K. Ceiling—A 2'× 4' acoustical "lay-in" ceiling throughout the Premises (height to be determined by Landlord).
L. Sprinkler work—A complete sprinkler system for the Premises. Any modifications to accommodate Tenant's design shall be performed by Landlord's sprinkler contractor at Tenant's expense.
M. Electrical service conduit with feeder wire—Only one single service will be permitted. Service shall be sized based upon Landlord's allotted load. Electrical service shall be 277/480 volt, three phase, four wire or, at Landlord's option, 120/208 volt service.

N. Electrical panel(s) and transformer—Landlord shall provide panel(s) and transformer for the combined power and lighting for Landlord's Work. Tenant shall, at Tenant's expense, install any subsequent transformer(s) or panels needed for Tenant's Work. Any upgrade to service size will be at Tenant's expense.
O. Electrical distribution—Landlord shall provide one duplex outlet per 20 linear feet (approx.) of wall in the sales area mounted 12" to 18" above the floor, one duplex outlet mounted 4" to 6" above the floor at the electrical panel location.
P. Lighting. Landlord to provide 2' × 4' recessed florescent lighting with acrylic prismatic lenses throughout the Premises.
Q. Telephone conduit with pull string—Landlord shall install empty conduit with pull string to Premises from telephone panel. Tenant shall, at Tenant's expense, provide all wire and equipment and accessories required for the Premises.
R. Exit and emergency lighting—As required by Code.
S. Rear exit door—If required by Code, Landlord shall, at a location to be determined by Landlord, install one rear exit door per project specifications keyed for master key to all spaces. Door plaque and rekeying by Tenant.
T. Blocking in exterior wall for signage. Sign band as specified in the Shell Building drawings.
U. Condensate Drains. As required by Code or Tenant's approved plans.

ARTICLE II—TENANT'S WORK AT TENANT'S EXPENSE

Unless otherwise specifically identified as Landlord's Work, Tenant shall complete all work required to place the Premises in a finished condition ready to open for business at the Tenant's own expense. Tenant's Work includes, but is not limited to, the following:

A. Demising Wall Finish—Tenant shall primer and paint/finish.
B. Stockroom Partition—Tenant shall install a stockroom partition to separate the sales area from the stockroom with a door. Wall shall be gypsum board (as required by Code).
C. Interior Partitions—Tenant shall install all interior partitions which shall receive ½" gypsum board finish on 20-gauge 3 5/8" metal studs 16" O.C.
D. Roof—Tenant shall, at Tenant's expense, contract directly with Landlord's roofing contractor for all Tenant's roof work.
E. Grease trap (if applicable)—Tenant shall provide a grease trap for the Premises at a location to be determined by Landlord.
F. Time clock—Tenant shall install a time-clock to control storefront sign and display window lighting. If Landlord has provided a control circuit, Tenant shall utilize the control circuit to actuate sign and display lighting.

G. Floor finish—Tenant to finish the floor in all areas that are accessible to the public at Tenant's expense.
H. Wall finish—Tenant to finish all interior walls with primer and paint, wall covering, tile, etc. at Tenant's expense.
I. Architectural and Engineering fees—Landlord shall pay all A&E fees for Landlord's Work. Tenant shall pay for Tenant's Work.
J. Awning (if allowed by project criteria)—Design and installation by Tenant at Tenant's expense.
K. Under-awning/canopy blade sign (if allowed by project criteria)—Design and installation by Tenant at Tenant's expense.
L. Primary storefront signage. Tenant shall provide and install a storefront identification sign for the Premises which may include, at Landlord's discretion, multiple signs (depending upon Tenant's storefront configuration) and Tenant's established national logo or insignia, if any. Storefront identification signs shall be limited to Tenant's Trade Name as approved in the Lease or as otherwise approved in writing by Landlord. Taglines, if approved at the sole discretion of the Landlord, shall be carefully reviewed for wording, size, style and fabrication. The storefront sign shall be illuminated (unless otherwise specifically approved, in writing, by Landlord).

Pad Deal

The Premises shall be delivered with Suitable Soil and/or Suitable Fill Material to the Proposed Grade. The depth of the Suitable Soil or Suitable Fill Material shall extend to the point of eliminating any influence from materials which are not Suitable Soil or Suitable Fill Material upon the support of Tenant's Building or other improvements or upon excavations for foundations, storm sewers, utilities or grease traps.

The Landlord's Land Surveyor will conduct an as-built survey, which shall be delivered to the Tenant, depicting and certifying both the horizontal and vertical locations of the Premises as being in compliance with Tenant's Approved Plans.

The Landlord's Geotechnical Engineer will conduct an investigation, the results of which shall be delivered to the Tenant, in reasonably acceptable report form, to classify the Suitable Soil and/or Fill Material on the Premises. The Geotechnical Engineer's investigation will determine the structural capabilities of the soil, as well as determine the most appropriate method to achieve the Site Delivery Specifications. The Geotechnical Engineer will also certify compliance with these Site Delivery Specifications.

If it is determined by the Geotechnical Engineer that any influences, including, but not limited to, seismic design considerations, will affect the support or structural integrity of the Tenant's Building, then the Premises will be delivered with the applicable measures to eliminate those influences.

Definitions

BUILDING PAD—The area where Tenant's proposed Building will be situated including up to ten (10) feet of the area which surrounds Tenant's proposed Building and the concrete dumpster pad.

PROPOSED GRADE—For the Building Pad, the Proposed Grade is eight (8) inches below the finished floor elevation as depicted on the final engineered site plans. For the Pavement Areas, the Proposed Grade is the pavement surface elevation, as depicted on the final engineered site plans, less asphalt and base thickness.

SUITABLE SOIL—Soil which is free of deleterious material, including, but not limited to, organic or frozen matter, expansive or compressible soils, rock, cemented sands, construction debris, landfill material and/or Hazardous Materials. Soil shall be low expansive with a maximum liquid limit (ASTM D-424) of 30 and a maximum plasticity index (ASTM D-424) of 15. Suitable Soil which, in its natural and undisturbed condition, is capable of supporting Suitable Fill Material and (a) Tenant's Building utilizing a conventional shallow foundation system without the use of special foundations such as piles, caissons, grade beams or other special supporting systems, and a conventional slab-on-grade floor without the need for special reinforcement or extra concrete thickness, and (b) the Pavement Area improvements utilizing a conventional asphaltic concrete pavement section typically used in the geographic area for a similar project.

FILL MATERIAL—Any material that has been, or will be, imported to the Premises.

SUITABLE FILL MATERIAL—Suitable Soil placed in horizontal layers not exceeding twelve (12) inches and compacted to not less than 95% maximum dry density as determined by the Standard Proctor (ASTM D-698) or 90% as determined by the Modified Proctor (ASTM D-1557) test procedure. The placement and compaction of each lift of fill shall be inspected, tested and approved by Landlord's geotechnical consultant before subsequent lifts can be placed and compacted.

PAVEMENT AREA—The areas located within the Premises exclusive of the Building Pad.

Conditions Precedent

The parties hereby acknowledge and agree that the obligation of Tenant under this Lease to lease the Premises and the obligation of Landlord to let same is subject to the satisfaction or waiver of the conditions precedent set forth in this Section, and that except as otherwise expressly provided herein, the sole remedy for failure of any said conditions precedent shall be to terminate this Lease pursuant to the procedures set forth in each Section. Note to drafter: ensure that all time periods are consistent with each other.

(a) Licenses, Permits and Approvals. Within ____________ days after the date Tenant's Plans are approved by Landlord, Tenant shall apply for and pursue the issuance of all governmental licenses, permits, approvals and authorizations necessary for

Tenant's construction and operation of the Project on the Premises, including, without limitation, building permits, signage permits, site use approval, zoning certificates, environmental and land use permits, water, drainage, sewer and utility certificates and any necessary approvals from state or local health, safety and transportation boards or authorities (the "Permits"), and shall act diligently to procure same. Landlord shall cooperate with Tenant and join in the execution of any applications(s) or other materials required of Tenant in connection with the foregoing; provided, however, that no interests of Landlord are prejudiced, Landlord does not incur any extraordinary cost or expense (unless Tenant promptly reimburses Landlord therefor), and Landlord has the right of final review and approval of all items submitted in connection therewith. In connection with the foregoing, Tenant shall notify Landlord promptly upon Tenant's receipt of all the Permits and shall provide copies of building, signage and zoning permits to Landlord. Should Tenant fail to obtain all required Permits within ____________ days after Landlord's approval of Tenant's Plans (provided Tenant submitted for the Permits as set forth herein and diligently pursued the issuance thereof), then Tenant shall have the right to terminate this Lease by delivering written notice to Landlord. In addition, if Tenant has not obtained its building Permits within one (1) year following the Execution Date, Landlord shall have the right to terminate this Lease by delivering written notice to Tenant. Should either Landlord or Tenant fail to deliver said termination notice in the manner required thereby within the time periods specified therein, then such party shall be deemed to have approved of this condition and waived any objection thereto.

(b) Survey.

i. Initial Preparation. Landlord shall provide Tenant with all existing utility locations within ____________ days following the Execution Date. Within forty-five (45) days after the Execution Date, Tenant, at its sole cost and expense, shall obtain an ALTA metes and bounds survey of the Premises prepared by a surveyor licensed in the State in which the Premises are located, the accuracy of which is to be certified to Landlord, Tenant, the title company designated herein, together with a legal description of the Premises. Prior to the deadline set forth hereinabove, Tenant shall cause: (i) sepia, mylar or other such reproducible copy and three (3) certified original prints of the Survey to be delivered to Landlord, and (ii) one (1) certified original print of the Survey to be delivered to the Title Company. On or prior to the deadline set forth hereinabove, Tenant shall deliver to Landlord any objections it may have to the Survey. If no notice is set by the deadline, Tenant shall be deemed to have approved the Survey. In the event notice of objections is timely received, Landlord shall use commercially reasonable efforts to cure the objections. If Landlord fails to cure the Survey objections within sixty (60) days following receipt of notice thereof, Tenant, may, as Tenant's sole and exclusive remedy, terminate this Lease upon ten (10) days prior written notice to Landlord, given within ten (10) days of the end of the sixty (60) day cure period. Should Tenant fail to deliver notice by the date provided herein, Tenant shall be deemed to have waived objections to the Survey.

ii. Field Drawings. Within sixty (60) days after the completion of the Project, Tenant, at its sole cost and expense, shall cause the Field Drawings (as hereinafter defined) to be revised to reflect the final, as-built conditions of the Premises (including, in detail, the location and square footage of the Building and Patio Area, Utility Facilities, and all other physical improvements made on and to the Premises and Utility Lines (as that term is defined in this Lease, if any, wherever located) and other such items as Landlord may reasonably request. Said Field Drawings shall be marked up by the Tenant, its contractor, subcontractors, employees or agents, and certified to Landlord, to demonstrate that the Building, Utility Facilities, Utility Lines and Project conform in all material respect to the approved Tenant's Plans and that the Building and the Patio Area, Project and all other physical improvements constructed or installed in or on the Premises are located entirely within the boundary of the Premises and do not encroach upon any property beyond the boundary of the Premises. For purposes of this subparagraph, the term "Field Drawings" shall mean Tenant's and such other plans used by Tenant, its contractors, subcontractors, employees and agents, in the performance of Tenant's Work.

(c) Title Report. Within ____________ days after the Execution Date, Landlord at Tenant's sole cost and expense, shall obtain a commitment to issue an ALTA leasehold title insurance policy insuring Tenant's leasehold estate in the Premises, Building and Patio Area (the "Title Report") from a title company of Tenant's choosing and reasonably acceptable to Landlord (the "Title Company"). Tenant shall have ____________ days after receipt of the last of the Title Report and all documents referenced as special exceptions therein to review same. If the status of title is objectionable to Tenant, Tenant shall provide written notice to Landlord within the ____________ day title review period specified herein (the "Title Objections"). Should Tenant fail to notify Landlord any Title Objections within said ____________ day time period, Tenant shall have deemed to have approved the Title Report and waived any objections thereto. If the Title Objections are timely received, Landlord shall, at its sole cost and expense, use commercially reasonable efforts to cure said Title Objections. If Landlord fails to cure said Title Objections within ____________ days following receipt of notice thereof, Tenant may, at its sole and exclusive remedy, terminate this Lease by delivering a written termination notice to Landlord within ____________ days after the end of the ____________ day cure period. From and after the date

Tenant has approved or is deemed to have approved the condition of title based upon its review of the Title Report, Landlord shall not, without Tenant's approval, take any action to change the condition of title except: (i) recording utility easements that will not affect the Premises or the Shopping Center; (ii) recording memoranda of leases that will not have a material and adverse impact on Tenant's operations at the Project; (iii) financing or re-financing the Shopping Center so long as Tenant receives a commercially reasonable non-disturbance agreement; and (iv) ground leasing or modifying existing ground leases so long as Tenant receives a commercially reasonable non-disturbance agreement.

(d) Soil Tests. Within ____________ days after the Execution Date, Tenant, at its sole cost and expense, shall determine whether the soil substrata and/or general soil condition of the Premises are reasonably satisfactory for construction of the Building, the Patio Area, and Project on the Premises. Tenant shall deliver, within ____________ days after the Execution Date, copies of all reports, studies and analyses prepared hereunder to Landlord for informational purposes. If Tenant causes any soil tests or analyses to be undertaken at any other time during the Lease Term, Tenant agrees to promptly deliver copies of all such reports, studies and analyses to Landlord. If Tenant reasonably determines that the soil substrata and/or general soil condition of the Premises are unsatisfactory for the Building, Patio Area and the Project, Tenant may terminate this Lease by giving written notice thereof to Landlord within said ____________ day period. If Tenant terminates this Lease pursuant to the provisions of this Section, Tenant shall restore the Premises to the same general condition in which it existed prior to the performance of such soil tests. Should Tenant fail to deliver said termination notice to Landlord in the manner required hereby within the time period specified herein, Tenant shall be deemed to have approved of this condition and waived any objections thereto.

(e) Environmental Testing. Within ____________ days after the Execution Date, Tenant, at its sole cost and expense, may cause the performance of a Phase I Environmental Assessment of the Premises by an environmental engineer/consultant licensed to perform environmental inspection/assessment services in the State in which the Premises is located, in order to determine whether there are Hazardous Materials (as that term is defined in this Lease) located in, on or about the Premises in quantities or locations which require remediation pursuant to applicable federal, state and local laws, statutes, rules, regulations and the like. In connection with the foregoing, Tenant shall deliver, within ____________ days following Tenant's receipt, copies of all final reports, studies and analyses prepared hereunder by consultants to Landlord; provided that these provisions shall not delay any reporting required by applicable law or court order. All such reports, analyses and studies shall be delivered by Tenant to Landlord without any representation or warranty. If Tenant reasonably determines that Hazardous Materials are present in, on or about the Premises as provided herein, and Landlord does not remove or remediate same as required by law within ____________ days after providing Landlord notice of the presence of such Hazardous Materials in, or about the Premises. Tenant may terminate this Lease by giving written notice to Landlord within ____________ days after Tenant receives written confirmation from Landlord that Landlord could not, or does not, elect to remediate such Hazardous Materials. If terminated, Tenant shall restore the Premises to the same general condition in which it existed prior to the performance of all environmental tests; provided that Tenant shall not be obligated to modify or remove any Hazardous Materials that are merely discovered by Tenant as part of its due diligence. If Tenant causes an environmental audit to be performed on the Premises and fails to deliver said termination notice to Landlord in the manner required hereby within the time period specified herein, Tenant shall have deemed to have approved of this condition and waived any objections thereto.

(f) Utility Verification. Within ____________ days after the Execution Date, Tenant, at its sole cost and expense, shall verify that all utilities required for operation of the Project (including, without limitation, natural gas, sanitary sewer, water, electricity, telephone and storm water facilities) are available to the Premises in adequate capacities for Tenant's use as set forth in this Lease. If Tenant determines that the utilities are inadequate, Tenant may deliver notice thereof to Landlord and Landlord shall have ____________ days to cure such inadequacies. Should Landlord fail to cure such inadequacies within the time period set forth herein, Tenant may terminate this Lease by giving notice thereof to Landlord within ____________ days after the end of the ____________ day cure period. Should Tenant fail to deliver said termination notice to Landlord in the manner required hereby and within the time period specified herein, Tenant shall have deemed to be approved this condition and waived any objections thereto.

(g) Liquor License. Within ____________ days after the Execution Date, Tenant shall have determined that a liquor license of the type required for the Project shall be reasonably available to Tenant from the appropriate governmental agency(ies). If Tenant fails to obtain the required liquor licenses, Tenant may terminate this Lease by giving notice thereof to Landlord within said ____________ day period. Should Tenant fail to deliver said termination notice to Landlord in the manner required hereby within the time period specified herein, Tenant shall have deemed to have approved of this condition and waived any objections thereto.

(h) Memorandum of Lease. Landlord shall, within ____________days after the Execution Date, deliver to Tenant a Memorandum of Lease in substantially the form attached hereto duly executed and acknowledged by Landlord. If Landlord fails to deliver such Memorandum of Lease within said ____________ day period, then

Tenant may thereupon terminate this Lease upon ____________ days prior written notice to Landlord, said notice to be given within ____________ days after the end of the ____________ day period. If Tenant fails to timely deliver such termination notice as provided above, Tenant shall be deemed to have waived its right to terminate the Lease for the failure of this condition.

Completion Date

Completion Date: The 180th day after the later of: (A) the date Landlord delivers possession of the Premises for commencement of Tenant's Work; or (B) the date on which Tenant obtains a building permit which permits it to commence Tenant's Work from the local governmental authority having jurisdiction over Tenant's construction in the Premises, provided that: (i) Tenant makes application for such permits within ten (10) days after the date Landlord has approved Tenant's Plans, (ii) thereafter Tenant diligently pursues and complies with all requirements imposed by said governmental authorities for the issuance of such permits, and (iii) Tenant submits a copy of the approved permit to Landlord within five (5) days after the date such permit was issued to Tenant. Tenant's failure to timely comply with any of the requirements under (B) above shall be deemed a waiver of same with respect to the determination of the Completion Date hereunder.

In addition, if after Tenant has applied for its building permit with the appropriate governmental authorities, it has not obtained such permit within ____________ days thereafter and such delay is not due to the fault of Tenant (for example, and not in limitation of the foregoing, incomplete or inaccurate submissions by Tenant or failure to timely submit or resubmit as provided in this Lease), then Tenant may within ten (10) days after expiration of such period notify Landlord of such delay, the reason for such delay and the expected date of obtaining such permit and should Tenant fail to so notify Landlord within such period of time, then Tenant shall be deemed to have waived this condition of the Completion Date relating to Tenant's receipt of such building permit.

Furthermore, if after Tenant has applied for its building permit with the appropriate governmental authorities, Tenant is required to resubmit its plans to the appropriate governmental authority and Tenant fails to make the resubmission within ten (10) days after notification of the required resubmittal, then Tenant shall be deemed to have waived this condition of the Completion Date relating to Tenant's receipt of such building permit.

Cash Allowance

Landlord shall pay to Tenant as Landlord's Contribution, if any, for Tenant's Work the sum equal to the lesser of (i) $____________ per square foot of Store Floor Area, or (ii) the Actual Net Cost (as defined below) of Tenant's Work (excluding trade fixtures, furniture and furnishings or other personal property), and no more, subject to Landlord's right to deduct any Minimum Rent, Percentage Rent, additional rent, expenditures by Landlord pursuant to the Lease, or other amounts owed by Tenant to Landlord pursuant to the terms of this Lease as of the date of payment. Landlord's Contribution shall be used only for alterations, improvements, fixtures and equipment that become part of or attached or affixed to the Premises ("Permanent Improvements"), but excluding trade fixtures, furniture and furnishings or other personal property. The "Actual Net Cost" of work as used above shall be the actual costs paid by the Tenant to the General Contractor or other parties for completion of Tenant's Work within the Premises, less all discounts, rebates, refunds and salvage, if any. Notwithstanding the foregoing, Landlord shall remit Landlord's Contribution to Tenant as follows:

1. Landlord shall pay fifty percent (50%) of the Landlord's Contribution within thirty (30) days after Tenant has completed fifty percent (50%) of Tenant's Work and Tenant has submitted items (i)–(v) and (xi) below.
2. The remaining fifty percent (50%) of Landlord's Contribution shall be paid within thirty (30) days after Tenant has completed all of Tenant's Work in strict accordance with this Lease and Tenant's Plans as approved by Landlord by the Required Completion Date, PROVIDED no default in, breach of, or failure to perform, this Lease by Tenant exists beyond any applicable cure and/or notice period; Tenant has paid or reimbursed Landlord all amounts owed to Landlord pursuant to this Lease; Tenant has opened its store for business; Tenant has executed such other instruments and documents as are required under this Lease or required by Landlord's mortgagee to be executed pursuant to this Lease, and has furnished Landlord all of the items (vi)–(x) below.
    i. Schedule of Values. Tenant shall deliver to Landlord a schedule of values in a form reasonably acceptable to Landlord consisting of a complete and accurate list of all contractors, subcontractors, materialmen, suppliers or other persons who will furnish work, labor, materials, equipment or supplies in connection with Tenant's Work, showing quantities and dollar amounts of Tenant's or its general contractor's contracts with said parties in connection with Tenant's Work. Such schedule of values shall be updated with each Application for Payment. In addition, Tenant shall provide a representation by Tenant that Tenant will expend at least ____________ ("Tenant's Funds") for the Permanent Improvements and an acknowledgement that Landlord has relied on such representation as material consideration for its agreement to pay a Landlord's Contribution in the amount set forth above. Prior to the initial payment by Landlord, Tenant shall provide:
        a. receipts showing payments for the Permanent Improvements totaling the amount of Tenant's Funds, or

b. an Escrow Agreement demonstrating the deposit of an amount equal to Tenant's Funds into an escrow account pursuant to the terms and conditions set forth below.

ii. Application for Payment. Submission of standard AIA Contractor's Application for Payment form signed and notarized on behalf of Tenant and/or its General Contractor.

iii. Tenant and General Contractor Affidavits. Affidavits stating that the required percentage of Tenant's Work has been completed.

iv. Certificate for Architect or General Contractor. Certificate stating that the required percentage of Tenant's Work has been completed.

v. Partial Waivers of Lien. Evidence satisfactory to Landlord that the requisite portion of Tenant's Work has been paid for (including copies of paid invoices, receipts, purchase orders or other proof evidencing payment for Tenant's Work), together with proof that any and all liens therefor that have been recorded or noticed, or have attached or may attach, have been discharged of record or waived (lien waivers), and that no security interests relating thereto are outstanding. Unless a lien has been recorded or noticed, Tenant shall be required to submit lien waivers only from contractors who supplied labor or materials in excess of $5,000.00.

vi. Proof of Payment. Evidence reasonably satisfactory to Landlord that all of Tenant's Work has been completed and paid for in full (including copies of paid invoices, receipts, purchase orders or other proof evidencing payment for Tenant's Work), together with proof that any and all liens therefor that have been recorded or noticed, or have attached or may attach, have been discharged of record or waived (lien waivers), and that no security interests relating thereto are outstanding.

vii. Tenant's Affidavit: An affidavit from Tenant listing all contractors and any material suppliers in the employ of said Tenant who have provided goods or services for the completion of Tenant's Work in the Premises.

viii. Tenant Contractor's Affidavit: An affidavit from Tenant's general contractor or contractors listing all parties who have furnished materials or labor or services to that contractor for completion of Tenant's Work in the Premises.

ix. Certificate of Occupancy: Copies of all certificates and other approvals with respect to Tenant's Work that may be required from any government authority and any board of fire underwriters or similar body for the use and occupancy of the Premises.

x. Permanent Improvement Affidavit: An affidavit to Landlord stating that Landlord's Contribution was used solely by Tenant for such Permanent Improvements.

Examination of Records. Tenant shall provide in its construction contracts (to include an acknowledgement by the General Contractor to Landlord of its agreement to comply) that Landlord and its accountants shall be permitted to review, audit and copy the records of Tenant, its General Contractor, and all subcontractors with respect to any Tenant's Work in the Premises or preparation for such work upon reasonable notice and during normal business working hours at any time prior to, or within one hundred twenty (120) days after, final payment of Landlord's Contribution. "Records" shall include any and all information, materials and data of every kind and character (hard copy as well as computer readable data) that may, in Landlord's judgment, have any bearing on or pertain to Tenant's Work required hereunder, the General Contractor's compliance with the Tenant's Plans, and the accuracy of Tenant's and General Contractor's representations regarding payments for services performed or materials provided. If an audit or examination in accordance with this provision discloses (i) the failure of Tenant or its General Contractor to make payments promptly and properly to its subcontractors, materialmen or suppliers for labor, materials, or equipment or (ii) Tenant's failure to perform Tenant's Work in accordance with the plans and specifications approved by Landlord including, without limitation, the quality of the work or materials, Landlord may suspend all further payments due hereunder or may, but shall not be obligated or required to, make direct payment of any part or all of such bills on behalf of Tenant or the general contractor, not to exceed the Landlord's Contribution, or payment by joint check to Tenant, the general contractor and any subcontractor, materialmen or supplier, charging all such direct or joint payments for labor, materials, equipment and services against the Landlord's Contribution and the progress payments provided for herein.

Free Rent Allowance

Notwithstanding anything herein to the contrary, commencing the date Tenant has initially opened for business and provided no default in, breach of, or failure to perform, this Lease by Tenant exists beyond any applicable cure and/or notice period Tenant may retain, as Landlord's contribution toward Tenant's alterations, improvements, fixtures and equipment that become part of or attached or affixed to the Premises (hereinafter called "Permanent Improvements"), but excluding trade fixtures, furniture and furnishings or other personal property, one hundred percent (100%) of the Minimum Rent otherwise payable to Landlord until such time as the total sum retained equals $____________; provided, however, Tenant shall pay all additional rent during such period. Thereafter, no other sums otherwise payable as Minimum Rent may be retained by Tenant. The Permanent Improvements are the property of Landlord and shall remain so after the expiration of the Lease. Upon Tenant's completion of such work, Tenant shall furnish an affidavit to Landlord stating that Landlord's contribution was used solely for such Permanent Improvements together with supporting documentation showing that Tenant spent at least $____________ on Permanent Improvements.

IV.

Exhibits for Restaurant Leases

Access, Visibility, and Protected Zones

Notwithstanding anything to the contrary contained herein or elsewhere in this Lease, (i) Landlord shall not permit a kiosk, cart, or other similar item to be situated in front of the Premises; (ii) Landlord shall not take any action in the Shopping Center that will have a materially adverse impact on access to the Premises or have a materially adverse impact on the visibility of the Premises and Tenant's signage, will reduce the number of parking stalls in the Center to be less than that required by applicable government code or will have a material and adverse impact of ingress to and egress from the Premises; and (iii) no part of the Premises or Protected Area will be changed (including without limitation, the addition of buildings within the Protected Area), parking in the Protected Area shall not be reduced and parking in the Shopping Center shall not be reduced below that required by code and access and/or visibility thereto from adjacent public roadways or adjacent Shopping Center service roads will not be materially adversely affected, except as a result of casualty or condemnation, without the prior written consent of Tenant, which shall not be unreasonably withheld. In the event Landlord violates the foregoing provision, then following six (6) months written notice to Landlord, as applicable, and such party's failure to cure, Tenant shall have the right to terminate this Lease.

To-Go Parking

Notwithstanding anything to the contrary in this Lease, subject to governmental compliance, Landlord will provide to Tenant, and Tenant will have the right to use, at no additional charge the ____________ non-exclusive parking spaces (the "Reserved Spaces") for "pick up" and "to go" customer parking for the Shopping Center generally and with signage identifying the ____________ reserved but non-exclusive spaces as dedicated to parking for fifteen (15) minutes or less. The Reserved Spaces will be located within the area depicted as Tenant's "To-Go" Parking Spaces on the To-Go exhibit attached to this

Lease. If Landlord receives notice from another tenant or occupant in the Shopping Center stating that Tenant's Reserved Spaces violate a restriction contained in such tenant's or occupant's lease and such lease or other agreement and the applicable restriction were entered into prior to the Effective Date of this Lease, (i) Landlord shall provide Tenant with a copy of such letter and the applicable provision from such tenant's or occupant's lease or other agreement and while such lease or other agreement remain binding upon Landlord, (ii) Tenant shall not have the right to such Reserved Spaces, and (iii) Landlord shall use reasonable efforts to relocate said Reserved spaces to a location reasonably satisfactory to Landlord and Tenant.

Late Lighting

Landlord agrees to keep all parking areas in the Shopping Center on or proximate to the Premises adequately lighted during hours after dark for business, for thirty (30) minutes before and one (1) hour after such business hours, and in the evenings from dusk until 2:00 a.m. Landlord shall, upon not less than seventy-two (72) hours prior written request from Tenant, light the parking areas on or proximate to the Premises, if not separately metered and controlled by Tenant, either before or after such hours if Tenant agrees in advance to pay all costs associated with the extended lighting hours.

Valet Parking

Landlord may, but shall not be obligated to, operate or cause to be operated a valet parking service for the customers of the Shopping Center. If Landlord elects to operate a valet parking service, such service shall be performed in a professional and efficient manner, and Landlord shall have the right, but not the obligation, to charge its customers for the use of such valet parking. If Landlord does not operate a valet parking service, then subject to Tenant's ability to obtain all required governmental approvals, Tenant shall be permitted to operate or cause to be operated a valet parking service for the exclusive use of Tenant's patrons.

Staging Area

During the performance of Tenant's Work, Tenant shall have the use of a staging area consisting of approximately ____________ square feet to confine the storage of equipment and materials and the staging of its construction within a portion of to that certain staging area identified as such on the Site Plan of the Shopping Center (the "Staging Area"). Landlord shall make the Staging Area available to Tenant's contractors and subcontractors throughout the performance of Tenant's Work; provided, however, at

Landlord's request, Tenant shall relocate the Staging Area no more than one (1) time during the performance of Tenant's Work to an area reasonably satisfactory to Tenant, and Tenant shall use commercially reasonable efforts to reduce the size of the Staging Area as construction progresses and less area is required for construction staging. Tenant shall keep the Staging Area neat, clean, secure and in good order, condition and repair. Tenant acknowledges that the Staging Area will be located on existing areas in the Shopping Center and Landlord shall have no obligation to upgrade, reinforce or otherwise provide a construction grade surface in the Staging Area except that the surface shall be a clean hard surface. Tenant shall repair any damage to the Staging Area occurring during Tenant's occupancy or possession thereof. Notwithstanding the foregoing, Tenant may not use the Staging Area between the Friday immediately following Thanksgiving Day and December 31, provided that Tenant may store its equipment and materials inside the Premises, or if it is unable to do so, Landlord and Tenant shall work together in good faith to identify a location in reasonable proximity to the Premises for Tenant to store its equipment and materials in a closed container in an area at the Shopping Center that does not impact any parking or ingress and egress to and from the Premises (i.e., in Tenant's loading dock area or other areas that are outside of Shopping Center customer parking).

In the event Tenant operates or causes to be operated such valet parking service for its patrons, such valet area(s) shall initially be located in the area shown on the Valet Exhibit attached to this Lease. Landlord shall grant non-exclusive parking rights to Tenant, for Tenant's valet service, for not less than ____________spaces without additional charge to Tenant. Such valet parking shall have a non-exclusive pick-up/drop-off area located in the area shown as "Valet Drop-Off" on the Valet Exhibit attached to this Lease. If Tenant elects, it may utilize the area shown as the "Optional Valet Drop-Off" on the Valet Exhibit attached to this Lease as a non-exclusive pick-up/drop-off area, in addition to, or in lieu, the "Valet Drop-Off."

In the event Tenant operates or causes to be operated such valet parking service for its patrons, it shall make commercially reasonable efforts to utilize Landlord's current vendor to operate such service but shall not be required to do so if such vendor is unable to deliver valet services in the manner and at a cost reasonably acceptable to Tenant. Tenant (or its valet parking contractor) shall have the right, but not the obligation, to charge it customers for the use of such valet parking. Landlord shall have the right to relocate the valet parking area to another parking area in the Shopping Center on thirty (30) days' written notice to Tenant, provided that such new valet parking area is within a reasonable return time from the Premises and provided further that the total number of spaces available is not less than the ____________ spaces on the non-exclusive basis.

Trash Area

Landlord shall provide convenient areas located within reasonable proximity to the Premises as shown on the Trash Exhibit attached to this Lease as Trash Area for Tenant's non-exclusive use that are sufficient in size to accommodate a dumpster and any other waste receptacles (including recycling receptacle(s) and receptacle(s) for collection of Tenant's food scraps) and meets with all applicable codes. Landlord shall, at Tenant's expense, provide trash and waste collection services which shall occur no less than seven (7) days per week. Landlord agrees that charges for trash and waste collection services shall be based on a per square foot basis of the Premises and that charges for trash shall be competitive for like providers of comparable quality in the metropolitan area where the Shopping Center is located.

V.

The Emergence of Grocerants

Grocerant Use Clause

Subject to existing exclusive use rights and prohibited uses set forth on Exhibit "___" attached hereto, the Demised Premises shall be used only for the purpose of the operation of a grocery store and/or supermarket under the trade name ____________ (or such other trade name used by Tenant in a majority of its other stores) (the "Permitted Use"). The Permitted Use may include, without limitation, (A) the sale of products, foods, merchandise, services and items generally sold in supermarkets or grocery stores including, without limitation, produce, meat, poultry, seafood, dairy, cereals, grains, fruits and vegetables, frozen foods, grocery products, household items, bulk foods, gourmet foods, bakery goods, prepared foods, alcoholic beverages (including wine, beer and package (i.e., "hard") liquor products and including for on or off premises consumption), vitamins, body care products, cosmetics, health care items, beauty aids, plants, flowers, books, magazines, bed sheets, towels and other household linens, clothing, medicinal herbs, naturopathic and homeopathic remedies, nutritional supplements, smoothies and/or fresh fruit drinks, and any other product, food, merchandise, services, or item sold in other supermarkets or grocery stores operated by ____________, or by entities owned or controlled by ____________, (B) the operation of an in-store bakery, brew pub, bar, café and/or a delicatessen style or sit down style restaurant, including the cooking required therefor, coffee bar and/or juice bar (Tenant may have such number of seats for Tenant's customers as Tenant deems necessary or desirable and, if required by applicable law with respect to an in-store brew pub or bar, a separate entrance to the brew pub or bar), (C) providing services ancillary or complementary to the foregoing including, without limitation, cooking demonstrations and cooking classes, and providing chair massages, and (D) the sale of any other products, foods, merchandise, and items and/or the provision of any other services or the conduct of any other activity that Tenant may from time to time deem to be desirable that are consistent with that of a first class retail shopping center, including those that may arise from future innovations to or changes in Tenant's business.

Food Hall Use Clause

The Premises shall be occupied and used by Tenant and any permitted successors, assigns, and sublessees, primarily for the purpose of conducting therein the business of an Italian/Western European eatery and market incorporating one or more of the following concepts: (i) restaurant(s) and food services for takeout/off-premises consumption (e.g., café, tavern and/or tasting room, delivery service, catering, banqueting and on-premises consumption, with beer wine and distilled spirits, including full-service restaurant(s)); (ii) a gourmet food market offering gourmet Italian foods and goods, private-label merchandise, sealed bottles of beer, wine, and distilled spirits and gift items and baskets; (iii) kitchen merchandise and food preparation gadgets , and cookbooks and books relating thereto; (iv) such other merchandise as may be warranted to enhance the central theme of the project, (v) cooking demonstrations; (vi) travel-related products; (vii) merchandise that enhances the brand (e.g., with logos, such as clothing, aprons, home-goods, etc.); and (viii) ancillary entertainment related to all of the above; (ix) wine shop and an urban winery and/or winery and/or micro-winery; and (x) a specialty restaurant with changing chefs/concept as core attraction/feature. Provided Tenant maintains proper licensing, Tenant may sell and/or serve beer, wine and distilled spirits for on-Premises and off-Premises consumption. Any proposed change of such permitted use or other material change to the retail marketing orientation or quality of operation of the business within the Premises (whether by Tenant or by any proposed assignee, subtenant or transferee) are subject to the advance written approval of Landlord in its commercially reasonable discretion. Landlord may withhold its approval if Tenant has not demonstrated to Landlord's commercially reasonable satisfaction that the proposed use, retail marketing orientation and/or quality of operation is compatible (in Landlord's commercially reasonable judgment) with other business operations (including Landlord's) conducted or permitted within the Development. At all times during the Lease Term, Tenant shall use commercially reasonable efforts to operate either an urban winery and/or winery and/or micro-winery in some portion of the Premises and shall obtain and maintain all federal and state licenses required for said operation. Notwithstanding the foregoing, so long as Tenant maintains one or more liquor licenses permitting Tenant to legally operate its business within the Premises, Tenant's failure to operate an urban winery or micro-winery within the Premises shall not be deemed an event of default under this Lease.

PART TWO

Franchises

So your cousin, dad, or friend has come to you and said that he is going to buy a franchise opportunity that has a brick-and-mortar/storefront location. After questioning his sanity, you realize that setting up a franchise operation involves many moving parts. Think of a franchise as a square dance with four main players in addition to a fiddler, a caller, and other dancers. You and your client will spend a great deal of time early on doing the do-si-do and then maybe doing an allemande left and then right before you ever get to the punch and cookies.

The main players are your client/franchisee/tenant, the landlord, the franchisor, and the bank. To properly represent for your client, you need to understand the roles of the other three players and to negotiate contracts/agreements with them along with the other players at the dance. You will need to employ good business skills, negotiating skills, and effective counsel.

If your client comes to you and says that he is opening a McDonald's franchise, don't read the rest of this section, but hire an attorney who specializes in complex franchise matters. However, this section will help guide you through most well-known national franchise chains with brick-and-mortar locations. There are tens of thousands of franchise opportunities, many of them not requiring lease negotiations, with the franchise operation being located in your client's basement or in a small office setting. However, this book focuses on restaurants, and this section will concentrate on restaurant franchise negotiations, although many of the concepts set forth in this section are applicable to other franchise operations located in shopping centers or stand-alone buildings.

Unless your client has money to spare or wants to invest his entire 401(k) savings, your client will likely need a Small Business Administration (SBA) loan to fund the buildout, startup cash flow needs, and franchise fee.

By the time your client approaches you to help him get his operation up and running, he has settled on a franchisor and has applied to become a franchisee. No legal or business positions are lost at this point, as vetting by the franchisor is often a long and arduous process. Think of it as buying a house and applying for a mortgage, with many more questions regarding your client's background and ability to run a business. After being preliminarily qualified as a franchisee, your client must negotiate a loan with the bank, which is akin to buying a house and giving up one's firstborn son.

Depending on your client's business and real estate skills, the franchisor may offer a variety of levels of services to assist him in finding a location. This is where your due diligence and thoroughness come into play. You must select the right town, the right location for traffic, the right landlord, and a host of other variables that can make or break your client's business. Then your client must select the proper bank. Just because your client has been a customer at XYZ bank for 30 years doesn't mean that lending institution is the best choice for applying for an SBA loan.

Other players at the square dance include the caller, which may be a manager if your client is not going to manage the location or if your client has multiple locations. The fiddler might be the construction company that will build out the space. Other dancers are more on the operational side, such as vendors for your products, service contractors, and a CPA. This section will not focus on the other players, which are mostly operational in nature, as the franchisor and groups of franchisees are able to assist your client in operating its business. Most quality franchisors have a vested interest in the success of your client's business. That is not to say that certain franchisors have, in the past or even today, made most of their money from selling franchise locations and collecting the up-front fees, with little regard to helping in the success of your client's business. Extensive online research can uncover most of those unscrupulous franchisors. It is best that your client steer clear from them. Fortunately, you and your client have access to the franchise disclosure document (FDD). By law, it is provided by the franchisor and is consistent across the board, setting forth the franchise fee, other fees paid to the franchisor, operational requirements, and a variety of other terms, conditions, and relationships of the franchisor.

Remember, your client is buying a system from the franchisor. Your client needs to feel comfortable in the clothes provided by the franchisor. He will be wearing them a long time. If your client is not scared off at this point, let's get started with discussing the four major players, including your client.

Chapter 6

Your Client

The basis of many successful franchise operations is consistency of look, consistency of operation, and consistency of product. This isn't like going to Burger King, where you can "have it your way." A successful franchisor will require the franchisee to "do it *their* way." The newer the franchisor and franchise concept, the less ingrained the franchisor will be in its requirements and the more opportunity your client will have in working with the franchisor to deviate from the franchise manual.

So there is a trade-off between becoming a franchisee for a new franchisor with a new concept versus becoming a franchisee of a more established and successful franchisor. Assuming that your client consults with you prior to the dance starting, you need to assess your client's ability to operate in a franchise environment. If you have a Type A client, he may butt heads with the franchisor. Your client may not be able to establish a good relationship with the franchisor, or he may find that the franchisor terminated the franchise agreement because of your client's inability to adhere to the operation manual. As Ray Kroc determined early on with McDonald's, the success of its operation depends on its franchisees complying strictly with the methods established by McDonald's headquarters. And we all know how successful McDonald's has become partially because of its insistence upon strict compliance with those methods.

You also must assess the financial well-being of your client. Many franchise operations fail, especially restaurants. Although the failure rate of franchise restaurants is less than the 9-out-of-10 failure rate of mom-and-pop restaurant businesses, the opportunity for failure is strong. You need to assess your client's ability to withstand the operational relationship with the franchisor, in addition to assessing your client's ability to meet the financial requirements of both the franchisor and the bank. Although you are paid to represent your client and his wishes, it is not a good idea to allow your client to enter into a business without him being apprised of the financial risks that are in front of him. If your client is putting all of his retirement money into this operation, he must be advised of the risks involved and the possible outcome if the operation fails. This outcome includes not only what the franchisor will extract from your client but also what the bank will extract. Most franchisor websites and FDDs establish total net worth and tangible net worth requirements that your client must meet in order to be considered as a franchisee. You must assess whether your client meets these criteria.

You also must assess whether your client has the business skills to run a business. Some franchisors help out more than others in assisting a franchisee in operating the business. Most of them provide some sort of training program that may last anywhere from a few days or weeks to a couple months, but once you are out in the field, you are on your own. Many franchisors have regional employees that make regular visits to the operation to answer questions and to assess how the business is doing. Fortunately, in this day and age of computers, daily record keeping and input is easy to establish, and it is easy for the franchisor to assess how the business is faring. Unfortunately, the numbers don't tell everything, so the franchisor may not know whether external factors are causing difficulties or an operational issue exists. If your client is going to operate the business himself, he should have the business wherewithal to follow the franchise manual, perform banking operations, keep track of inventory, have the interpersonal skills needed to deal with any employees, and put in long hours to ensure the success of the business. A person needs plenty of stamina to operate a successful business, whether it be a restaurant or a cell phone store or another business (franchise or not). A client near retirement age might do better operating a less demanding franchise than a restaurant that is open for breakfast, lunch, and dinner.

Your client may be someone you have known for a while and worked with before, or he may be someone who walked in off the street. However, as you can see from the above discussion, you need to spend time with the client and get to know him so that you can advise him properly on his ability to run a successful franchise business. As there are so many franchise opportunities available, by getting to know your client, you can direct him into a business that best fits his financial profile and risk aversion, business acumen, and lifestyle choices.

Chapter 7

Choosing a Landlord and Location

Now that you are done playing Dr. Phil, you can play attorney. Most of the remainder of this section of the book will focus on transactional work: negotiating with a variety of players, including government authorities, the landlord, the franchisor, managers (if any), and the bank. This chapter will concentrate on the location and the landlord.

Site selection is of prime importance. The franchisor will want to approve the site your client selects. Depending on your client's sophistication and the sophistication of the franchisor, however, you will spend much time vetting the site. If your client selects a quality landlord, much of your due diligence on site selection can be provided by the landlord. Even in the cases of large national landlords, however, your client still must vet the municipality, the location, and the shopping center to ensure that he can operate his franchise at the location selected.

Whether your client has selected a stand-alone building or a location within a multitenant building, even though the building may be occupied by only two tenants, it is necessary to determine whether local code will allow the operation of your client's franchise as dictated by the franchisor's franchise requirements. Unless your client is working with a sophisticated franchisor, your client will need to ensure himself and the franchisor that your client (1) can use the required trade dress, (2) has appropriate ingress and egress, (3) has ample parking, and (4) knows of nothing pending that will impair your client's operation of the franchised business, such as change of traffic patterns (right-in/right-out entrance versus full turning movements) or a change from a highway to a limited-access highway.

For instance, if your client is going to operate a franchise business with a national logo or national colors or even a trade dress that includes awnings or other exterior improvements, your client must know that the location selected allows such items under local code and that the same are not prohibited or limited by any restrictive easement agreement, declaration, or other agreement, covenant, and restriction or under the rules of the landlord. For example, your client intends to go into a new power center, but only certain sign colors and sign designs are allowed by the local jurisdiction, whether that jurisdiction be the government or some quasi-government entity, or the landlord may prohibit certain signs or sign designs that are included in the franchise sign package. For instance, if you want to open a Jimmy John's restaurant, the franchisor's sign package includes a variety of open-faced neon signs that are to be placed in the storefront windows. Many jurisdictions and landlords prohibit the use of such signage in windows. You should request the landlord's sign criteria as soon as possible in your negotiations. You also want to make sure that your client's grand opening package is allowed within the jurisdiction or shopping center. All of this vetting will save time and heartache during or even after the negotiation process. If you must obtain a variance for a sign or an awning design from the local government, you will invest significant time and money in trying to obtain that variance, with no assurance you will obtain one. You and your client will have to obtain approval from the franchisor for any change in the design package.

Other items for your due diligence with respect to the location include confirming the availability of adequate parking, drop-off lanes, drive-through opportunities, to-go parking spots, and pylon signage, just to name a few. Hopefully, your client will bring you into the site selection process early so that you can minimize or eliminate surprises during the lease negotiation process. What may look like a great location may be a disaster if your client cannot satisfy the franchisor's needs or his own. A less attractive center across the street may better suit your client's needs.

Now that your client has selected the site, the franchisor will generally need to approve the location. Some franchisors are more involved than others in the site selection process. Once the franchisor has approved the location, your client will be able to negotiate a lease agreement with the landlord. The first step in that negotiation should be to negotiate an LOI. The LOI may run many pages, depending on the landlord. The LOI is the basis for the lease agreement. Depending on state law and the terms of the LOI, it should be non-binding. Nevertheless, many landlords will want to conform the lease agreement strictly to the LOI. Your client should expect the same treatment from the landlord. Therefore, it is important during the LOI stage to be clear about what you and your client want included in the lease agreement. Note that many franchisors will expect the lease to include an exclusive use provision, the build-out/work letter and sign package, and certain other rights of the franchisor. It is also advisable to obtain the franchisor's approval of the LOI during the LOI negotiation stage. One pet peeve of a landlord is to negotiate a lease extensively only to learn that a franchisor requires a rider that significantly modifies the lease agreement. It is best that your client allow you to review the LOI and compare it against the franchisor's requirements listed in any rider and the franchise agreement.

Of the many clauses your client and the franchisor may want to include in the lease, several are consistent across the board. First of those is the exclusive use provision. Because both your client and the franchisor are investing heavily in the buildout and operation of the business, your client should request an exclusive use provision drafted as broadly as possible for its particular use. For example, if your client wants to operate a Mexican restaurant, he would want to be granted an exclusive for the sale of Mexican food within the shopping center. The term *Shopping Center* should include any outlots owned by the landlord or its affiliates. The exclusive should be drafted as broadly as possible. An example of a broadly defined exclusive would be that another tenant's sales of Mexican food within the shopping center could not exceed 10% of its gross sales. Of course, the landlord will want to define the exclusive as narrowly as possible.

Another standard clause in most leases with franchisees is the right to assign the lease to the franchisor or to another franchisee. Landlords will typically allow an assignment to the franchisor so long as the franchisor assumes the lease in writing, cures any defaults under the lease, provides notice to the landlord within a certain number of days of such assignment, and remains liable under the lease even if the lease is reassigned. This assignment can generally be made without approval of the landlord or payment of any assignment fee. Typically, the franchisor will not want to be liable to cure any defaults of the franchisee or remain liable under the lease following a subsequent assignment, so this lease provision may be somewhat heavily negotiated. The franchisor will typically want to be able to assign the lease to another franchisee without the landlord's approval or payment of an assignment fee. A landlord often resists this transfer because it wants a qualified operator to run the business within its shopping center. Landlords will want approval over any assignment to a franchisee. However, you may be able to negotiate terms that if the new franchisee meets some basic level of expertise and financial net worth, the lease may be assigned from either the franchisee or your client without the landlord's approval or payment of an assignment fee. Example A provides an example of an assignment clause to a franchisor; Example B provides an example of an assignment from a franchisor to another franchisee.

Another right that franchisors will require in a lease is the right to inspect the premises at any time and to remove any proprietary marks of the franchisor. This clause is generally invoked if the franchise agreement between the franchisee and the franchisor has been terminated. Example C provides an example of a right to inspect clause.

The right to de-identify the premises may include extensive work, such as changing the storefront elevation of the building, changing the color of the building, and removing any recognizable design and logo features from the premises. For instance, if your client operates a Checkers restaurant, the building and site is essentially one giant logo. At the end of the term of the lease agreement or the franchise agreement, as the case may be, Checkers corporate wants the right to completely de-identify the building. The landlord needs to be aware of such requirements of a franchisor, and an appropriate cause should be included in the lease. Typical de-identification clauses are shown in Example D.

Another clause that is less onerous but still of concern to your client, the franchisor, and the landlord is the franchisor's request to receive any notification sent by the landlord to your client, especially notification of any event of default or breach of lease. Typically landlords want to limit this notification to any event of default and resist sending all notices to your client/tenant because these notices are often immaterial to the relationship between the franchisor and the franchisee. If the landlord agrees to provide notice to the franchisor, a proper address for the franchisor should be included in the lease or the rider to the lease, with rights to change the address upon notice to landlord. One good lease drafting practice is to include a clause within the body of the lease stating that a rider is attached to the lease and shall control over any language contained within the body of the lease.

A franchisor also asks the landlord to provide the franchisor with any sales and/or financial reports the landlord may receive from your client. The landlord should resist this provision because no privity between the landlord and the franchisor is created by the lease. Most franchise agreements between the franchisor and the franchisee already require the franchisee to report such gross sales and financial figures to the franchisor. It should be up to the franchisor to determine the validity and completeness of such reporting, and the landlord should be absolved of any requirement to provide this documentation.

Another lease clause often requested by the franchisor is the right of the franchisee to change its menu items and even its general food product category. Often franchisors have restaurants with more than one food category. An example is Focus Brands that currently includes Moe's Southwest Grill, which is a Southwestern/Mexican concept, and McAlister's Deli, which is a fast-casual restaurant serving American foods. The franchisor may request the right of the franchisee to be able to switch from one category to another. Landlords typically resist this right as they want to control the use of a tenant to prevent duplication of use within the shopping center. A compromise would be to limit the change of use to another use as long as the landlord has not granted another tenant in the shopping center an exclusive.

If the landlord requires a radius restriction within the lease that prevents another operation of the same name or similar use within a certain trade area (generally expressed in a number of miles from the shopping center), that radius restriction should match the one provided in the franchise agreement between the franchisor and franchisee. If the landlord wants the radius restriction of 5 miles for any similar use or under the same trade name and the franchise agreement between the franchisor and franchisee limits that trade area restriction to only 2 miles, the opening of another restaurant outside the franchisor's restricted area but within the limits of the landlord's restriction would be a violation of the lease. You might say that the violation would not occur because another franchisee or the franchisor, not your client, would open the business. However, if the lease is later assigned to the franchisor or to another franchisee with locations in the radius area, the assignee might be in violation of the radius restriction. Therefore, the radius restriction in the lease should match the radius restriction in the franchise agreement.

A large contentious area of the lease is the required buildout of the premises by the franchisor. In addition to providing consistent product across its franchise platform, a franchisor is also selling the identification of its brand. Almost everyone knows the Golden Arches of McDonald's or the blue-and-white circular logo of AT&T. The design of the storefront and the premises is extremely important to the franchisor and to the success of your client's business. If your client has the only building within a particular area, identification of his store is less important than if he is in a row of 15, 20 or more stores with similar size signs and similar storefronts. Therefore, negotiating the identification features of the franchisor within the store and on the storefront, including the storefront sign, is very important to the franchisor and your client. Many franchisors require identifying design features other than the storefront sign, such as awnings, colors of doors and the storefront, and architectural design and features. It is important that the landlord approve the design of the buildout and the sign package found in the lease. Other buildout requirements that need to be included in the lease are the adequacy of utilities; dumpster locations; the condition of the floor slab, especially if the floor is to remain uncovered and stained; air-conditioning capacities; and restroom availability. Many of these items would be negotiated in any lease. However, the franchisor may require certain design requirements over and above standard retail, and the nature of your client's business may also require certain special requirements, especially if it is a restaurant.

EXAMPLES

Example A: Assignment to a Franchisor

Should Franchisor become an Assignee of this Lease, so long as Assignee is open and operating in the Premises and is not in monetary default beyond any applicable cure period as of the effective date of the assignment, Assignee shall have the right to assign this Lease to any entity owned or controlled by Assignee (or any franchisee of Assignee) without payment of any assignment fee and without triggering any right of Landlord to terminate this Lease and recapture possession of the Premises, provided that: (i) such entity agrees in writing to assume all the obligations to be performed by Assignee; (ii) Assignee agrees in writing to guarantee the prompt performance of all terms, conditions and covenants in this Lease to be performed by such entity pursuant to the foregoing assumption; (iii) such assignment shall be for the same Permitted Use set forth in Section ________ of this Lease; and (iv) Landlord receives an executed copy of any such assignment within ten (10) days of the date of such assignment.

Example B: Assignment to a Franchisee

Notwithstanding anything in this Lease to the contrary, Tenant shall have the right, without the necessity of obtaining Landlord's consent, without payment of any assignment fee and without triggering any right of Landlord to terminate this Lease and recapture possession of the Premises, to assign this Lease or sublet the Premises to a franchisee or licensee of Tenant upon the following conditions: (a) Tenant shall not be in default under the Lease beyond any applicable cure period on the effective date of the assignment or sublease; (b) on or before the effective date of the assignment or sublease, Tenant shall (w) notify Landlord in writing of (i) the effective date of the assignment or sublease, (ii) the facts placing such assignment or sublease within the provisions of this paragraph, and (iii) any changes to the address for billings and legal notices sent to Tenant, the assignee or sublessee; (x) provide Landlord with a written assumption agreement wherein such assignee or sublessee agrees to assume in writing for the benefit of Landlord all of Tenant's obligations under the Lease; (y) provide Landlord with evidence reasonably satisfactory to Landlord that the franchisee or licensee satisfies the minimum requirements for a franchisee or licensee of the franchisor or licensor, including without limitation net worth requirements; and (z) provide evidence reasonably satisfactory to Landlord that such franchisee or licensee is a legal entity in good standing in the state of its origin and is authorized to do business in the state in which the Center is located; (c) the franchisee or licensee shall occupy the Premises and conduct its business under the trade name and business set forth elsewhere in this Lease; (d) the assignment or sublease shall be effective only so long as Tenant maintains direct control and supervision over such franchisee; (e) in no event shall the franchisee or licensee be permitted to assign this lease or sublet its interest in the Premises without Landlord's consent to any party other than the franchisor and then only if the franchisor or licensor cures any defaults under the Lease. In no event shall Tenant be released from any liability under this Lease as a result of such assignment or sublease.

Example C: Franchisor's Right to Inspect the Premises

Franchisor has a right to enter the Premises at any time and without trespass to inspect the Premises for compliance with Franchisor's Franchise Agreement with Tenant. Franchisor has the right to require Tenant to remodel, equip, paint and decorate the interior of the Premises and to display such proprietary marks and signs on the interior of the Premises as Tenant is reasonably required to display pursuant to the Franchise Agreement and any successor Franchise Agreement under which Tenant may operate a restaurant in the Premises; provided, however, that any remodel of the exterior of the building and/or its signs shall be subject to Landlord's prior approval, which shall not be unreasonably withheld, conditioned or delayed.

Example D: De-identification Clauses

For fifteen (15) days after the expiration or termination of the Lease, Landlord agrees that Franchisor shall have the right to enter the Premises to make any removals, modifications or alterations necessary, including modifications to the building in which the Premises are located, in Franchisor's sole discretion to protect its franchise system, trademarks, trade names, trade dress and other intellectual property without being guilty of trespass or any other tort or crime provided Franchisor promptly repairs any damage to the Premises caused by such modifications or alterations.

Landlord agrees upon the expiration or termination of the Franchise Agreement to relinquish to Franchisor any and all liens or other ownership interests, whether by operation of law or otherwise, in and to any tangible property bearing Franchisor's trademarks, service marks or trade dress.

Chapter 8

Experienced Manager

Another participant in a square dance is the caller. The caller in a store setting is the manager. If your client intends to manage the business himself or with another family member, this chapter may be of somewhat less importance than if your client hires a manager for the store. In a restaurant setting, unless your client has unlimited stamina, he will need someone to assist in managing the business.

In the FDD, your client will have received a basic operating statement showing the breakdown of the anticipated costs and profits of the business. An experienced manager can assist in keeping the costs below what is shown in the FDD, thereby increasing profits for the business. An experienced manager will know the ins and outs of building a crew if the business requires one and dealing with reporting to the franchisor; purchasing supplies and/or goods; dealing with the government regarding taxes, wages, and insurance benefits; and overseeing other aspects of running a franchise business. If your client hires a manager to run or assist in running the business, that manager should have experience in the same business as your client's.

Many franchisors require franchisees to attend classes at the franchise headquarters to prepare them for operating a business. However, a course of three weeks or three months cannot prepare an inexperienced operator to run a business, especially a restaurant. In addition, and especially in a restaurant setting, the hours are long, arduous, and often outside the stamina of a normal human being. Even if a restaurant opens at 11 a.m. for business, food preparation must occur early, deliveries of goods and food items are often made early in the morning, and restaurants generally stay open until at least 9 p.m. Other franchise operations may be less demanding than that of a restaurant or other food service franchise, and hiring an experienced manager may not be as critical as it is in a restaurant setting.

There are many ways of compensating a manager for the business. He can be provided a salary, a bonus, a "piece of the pie," or a combination of any of those. A good restaurant manager might be offered a base salary plus a bonus if he meets certain financial targets with respect to costs of wages, costs of food, and/or profitability. Your client should be cautioned that just because brother Billy worked at a fast-food restaurant 15 years ago in high school, that experience may or may not translate into a quality restaurant manager. If your client is lucky to get a manager who is experienced with the franchisor, it will save in up-front training costs and provide your client a jump start on making the business profitable. The manager should be brought on early in the development of any business, especially a restaurant, to help coordinate buildout, hiring, and grand opening activities.

The franchisor will control most of the design of the premises, the menu, the number of crew members required for each shift, advertising, grand opening activities, financial reporting, and other aspects of the franchise business. Some franchisors are more involved in the franchisee's business than others. For instance, in some cases, your client may have to purchase all of the food and/or merchandise directly from the franchisor. Often your client is required to purchase fixtures from a preferred vendor of the franchisor. Some franchisors, however, are less restrictive and allow franchisees to use local vendors to plan and build out the premises. That is less likely with a restaurant and more likely in a goods or services store. Remember that the franchisor typically has a brand it is selling and that brand recognition is critical for customer recognition.

It would be wise for your client to enter into an employment contract with any manager he hires to help run the business. That employment contract should spell out the basics of term, wages, bonuses, benefits, and any other items normally found in an employment contract. The employment contract should also contain a non-compete clause (your client does not want the manager leaving the franchise for a competing use) and a nonsolicitation provision so that the manager does not steal your client's best workers.

A third special clause in the employment contract should allow your client to obtain and maintain a key man life insurance policy on the manager. Because a quality manager is of utmost importance to the operation of any business, it would be devastating, especially in a retail environment, if a quality manager suddenly died. The employment agreement should contain a requirement that the manager is to cooperate with the franchisee to obtain a key man life insurance.

As stated earlier, performance bonuses might be written into the employment contract. Performance bonuses could relate to any line items of a store operation–wages; cost of goods sold; occupancy costs such as maintenance, expendables, and utility costs; and a bonus for longevity. A happy manager is someone who can exponentially enhance your client's business and provide your client peace of mind and assurances of success in his business operation.

A sample employment contract for the manager of a fast-casual restaurant is provided. It contains the basics of what was just mentioned but could be enhanced with other provisions.

Any manager must be able to deal with all kinds of outside vendors and with the franchisor. In a restaurant setting, outside vendors include raw food vendors, drink vendors, advertising people, government health inspectors, cleaning and maintenance companies (e.g., janitorial, pest control, and trash services), and a variety of other operational service and goods providers. An experienced manager in the same business area as your client's operation will provide better control and assurances of profitability.

An experienced manager will also be able to provide training to employees. Almost all franchisors want your client to do it their way. By having experience in the industry in which your client has a franchise operation, the manager will hit the ground running. Franchisors provide a plethora of information regarding procedures for running the business; however, franchisors cannot provide too much information without running the risk of joint employer liability. Learning how to run a business without having had experience is difficult, but it is much more difficult unless your client has someone there to help every step of the way. Some franchisors provide oversight early in the franchise operations. Your client should find out how much oversight he can expect from the franchisor during the startup of the company. Most franchisors have regional management and district management that can provide assistance where needed. However, if the franchisor is just starting out in the territory or has a large number of stores, the franchisor's personnel may not have the time to provide your client with the tools needed to learn the business from the ground up.

If your client is operating in a small town with a limited customer base, one bad experience can lead to disaster. In more of metropolitan area where people do not talk to each other often, a bad customer experience is a learning experience but may not be as devastating as in a small town. It is crucial that your client get off to a good start. If he does not elect to hire an experienced manager, you, as counsel to your client, should stress that he train as much as possible with the franchisor and learn as much as he can from other franchisees in the system. Each FDD includes a list of all of the franchisees of the franchisor, including addresses and telephone numbers. Your client has the opportunity to converse with these people as to what to expect from the franchisor and learn any "tricks of the trade" in order to get the franchise business operating efficiently and to ensure quick profitability.

Even though many businesses fail due to location, economic downturn, or other external factors, the biggest reason most businesses fail is due to bad management. An experienced manager can help prevent a disaster and can control the music being played at the square dance.

EMPLOYMENT AGREEMENT

THIS AGREEMENT (the "Agreement") made as of the ____ day of ________________, 20__, between ________________, a(n) ________________________________ (the "Employer") and__________________, an individual resident of ___________________ (the "Employee"). The Employer and the Employee may hereafter be individually referred to as a "Party" or together as the "Parties."

Recitals

WHEREAS, the Employer, through its operations and the operations of affiliates of the Employer, owns and manages restaurants; and

WHEREAS, the Employer has determined that the services of Employee, his professional expertise and experience, and his knowledge of the restaurant industry are of value to the Employer, and the Employee desires to provide services to the Employer; and

NOW, THEREFORE, in consideration of the foregoing and the mutual covenants contained herein, the Parties agree as follows:

1. Employment. The Employer offers to employ the Employee and the Employee accepts employment with the Employer on a full-time basis upon the terms and conditions hereinafter set forth. The term "full-time basis," as used herein, shall mean sufficient hours required to perform the duties outlined in Section 3 and the normal week for individuals in comparable restaurant positions in the industry.
2. Term. This Agreement and the Employee's employment under it shall be effective on _____________, 20__ (the "Commencement Date") and shall end on the last day of the initial ten (10) year agreement with [FRANCHISOR], or its successor or assign, (the "Franchisor") to own and operate ________________ franchised restaurants (the "Franchise Agreement") (the "Initial Term"). Provided, however, this Agreement shall be automatically extended through the end of the Extension Term unless this Agreement is terminated pursuant to the provisions of Section 11. The term "Extension Term" for purposes of this Agreement shall mean a period of extension of the Franchise Agreement with Franchisor as negotiated by the Employer.
3. Duties. The Employee is engaged by Employer to an executive capacity as the General Manager Operator of __________________ restaurants ("______"). The Employee shall be located in ______________________, or such other location as the Parties shall agree and shall report to the Chief Operating Officer of the Employer (the "COO") with respect to the performance of his duties and shall be subject to the direction and control of the COO. Any material change by the Employer in the duties

of the Employee as described above without the written consent of the COO shall be considered a termination of this Agreement without cause pursuant to Section 11(d). In carrying out the duties as required herein, the Employee shall comply with all Employer and franchisor policies, procedures, rules and regulation, both written and oral, as are announced by Employer from time to time. It is also understood and agreed to by the Employee that his assignment, duties and responsibilities and reporting arrangements may be changed by Employer at any time.

4. Extent of Services. The Employee, subject to the direction and control of the COO, shall have the power and authority commensurate with this executive status and necessary to perform his duties hereunder. The Employee shall devote his entire employable time, attention and best efforts to the business of the Employer, and shall not, without the consent of the Employer, during the term of this Agreement, as may be extended from time to time, be actively engaged in any other business activity in any capacity, in promoting, undertaking or carrying on any other business that competes with the Employer or an affiliate of the Employer or could reasonably interfere with his duties to Employer without Employer's prior written permission, whether or not such business activity is pursued for gain, profit or other pecuniary advantage; however, this shall not be construed as preventing the Employee from investing his assets in such form or manner as will not require any services on the part of the Employee in the operation of the affairs of any company in which such investments are made.
5. Compensation and Expenses.
   a. Base Salary. For all services rendered for the Employer pursuant to this Agreement, until the termination of this Agreement, the Employee shall receive a Base Salary of ________________ and 00/100 Dollars ($________________) per year, payable in bi-weekly installments. The salary of the Employee (and all other payments taxed as compensation) shall be subject to the withholding of taxes. The Employee may receive increases in his Base Salary from time to time, based on his performance in his executive and management capacity. The amounts of such increases in Base Salary shall approved by the COO.
   b. Bonus. In addition to Base Salary, the Employer may, at any time and from time to time, pay Employee a bonus. Employer shall receive a bonus based on maintaining the "Premises Costs" at ____________ percent (___%) or less of "Gross Sales" from the operation of a certain _________. "Premises Costs" shall be defined as costs for wages and associated benefits and taxes (other than those of Employer), costs of food and of utilities and outside services. Gross Sales shall be defined as the sale prices of all goods, wares, food and merchandise sold at or from the ______________ for cash, credit or otherwise, without reserve for deduction for uncollected amounts less exchanges of merchandise between Employer's stores made only for the convenient operation

of the Employer's restaurants, returns to suppliers, refunds to customers, sales of fixtures, machinery and equipment after use in the restaurant and sales, excise or similar tax imposed by governmental authority and collected from customers at the restaurant and paid out by Employer.

c. Expense Reimbursement. The Employee shall receive reimbursement for all reasonable expenses approved by the COO that the Employee incurs for improving and promoting the Employer's business, pursuant to the Employer's expense reimbursement policies as applicable from time to time.

d. Secondment. The Employer may employ the Employee through one or more entities affiliated with Employer for purposes of payroll and benefits administration on such terms as may be agreed between the Employer and the Employee, consistent herewith.

6. Fringe Benefits.

a. Employee Benefits. The Employer shall, at its expense, provide the Employee with an annual benefit of _______________ and 00/100 Dollars ($_______________) for Employee's automobile expenses, health insurance and cellular telephone, said amount payable in advance in equal month installments. Such amount may be increased on each anniversary of the Commencement Date by an amount determined by the Employer.

b. Vacation. The Employee shall be entitled to _____ (__) weeks' vacation with pay each year during the term of this Agreement.

7. Ownership. In addition to the salary compensation described above, the Employee shall receive a _________ percent (_____%) ownership equity stake in the first (1st) ____________ located in ______________________. The Employee shall receive a ______________ percent (___%) ownership equity in any future _______________ restaurants in which Employee is directly involved in opening and operating after the first (1st) restaurant is successfully open and operating. **[DELETE IF NO OWNERSHIP]**

8. Disclosure of Information. The Employee acknowledges that in and as a result of his employment with the Employer, he will be making use of, acquiring and/or adding confidential information for the Employer and its affiliated entities of a special and unique nature and value. As a material inducement to the Employer to enter into this Agreement and to pay the Employee the compensation stated in Section 5 and Section 7, as well as any additional benefits stated herein, the Employee covenants and agrees that he shall not, at any time during or following the term of his employment, directly or indirectly, divulge or disclose for any purpose whatsoever, any confidential information that has been obtained by or disclosed to him as a result of this employment with the Employer, except to the extent that such confidential information (a) becomes a matter of public record or is published in a newspaper,

magazine or other periodical available to the general public, other than as a result of any act or omission of the Employee, (b) is required to be disclosed by any law, regulation or order of any court or regulatory commission, department or agency, provided that the Employee gives prompt notice or such requirement to the Employer or its applicable affiliate to enable the Employer to seek an appropriate protective order, or (c) is necessary to perform properly the Employee's duties under this Agreement. Upon the termination of this Agreement, the Employee shall return all material obtained from or belonging to the Employer which he may have in his possession or control. Confidential information includes, without limitation, any and all trade secrets, confidential, private or secret information of the Employer including without limitation (i) business and financial information of the Employer, (ii) business methods and practices of the Employer, (iii) marketing strategies of the Employer, and (iv) such information as the Employer may from time to time designate as being confidential. Employee agrees that he will not copy any confidential information of the Employer including any curriculum belonging to the Employer nor remove same from the Employer's premises without the express written permission of the Employer, except as required as part of his duties hereunder. Employee recognizes and acknowledges that a breach of this provision may result in the termination of employment and/or the institution of legal proceedings.

9. <u>Covenants Against Solicitation</u>. The Employee acknowledges that the services he is to render to the Employer are of a special and unusual character, with a unique value to the Employer, the loss of which cannot be adequately be compensated by damages or an action at law. In view of the unique value to the Employer of the services of the Employee for which the Employer has contracted hereunder, because of the confidential information to be obtained by, or disclosed to, the Employee as hereinabove set forth, and as a material inducement to the Employer to enter into this Agreement and to pay the Employee the compensation stated in Section 5 and Section 7, as well as any additional benefits stated herein, and other good and valuable consideration, the Employee covenants and agrees that throughout the period the Employee remains employed hereunder and for two (2) years thereafter, the Employee shall not, directly or indirectly, anywhere in the State of ______________, a state in which Employer or an affiliate of Employer operates a restaurant or a franchise territory awarded to or to which Employer has signed an agreement to operate a restaurant with a franchisor or is engaged in negotiations with a franchisor to operate a restaurant (a) solicit or attempt to convert to other corporations or entities, persons or other entities providing the same or similar products or services provided by the Employer and its affiliates; or (b) solicit for employment or employ any employee of the Employer or any of its affiliates; or (c) retain as an independent contractor or agent any such person or entity.

The Employee further agrees that should he be approached by a person who is or has been an employee of the Employer during the period described above, the Employee will not offer to or employ or retain as an independent contractor or agent any such person for a period of two (2) years following the termination of employment with Employer or an affiliate of Employer.

10. Non-Competition. The Employee agrees that he will not, without the prior written consent of the Employer, at any time during employment with the Employer or an affiliate of Employer and for a period of two (2) years following the termination of employment however caused (whether employment is terminated by Employee or the Employer and whether with or without cause or in breach of this Agreement) either individually or in partnership or jointly or in conjunction with any person as a principal, agent, employee, shareholder (other than a holding of shares listed on a United States or Canadian stock exchange that does not exceed five percent (5%) of the outstanding shares so listed) or in any other manner or capacity whatsoever carry on, be engaged in, or be concerned with or interested in or advise, lend money to, guaranty the debts or obligations of or permit his name or any part thereof to be used or employed by any person or entity engaged in or concerned with the aspect of business in which the Employee is engaged within the State of ____________, a state in which Employer or an affiliate of Employer operates a restaurant or a franchise territory awarded to or to which Employer has signed an agreement to operate a restaurant with a franchisor or is engaged in negotiations with a franchisor to operate a restaurant.
11. Termination.
    a. Termination by the Employee. The Employee may terminate this Agreement at any time and for any reason upon at least one hundred eighty (180) days written notice to the Employer.
    b. Termination by the Employer for Death or Disability. The Employer may terminate this Agreement upon the death or permanent disability of the Employee. For purposes of this Section 11(b), permanently disabled shall be defined as a disability that has continued or is reasonably expected, based on the opinion of two (2) physicians licensed in the State of ______________ after a physical examination of the Employee, to continue for at least one (1) year.
    c. Termination by the Employer With Just Cause. The Employer may terminate this Agreement at any time with Just Cause. For purposes of this Section 11(c), "Just Cause" shall mean:
        i. a material breach by Employee of this Agreement, the commission of gross negligence, or willful malfeasance or fraud or dishonesty of a substantial nature in performing the Employee's services on behalf of the Employer, which breach is in each case (A) willful and deliberate on the Employee's part and committed in bad faith or without reasonable belief

that such breach is in the best interest of the Employer and (B) repeated by the Employee after receipt of written notice from the Employer specifying such breach;

ii. The Employee's conviction by a court of law, or admission that he is guilty of a felony; or

iii. The Employee's absence from his employment, for reasons other than health, for a period of more than one (1) week without the prior written consent of the Employer.

d. Termination by the Employer Without Just Cause. The Employer may terminate the Employee at any time without Just Cause.

e. Payment Upon Termination. If the Employee is terminated under (a), (b) or (c) above, the Employee shall be entitled to receive his Base Salary, as provided in Section 5(a) which is accrued but unpaid at the date of termination and all other unpaid amounts previously accrued or awarded pursuant to any other provision of this Agreement. If the Employee is terminated under (d) above, the Employee shall be paid the balance of the compensation due hereunder for a period of __________ (___) days.

12. Key Man Insurance. The Employer shall secure so-called Key Man Insurance on the Employee in amounts and with terms determined by the Employer. Employee shall cooperate with Employer and Employer's insurance provider in obtaining such insurance.

13. Miscellaneous.

a. Entire Undertaking. This Agreement sets forth the entire agreement and understanding between the Parties as to the matters contained in it, and merges and supersedes all prior discussion, agreement, and understanding of every kind and nature among them.

b. Amendments. Any modification or amendment to this Agreement shall become effective only if it is in writing and executed by both Parties.

c. Binding Effect. This Agreement shall be binding upon, and inure to the benefit of, the Parties and their respective legal representatives, trustees, receivers, successors and permitted assigns.

d. Assignment. The Employee may not assign this Agreement or any provision of this Agreement to any other person or entity without the consent of the Employer. The Employer may assign this Agreement to any entity or person without the consent of the Employee.

e. Notices. All notices, requests, demands and other communication provided for in this Agreement shall be in writing and shall be deemed to have been given at the time when personally delivered, or mailed by registered or certified mail, return receipt requested, or delivered by a national overnight courier, to the address of the other Party as such Party shall from time to time provide, however, that any notice of change of address shall be effective only upon receipt by addressee.

f. Invalidity of Provision. If any provision or the application of any provision of this Agreement to any person or circumstance is held invalid, illegal or unenforceable, the remainder of this Agreement and the application of such provision to other persons or circumstances shall not be affected, and the remaining provisions of this Agreement shall be unimpaired, and the invalid, illegal or unenforceable provision shall be replaced by a mutually acceptable valid legal and enforceable provision which comes closest to the intent of the Parties.

g. Governing Law. This Agreement shall be construed and governed by the laws of the State of ________________ and any dispute arising out of or relating to this Agreement shall be exclusively resolved in the courts of the County of ____________, State of ____________. All Parties to this Agreement consent to such jurisdiction.

h. Headings. The headings of this section of this Agreement are inserted for convenience only and in no way define, limit, or prescribe the intent of this Agreement.

i. Waiver. Waiver by either Party of a breach of any provision of this Agreement shall not operate or be construed as a waiver of any subsequent breach by either Party.

j. Execution Procedure. This Agreement and its amendment may be executed in multiple copies, with each multiple copy to be deemed an original, but all multiple copies together constituting one and the same instrument.

k. Interpretation. The Employer prepared this Agreement for the convenience of the Parties and each Party has had the opportunity to review and comment upon its provisions and seek professional advice. As a result, this Agreement shall not be interpreted in favor of or against any Party for having prepared it.

l. Costs and Attorney Fees on Breach. If any action is brought by either Party under this Agreement by reason of any claim or cause of action against the other, arising out of or in connection with any breach or other nonperformance of the provisions of this Agreement, then any party which is successful upon any final determination of any such claim or cause of action shall be entitled to reasonable preparation, investigation and court costs and reasonable attorney's fees, as are fixed by a court of competent jurisdiction.

IN WITNESS WHEREOF, the Parties have entered into this Agreement as of the day, month and year first above written.

EMPLOYER: ______________________________,
a(n) ______________________________
By: ______________________________
Name: ______________________________
Its: ______________________________

EMPLOYEE: ______________________________,
an adult individual

____

Chapter 9

Architect and General Contractor

Every square dance needs music. For this dance, two players are needed—a fiddler and a banjo picker. The fiddler is the general contractor, and the banjo picker is the architect. Although neither player will be used all the way to the end of the franchise operation, both are very important to get everyone dancing.

Your client, as the franchisee, will work closely with the architect and the general contractor to design and build out the franchise location. In addition, if your client has employed a manager, that person will also be involved with the architect and general contractor, especially the general contractor.

Remember, this is not "Have it your way." The franchisor has very specific and rigid requirements regarding the look of the franchise location. The architect will work closely with the franchisor's architect and design team to create a store that is acceptable to the franchisor and provides the kind of identification necessary to ensure that customers of the franchisor have a similar experience and a consistent look whenever they are in one of the franchisor's locations.

When selecting the architect, the architect should be familiar with and have experience in the business of the franchisee, especially if the franchisee is opening a restaurant. The architect needs to be familiar with local code, state code, quasi-jurisdictional requirements and restrictions, and other design requirements of the local jurisdiction. Landlords often establish restrictions on design and signage of the premises, which may be contrary to the look and design the franchisor requires. It is important that your client and/or the architect request such rules and regulations from the landlord before they begin plan preparation.

The franchisor will provide the architect with a set of prototypical plans for its use prior to the architect commencing any drawings. The architect should review these prototypical plans against the landlord restrictions and any government requirements to find any differences between the plans and what the franchisee can build. Often plans, either prototypical or approved, are attached to the lease along with approved signage or signage restrictions included therein. It is important that you, as the attorney for your client, negotiate out any inconsistencies between the requirements of the franchisor and the requirements of the landlord. The architect should be responsible for pointing out the differences in building codes and zoning laws and the franchisor's requirements.

One area of significant concern to landlords is the look of the storefront of the premises. Certain landlords have very specific criteria as to what type of signage is allowed. Often exposed neon signs, any flashing signs such as "OPEN" or "HOT NOW," and lighting are highly regulated by the landlord. Quasi-governmental or governmental agencies may also prohibit the use of the franchisor's design criteria. Certain landlords require pin-mounted signs, whereas other landlords require signs mounted on a raceway. Some landlords will not allow poster signs in the front window of the premises, but other landlords will allow such signage if it covers no more than a certain percentage of the glass and is professionally prepared. Lighting of the storefront sign may be required or restricted by the landlord, such as gooseneck lighting, backlit or halo lighting, or internally lit letters. Generally, landlords will not allow box signs, and if that is a requirement of the franchisor, it must be worked out in the lease negotiation phase. Your client does not want any surprises after the lease is executed with the landlord. In addition to time and money spent resolving such issues, your client may not be able to obtain the necessary changes to the landlord or governmental criteria necessary to obtain the look the franchisor requires.

If the landlord requirements or the zoning restrictions or building codes require changes to the prototypical plans provided by the franchisor, the architect must speak with the franchisor's design team to work out any differences. Most franchisors have alternative design criteria such that most buildouts can be completed adhering to landlord's criteria and governmental requirements. However, if the franchisor will not accept such differences, your client must apply for a zoning variance. Zoning variances require a delay in the start and/or completion of the buildout plans, your client's opening, and significant legal fees and architectural fees. Moreover, there is no assurance that your client will obtain the required variances for the buildout. Your architect and the franchisor's design team must work diligently to resolve any differences early in the dance. If the franchisor simply cannot live with restrictions placed on it by the government and/or the landlord, a change of location will be required. This all costs time and money.

The architect should be registered in the state in which the premises are located. It will need to stamp the plans prior to submittal to the state for approval. You should check the architect's errors and omissions insurance to make sure it is adequate to protect your client should any issues arise during the design and/or buildout stage. Sometimes architects from a different jurisdiction hire a local architect to file-stamp the plans prior to submission. This practice is not recommended because the contracted architect does not review the plans carefully prior to putting its stamp on it and therefore may not point out any issues with governmental requirements.

The contract with the architect will most likely be an AIA contract for architects. It is very difficult to negotiate any major revisions into said contract; however, it is important to make sure the contract includes a submission date for plans, requires the architect to carry errors and omissions insurance coverage, and includes any procedures necessary for filing variances or working with the landlord and/or franchisor's design team in case issues arise.

Once the plans are submitted to the state for approval, the architect must be ready to respond quickly to any changes requested by the governmental jurisdiction. In some states, such as Florida, the plans for a restaurant must be submitted to both the health department, which is located in Orlando, and the agency for state permits, which is located in Tallahassee. In some jurisdictions, it is advisable to hire a permit expediter to marshal the plans through the different agencies necessary for plan approval. A permit expediter can often shorten the lead time for permit approval significantly. Typical plan approval varies widely from jurisdiction to jurisdiction, but a good rule of thumb is to allow at least 4 to 8 weeks.

If the landlord wants to review and approve the plans, the architect should submit the 85% complete set of plans to the landlord for preliminary approval. This set of plans will include most of the design work and the mechanical, electrical, and plumbing plans. After the landlord approves these preliminary plans, the architect can complete the set of drawings. Once completed, the plans are submitted to the landlord for approval and to the government agency, often simultaneously.

Your client can submit these preliminary plans to its prospective general contractors so that they can start reviewing the specifications for bidding purposes. Once the plans are formally approved by the landlord and, if necessary, the franchisor's design team, your client can put the work out for bid with general contractors for the buildout of the premises. It is wise to solicit bids from at least three general contractors.

Often the franchisee and/or general contractor is required to purchase equipment from a preferred vendor of the franchisor. In such case, the general contractor must be provided by either the architect or the franchisor's design team with the names and numbers of the preferred vendors. If the franchise agreement requires the franchisee to purchase such equipment directly from a preferred vendor to be supplied to the general contractor, be advised that the warranties on such equipment and even the warranties on the installation thereof may be an issue for the general contractor. Therefore, it is best to resolve those issues in the construction contract with the general contractor.

Once the bids are received, your client should compare those bids to the approximate buildout cost provided by the franchisor. If the bids are significantly higher or lower than what is expected, your client must determine why. Often the franchisor's design team and/or the architect can assist in this analysis. If a bid comes in significantly lower than what is expected, it should send up a red flag that the contractor failed to bid all of the work or made a mistake. In analyzing the bids, a good owner compares all of the line items for the work to be accomplished. Upon selection of the general contractor, your client may point out to the general contractor lower subcontractor bids for certain work that could be substituted for subcontractors on the general contractor's initial bid. This process can often save your client as much as 10% or 15% percent of the construction costs.

The construction contract should formalize all of the requirements necessary for building out the premises. All change orders from that construction contract should be submitted in writing by the general contractor to your client and signed by your client prior to the general contractor moving forward. Also, some construction contracts place the burden of code compliance on the general contractor, irrespective of the architect's plans. A sample construction contract is included at the end of this chapter. It is wise to have the general contractor provide you with a critical path chart showing all phases of the work and when the contractor is expected to start and complete the work. If preferred vendors are involved, it is necessary that the equipment arrive on time and to specifications. Depending on the relationship between the general contractor and the franchisee, one or both should be responsible for ensuring that the equipment is delivered on time.

The general contractor must comply strictly with the plans and specifications set forth in the approved plans. Remember, the franchisor is depending on your client to provide a consistent look for the franchisor. Any deviations from the approved plans and specifications that are material to the look and/or design of the premises should be approved by the franchisor's design team prior to making such changes.

During the construction phase, your client and its architect (if such requirement is set forth in its contract) should inspect the premises regularly to make sure the buildout is proceeding on schedule. There are many facets to opening the franchise location other than just the design or buildout. Your client, if it is a brick-and-mortar store, will more than likely prepare for a grand opening and preopening advertisement. Any delay in opening the store due to disruptions in construction and obtaining the certificate of occupancy can be devastating. If your client has seasonal dependencies, such as opening prior to the year-end holidays or Easter, any construction delays may cause your client to miss such window, in which case your client may be operating in the red for many months to come. Regular communication among the general contractor, the preferred vendors, any other parties, and your client should be encouraged.

Your client's lender may require inspection prior to funding the draws of the general contractor. Banks sometimes farm out the inspection to third-party vendors, and obtaining a timely inspection by the bank in a timely manner is often problematic. Even if the bank inspects the premises within a few days or a week after submission of a draw for payment by the general contractor, this delay in inspection and review of paperwork may delay the payment to the general contractor past the timing set forth in the construction contract. The general contractor should be aware of your client's funding vehicles, especially if there is an SBA loan.

Submission of draws should be carefully completed by the general contractor. All draws should include partial waivers of lien (or final waivers of lien if it's the final construction draw) and should be notarized by the subcontractors and/or materialmen. The actual construction draw should be notarized by the general contractor and should be detailed as to the percentage of work that is completed. The bank may provide its own waiver of lien form and/or other documentation required by the bank for payment. Depending on the bank, failure to dot one *i* or cross one *t* can a delay payment to the general contractor. It is necessary that your client understand what the bank needs for payment of each draw and should convey that fact to the general contractor prior to signing the construction contract.

Once the construction is complete, your client and architect should walk through the premises to create a punch list of any items of the construction work that need to be corrected. These punch list items should be corrected within approximately 10 days of submission to the general contractor. Often these punch list items do not delay obtaining a certificate of occupancy from the governmental jurisdiction. The certificate of occupancy should be submitted and obtained as soon as possible because franchisors often require a franchisee to obtain a certificate of occupancy 1 to 2 weeks prior to franchisor allowing the franchisee to open. If the franchisee has already arranged for preadvertisement and grand opening activities, a delay in opening due to not yet having received the certificate of occupancy may cost your client significant money. Your client does not want any surprises at the end. Once a certificate of occupancy has been obtained and the punch list items are completed, your client may proceed to opening.

The opening should be coordinated with any preadvertisement and grand opening activities that are required by the franchisor or contracted for by the franchisee. The franchisor will generally control any grand opening activities your client wants to have when the premises opens.

If everything proceeded as planned, the buildout with the general contractor should have gone smoothly. Although the architect's role in the square dance is over once the buildout is complete and accepted by your client, the general contractor must continue to fiddle for at least a year during the warranty period. Prior to final payment, the general contractor should transfer any warranties of equipment to your client and provide any other information the preferred vendors have. Your client should obtain a list with telephone numbers of all subcontractors and materialmen who supplied labor and/or materials to the premises in case the general contractor is unavailable for warranty issues. Once the warranty period ends for the general contractor, it is quite possible that your client may want to use the contractor and/or architect again if the franchisor requires any changes to the premises during the term of the franchise agreement. It is wise to maintain an even and smooth relationship with the general contractor. Also, if the franchise agreement allows for multiple locations, your client may want to use the same individuals for design and buildout as were used for the initial premises. These continued relationships will save time and money in the future.

Once open, with any luck, the music will continue to play for your client, the franchisee. Your client can switch to prerecorded music at this point and dismiss the architect and/or general contractor (except for warranty issues). Your role during this design and construction phase is to make sure the contracts are drafted properly; that any discrepancies in design are handled up front so that no surprises happen; that any zoning requirements are addressed; and that your client, the architect, the general contractor, and the bank all live in harmony. Delays cost time and money. Sometimes you act as a contract drafter and adviser; sometimes as a negotiator; and sometimes as a liaison between your client, the architect, the franchisor, the general contractor, and the lender. If everything goes well, you and your client will be rewarded with a profitable franchise operation. If you've done your job, your client may well open and operate many other franchise locations for this franchisor and/or others. LET THE MUSIC PLAY!

CONSTRUCTION CONTRACT

CONTRACT made this ___ day of ____________, 20__, by and between __________________, a ________________________ with an address of ___________ __________________ (hereinafter called "Owner") and ______________________, a ________________________ with an address of __________________________ (hereinafter called "Contractor").

PROJECT ______________________________________

(City, State) _________________________________

ARCHITECT __________________

____

____

PLANS AND SPECIFICATIONS Dated ______ and consisting of ______________ pages.

WITNESSETH

That for the consideration hereinafter named, the parties agree as follows:

SECTION 1. Contractor agrees to furnish all materials, tools, plans, equipment, heat, power, water, taxes, transportation, clean-up as directed by the Owner, and to perform and/or supply all labor and services of every kind whatsoever to fully complete, as required by all governmental authorities (local, state and national), as set forth in the plans and specifications and all addenda and alternates thereto, to the satisfaction of the Owner and/or Architect for the work described in the Plans and Specifications, copies of which are incorporated herein by reference. All of the Contractor's work shall be performed in strict compliance with the Plans and Specifications.

This Contract shall consist of the following component parts:

A. This Contract, including all addendums and exhibits.

B. Plans and Specifications prepared by the Architect and approved by Owner.

C. All addenda and alternates issued prior to execution of this Agreement

D. All modifications issued subsequent to the execution of this Agreement by written mutual consent of Contractor and Owner as shown on the Change Order form attached hereto as Exhibit "B."

This Contract together with the other documents enumerated in this Section 1, which said other documents are as fully a part of the Contract as if hereto attached or herein included.

Contractor specifically acknowledges inspecting, reading and understanding of the contents of the above listed component parts of this Contract and further acknowledges that any of the component parts not in his immediate possession are available for his inspection at the office of Owner.

SECTION 2. Contractor's strict performance hereunder must comply with all applicable laws as well as the provisions of this Contract and meet all the requirements, guarantees and provisions of the Plans and Specifications and have the approval of Owner, Architect and the inspecting agencies as said approvals are a condition precedent to the payment of any money hereunder by the Owner. Contractor shall give his personal supervision to the Project or have a competent superintendent, satisfactory to Owner, on the Project and available at all times with full authority to act for Contractor.

SECTION 3. Contractor agrees to make all necessary repairs to the above-described work being performed by him until accepted by Owner. Contractor unconditionally warrants and guarantees all labor and/or material and/or services employed and furnished by or to him in performing the work, and agrees to make good, upon demand by Owner, without costs to Owner, any and all defects due to workmanship and/or materials or any damages resulting therefrom which may appear at any time for twelve (12) months from and after completion and acceptance of the entire project by Owner. Nothing in this paragraph shall be construed to limit any warranty or guaranty on work to be performed by Contractor. Nothing herein shall in any way release Contractor for latent or hidden defects on the work performed by Contractor, and the failure of Owner to discover or reject defects which are latent or hidden within the twelve (12) month period will not act as a waiver of said defects.

SECTION 4. This Contract is subject to all the performance required and supervision, inspection and acceptance of Contractor's entire work in full by the Owner and/or Architect.

SECTION 5. Upon receipt of all required permits, Contractor shall commence work after being notified so to do by Owner and agrees to substantially complete all of the work included in this Contract on or before ________________.

On each Friday of every week during the term of this Contract, Contractor shall e-mail progress photographs of the site and project to: ________________. Failure to provide the aforementioned photographs may result in Owner's failure to make timely payments to Contractor as provided herein.

If, in Owner's sole opinion, Contractor is delaying work on the Project or is delaying the work of any other contractor or trade involved in the construction of the Project, or any part thereof, then Owner may, in addition to all other rights or remedies without waiver or prejudice to any other of Owner's rights or remedies, and after giving Contractor seventy-two (72) hours written notice, terminate this Contract and/or take possession of the premises and all materials, tools and appliances thereof and finish the work by whatever method Owner may deem expedient. In such case, Contractor shall not be entitled to receive any further payment until the work is completed. If the unpaid balance on Contractor's price shall exceed the expense of completing the work, including compensation for additional managerial and administrative services, such excess shall be paid to Contractor. If such expense shall exceed such unpaid balance, Contractor shall be liable for and shall pay the difference to the Owner, upon demand.

SECTION 6. For the work performed by Contractor, Owner shall pay Contractor $______________ (which amount includes Applicable State & Local Taxes).

A. On or before the date on which Contractor submits his first billing, Contractor shall furnish Owner a breakdown of the various items of construction covered by this Contract, including an itemized breakdown of the names, cost and scope of any construction, materials, supplies, labor and services supplied by any other person, firm or corporation, the total of which shall not exceed the contract price.

B. On the fifteenth (15th) day of each month after the commencement of construction, Contractor shall invoice Owner on the Application and Certificate for Payment, a statement setting forth in detail the percentage amount of work completed during the month as it pertains to each item of the construction and setting forth the name of the party performing labor and/or services and/or furnishing equipment and/or materials and all other materials reasonably requested by Owner. Contractor and each of its subcontractors and materialmen shall furnish Owner a Waiver of Liens and Claims form. A copy of said forms are attached hereto as Exhibit "A-1" and Exhibit "A-2," respectively.

Within fifteen (15) days after receipt by Owner of all the documents described in Section 6B above, Owner shall pay directly to Contractor (and at Owner's sole option to Contractor's subcontractors and materialmen and/or any person, firm or corporation supplying labor, material, supplies and equipment rental) monies due for costs and expenses attributable to materials, equipment, labor and services performed by Contractor and any subcontractors, laborers, suppliers of material, services or equipment used in construction of the improvements, 90% of the portion of the contract sum properly allocable to labor, material, equipment, services and supplies actually incorporated in the work for the period covered by the application for payment, less the aggregate of previous payments made by the Owner pursuant to this paragraph; provided that the work invoiced has been (a) performed, (b) used in the construction of the improvements and (c) approved by Owner.

In the event Contractor and Owner cannot agree as to the proper proportion of the contract which is completed, the parties hereto mutually agree that the Architect shall determine the percentage of completion and the amount properly due Contractor.

Final payment consisting of the entire unpaid balance of the contract sum shall be paid by Owner to Contractor, or at Owner's option, to the party or parties entitled to the funds, thirty-one (31) days after the later of (1) completion of all the work, Certification by Owner and/or Architect that the work is completed, (2) all punch list items prepared by Contractor, Owner and/or Architect have been completed, and (3) all warranties, shop drawings and as built drawings (as the case may be) have been delivered to Owner.

Prior to final payment, Contractor shall furnish to Owner a statement from Contractor and all subcontractors certifying and warranting that all liabilities and obligations for services, equipment, material and labor and all other indebtedness concerned with this Contract have been fully paid and satisfied and that there are no unsatisfied or outstanding claims which can be asserted against Owner or the real estate upon which the construction was performed.

SECTION 7. Contractor shall carry commercial general liability and property damage insurance with limits of not less than $1,000,000.00 for one person and $3,000,000.00 for one accident and property damage limits in the sum of $1,000,000.00 as protection against loss or damage that may be caused by operations of Contractor under this Contract. Contractor, as an independent Contractor, accepts exclusive liability for all contributions for Unemployment Compensation Insurance premiums, and like expenses. Contractor agrees to carry Worker's Compensation Insurance and to furnish Owner appropriate certificates of insurance for Worker's Compensation, commercial general liability and property damage insurance aforementioned in companies satisfactory to the Owner. Such certificates shall be furnished to Owner within ten (10) days after the execution of this Contract and each policy shall require ten (10) days' notice to Owner prior to the effective date of cancellation thereof. Contractor hereby indemnifies and holds harmless Owner from any and all liability, cost or expense (including attorney's fees and court costs) arising by reason of the injury to the person or property of (a) the Owner, its agents, employees, (b) Contractor or its subcontractors or (c) any other person or persons by reason of the performance of the work by said Contractor or by and on account of any act or omission of Contractor, his subcontractors, employees, servants or agents.

SECTION 8. The failure of Owner or Architect to discover or reject materials or the work not in accordance with this Contract shall not be deemed to be an acceptance nor a waiver of defects therein, nor shall any payment or partial or entire occupancy of the site be construed to be an acceptance of the work or of materials which are not in accordance with this Contract.

SECTION 9. Contractor shall keep each job clean and free from all rubbish, dust, debris and waste materials and shall daily remove same from the job and dispose of same off the project to the complete satisfaction of Architect and Owner.

SECTION 10. Contractor acknowledges and agrees that during its work under this Contract, the work of other crafts and trades may be required to be performed by other Contractors. Owner and/or Architect shall at all times have the right to direct and coordinate the work of others as well as the Contractor(s) so that performance of construction on the project shall at all times be properly and efficiently correlated. To that end, Contractor shall perform the various phases of the work herein contracted at the time or times and in the place or places as directed by Owner or Architect. Owner and/or Architect shall at all times have access to the building site to carry on, expedite and perform those portions of the work required to be done which are not included in this Contract.

SECTION 11. The Contractor shall furnish Owner and Architect samples of material, grade and quality, to be verified at cost of Contractor, and such materials, as approved by Owner and Architect, shall be used in the Project.

SECTION 12. Any alteration of or deviation from the Plans and Specifications or the terms and provisions of this Contract, whether involving extra costs for or of material or labor or otherwise, will be binding upon Owner only if set forth in writing and signed by Owner. It is expressly understood that agreements, change orders, or any other agreements whatsoever made with persons other than Owner are not binding upon the Owner and Contractor agrees not to present claims against Owner based on agreements by persons other than those mentioned above.

SECTION 13. Contractor, in the event of any dispute or controversy with Owner or any other contractor over any matter whatsoever, shall not cause any delay or cessation in or of its work or the work of any other contractor or the Owner, but shall proceed under this Contract with the performance of the work required hereby.

SECTION 14. Contractor agrees not to assign, sell or transfer or sublet or dispose of the whole or any part of this Contract or any rights hereunder or in connection herewith without the prior written consent of Owner.

SECTION 15. Owner may, in writing, require Contractor to immediately remove from the work any employee or agent of Contractor who Owner deems, in its sole discretion, to be incompetent, careless, insubordinate or otherwise objectionable.

SECTION 16. All notices or demands required or permitted under and by this Contract shall be in writing and shall be effective three (3) days after mailing through the United States Postal Service, certified, return receipt requested, and addressed to Contractor hereto at the address shown above or the next day if sent by overnight courier.

SECTION 17. If any part or the whole of the project is not built or if, for any reason, Owner and/or Architect cancels or any governmental authority directs a cessation of the work on all or any part of the said project, the above contract price shall be reduced in the proportion to which the canceled or incomplete portion relates to the entire project. In such event, Contractor shall and does hereby release and discharge Owner from any and all claims arising from such whole or partial termination hereof.

SECTION 18. Time is of the essence of this Contract. There are no representations, covenants, warranties, promises, agreements, conditions or undertakings, oral or written between Owner and Contractor other than as set forth herein. Except as otherwise provided, no subsequent alteration, amendment, change or addition to this Agreement shall be binding upon Owner or Contractor unless in writing and signed by them. If any provision or part hereof is adjudicated void or unenforceable, all remaining provisions hereof shall be valid, enforceable and effective. The rights and remedies of the owner hereunder are cumulative and the exercise of one shall not constitute a waiver of the others.

SECTION 19. If the Contractor fails to achieve substantial completion of the work within the time periods set forth in this Contract, the Owner shall be entitled to retain or recover from the Contractor, as liquidated damages and not as a penalty, $________ per day for the first fifteen (15) calendar days, and $___________ per day for the next fifteen (15) calendar days in which the actual time of performance exceeds the authorized time periods set forth in this Contract. Commencing upon the thirty-first day in which the actual time of performance exceeds the authorized time periods set forth in this Contract, the damages shall be $__________ per day until substantial completion has been achieved.

SECTION 20. Miscellaneous.

A. Owner will provide a building permit to Contractor.
B. Contractor is responsible for furnishing its own warehousing trailers.
C. Contractor is responsible for furnishing and installing temporary shelter as needed to assure completion of its scope of work.
D. Contractor will obtain all required licenses and inspections, at its sole expense.
E. Owner agrees to carry builder's risk insurance with extended coverage (including theft insurance) in an amount equal to the contract price which policy shall name Owner and Contractor as insured as their interests may appear.

IN WITNESS WHEREOF, the parties hereto have executed this Contract the day and year first above written.

OWNER:

___________________, a ___________________________

____

By: _______________________________

Its: _______________________________

CONTRACTOR:

____________________, a ___________________________

____

By: _______________________________

Its: _______________________________

EXHIBIT "A-1"

APPLICATION AND CERTIFICATE FOR PAYMENT

To Owner: | Project: | Application No.: | Distribution to:

From Contractor: | Via Architect: | Period To:

___ OWNER

___ ARCHITECT

Architects Project #:

___ CONTRACTOR

___ BANK

Contract For: | Application Date: | Contract Date: ___

CONTRACTOR'S APPLICATION FOR PAYMENT IN THE AMOUNT OF:

CHANGE ORDER SUMMARY

1 Original Contract Sum .... ___________

_ 2 Net change by Change Orders .... ___________

_ 3 Contract Sum to Date line 1(+–) 2 ... ___________

4 Total Completed & Stored to Date .. ___________

Approved this Month

5 Retainage: Prior: ___________

Number | Date Approved | Additions | Deductions

a. _____% of completed work |||||

| | | || b. _____% of Stored Materiall

|||||

||||| c. 10.00% of changes _________

||||| Total Retainage (Line 5a+5b+5c+Prior) _______________

TOTALS || This Statement _______________

Net Change by Change Orders

6 Total earned Less Retainage ... ___________

(Line 4 less Line 5 Total)

7 Less Previous Certificates for ... ___________

PAYMENT (line 6 from prior Certificate)

8 Current Payment Due .... ___________

9 Balance to Finish, in

Plus Retainage .... ___________

(Line 3 less Line 6)

This Certificate is not negotiable. The AMOUNT CERTIFIED is payable only to the Contractor named herein. Issuance, payment, and acceptance are without prejudice to any rights of the Owner or Contractor under this Contract.

AMOUNT CERTIFIED $_______________

(attach explanation if amount certified differs from the amount applied for)

The undersigned Contractor certifies that to the best of the Contractor's knowledge, information and belief the work covered by this Application for payment has been completed in accordance with the Contract Documents, that all amount have been paid by the Contractor for work for which previous Certificates for Payment were issued and payments received from the Owner, and that current payment shown herein is due.

CONTRACTOR:

By: ____________________ Date: ________

OWNER'S AGENT: CERTIFICATE FOR PAYMENT

In accordance with the Contract Documents, based on on-site observations and the data comprising the above application, the agent certifies to the Owner that to the best of the agent's knowledge, information and belief the work is in accordance with the Contract Documents, and the Contractor is entitle to payment of the AMOUNT CERTIFIED.

Certified By: ____________ Date: __________

State of: ___________ County of: ___________

Subscribed and sworn to before me this _____ day of

______________________ 20__

Notary Public: __________________________

My Commission expires: ___________________

EXHIBIT "A-2"

WAIVER OF LIENS AND CLAIMS

WHEREAS, the Contractor has been employed by Owner to furnish materials, labor and services for the construction of the improvements the Project;

NOW, THERFORE, the Contractor for and in consideration of the monies to be paid pursuant to the aforementioned request, does hereby waive, release and discharge any and all liens, rights, rights-of-lien, claims, demands, and actions whatsoever on or against said above described real estate and/or the improvements thereon and/or against the owners thereof, or against Contractor, on account of or by reason of labor, materials or services furnished or supplied to this date or which may be furnished by Contractor as respects the above described real estate and/or the improvements thereon. If permissible by law, Owner may assign this Waiver of Liens and Claims to any other party for the benefit of that party.

CONTRACTOR ______________________

____

By: ___________________________

Its: ___________________________

SUBSCRIBED AND SWORN to before me, this _____ day of ___________, 20___.

____

Notary Public

My Commission Expires: ______________

County of Residence: ______________

YOU WILL NOT BE PAID UNLESS:

i. All blanks are filled in or marked "N.A.," if not applicable.

ii. Both portions of this instrument are signed by an authorized person and his signature properly notarized.

EXHIBIT "B"

CHANGE ORDER

Project: **Change Order Number:**

Date:

Contractor: **Contract Date:**

The Contract is changed as follows:

The original Contract Amount was $________________

The net change by previously authorized Change Orders $________________

The Contract Amount prior to this Change Order was $________________

The Contract Amount will be (increased/decreased/unchanged)
by this Change Order in the amount of $________________

The new Contract Amount, including this Change Order will be $________________

The Completion Date will be (increased/decreased) by ________________days

The date of Substantial Completion as of the date of this Change Order is ____________

NOT VALID UNTIL SIGNED BY CONTRACTOR AND OWNER

Contractor: ________________ **Owner:** ________________

Address: ________________

____

By: ________________	By: ________________
Printed: ________________	Printed: ________________
Its: ________________	Its: ________________
Date: ________________	Date: ________________

Chapter 10

The Franchisor and the Franchise Agreement

Another member of your square dance quadrangle is the franchisor. This member controls your client's rights and operations of the franchise by means of the Franchise Agreement. The Franchise Agreement is attached to the FDD.

The bigger the franchisor, the more onerous the Franchise Agreement. You, as an attorney and zealous advocate for your client, will want to pounce on the Franchise Agreement to make it less one-sided and fairer for your client. Unfortunately, your opportunities for change are limited.

This chapter could have been a long one about making the Franchise Agreement a franchisee-friendly document. It is not. A few opportunities exist to improve the document for your client, but most franchisors will agree to few changes. The better the franchisor, the less likely you, as an attorney, will make large inroads in the language.

Fortunately for your client, Franchise Agreements are governed by federal law. In addition, about half of the states have some manner of governance over the Franchise Agreement. About one-third of the states require the franchisor to register with the respective Secretary of State, and in another 11 or so states the franchisor must file with the Secretary of State. Governance entails the rights of the franchisee in the franchise relationship with the franchisor. The FDD and the Franchise Agreement are governed under the Federal Franchise Rule (16 CFR 436), which can be found on the website of the Federal Trade Commission (https://www.ftc.gov). In addition, several associations exist to help franchisees navigate the Franchise Agreement. Two of note are the American Franchisee Association, whose website is www.franchisee.org, and the American Association of Franchisees & Dealers, whose website is https://www.aafd.org. The latter is a 501(c)(3) organization. However, these are just two of many groups that can assist you and your client in negotiating the Franchise Agreement. Some of the groups are pay for play, so be careful.

Most franchisors have carefully constructed their Franchise Agreement to keep control of the operation of the franchise while also providing significant assistance for the operation of the business. Because of federal laws, the franchisor must be evenhanded in its negotiations with its franchisees. All changes to the Franchise Agreement must be disclosed and set forth in the FDD. Franchisors typically do not want a long list of changes to their agreement to be published for everyone to read.

A well-structured franchisor will typically negotiate the same three or four items in the Franchise Agreement with the franchisee. Those typical items are:

1. the franchisee's right to receive notice of breach or default of the Franchise Agreement;
2. the right to closure clause;
3. the insurance clause; and
4. the personal guaranty.

In the notice rights clause, the franchisor often grants the franchisee a cure period. Of course, the franchisor has a cure period prior to being placed in default, but you must ask for one for the franchisee. In the right to close clause, the franchisor will use a reasonable standard for the franchisee's right to close the business during the term of the Franchise Agreement. Generally, any failure to be open is a default under the Franchise Agreement. In the insurance clause, the franchisor will often lower its insurance coverage limits in case of casualty or fire within the business. However, the franchisor will want to ensure that the franchisee has adequate insurance in case of casualty or fire so that the franchisee can rebuild the operation and reopen within a reasonable time. The guaranty clause can be often limited to a rolling guaranty or even eliminated depending on the financial strength of the franchisee.

There are many other clauses that you as a zealous advocate for your client wish to tackle. Many of these items deal with the unilateral control of the franchisor over the franchisee, such as location of other franchise operations in the immediate vicinity of your client's business, requirements that your client use a vendor of the franchisor's choosing without the ability to go to an outside source, the ability of the franchisor to make unilateral changes to the Franchise Agreement or the operations manual at any time, and lack of disclosure of use of advertising funds and other payments made to the franchisor by the franchisee. Remember, the franchisor must be evenhanded when dealing with all franchisees, but as long as it treats all franchisees equally, it can place demands on the franchisees that are self-serving but not illegal.

A quality franchisor will provide a more evenhanded document than will a franchisor that has a poor reputation in the marketplace. If your client receives a Franchise Agreement attached to the FDD that is very onerous, you should investigate the franchisor's relationship with existing franchisees. All existing franchisees with contact information are included in the FDD, so make use of this information provided to your client. Notwithstanding the foregoing, if you are negotiating a Franchise Agreement for a McDonald's or another large nationally known franchisor, many of these distasteful clauses may be in the Franchise Agreement and you will have little or no chance of making changes to that agreement. On the other hand, if the franchisor is small or has a bad reputation, the franchisor may be more flexible. If such a franchisor is not flexible, advise your client of the perils of the Franchise Agreement and of "getting in bed with the devil."

Often attached to the Franchise Agreement is a rider that the franchisee agrees to incorporate into the lease with the landlord. This will be the basis of the relationship among the franchisor, the franchisee, and the landlord and will give the franchisor rights under the lease even though it is not a party thereto. Unfortunately, the franchisor is a third-party beneficiary of the lease and not a tenant under it. Franchisors create this structure for liability reasons. This structure allows for reduced staffing costs of the franchisor and limits the franchisor's status as an employer of the franchisee's employees. The rider basically grants the franchisor the right to assume the lease and take over the business if the franchisee defaults under the Franchise Agreement or the Franchise Agreement is terminated. In case of the cessation of business at the location, it gives the franchisor the right to de-identify the premises. In other words, the franchisor will come in and take all of its trade dress and trademark items, as well as other items in the location that are identified with a business of the franchisor. Some riders are more detailed than others. Two such riders are attached as exhibits at the end of this chapter. The first is a simple rider from a franchisor. The other rider is more detailed, giving the franchisor more rights with respect to the location and the operation therein.

Note that the rider is attached to the Franchise Agreement. Once the Franchise Agreement is signed and the landlord will not accept the rider as attached, the franchisee is in breach of the Franchise Agreement. Fortunately, most franchisors understand this and will negotiate the rider; however, the negotiations of the rider can be quite contentious. Landlords do not like to get the rider at the end of lease negotiations because it actually amends the lease terms. Because almost all franchisors require a rider to a brick-and-mortar lease, it will save time and anguish if the rider is provided to the landlord early. Changes to the rider must be approved by the franchisor. Remember, once the lease is signed, the landlord is under no obligation to add the rider to the lease or make changes to the lease to satisfy the franchisor.

The landlord has a vested interest in controlling possession of the space and controlling who operates in the space. The landlord often wants to gain control of the space quickly if the operation goes dark and to limit any damage to the premises from removal of items therein. The landlord also wants to protect its revenue stream from the space. The landlord will want to maintain the character of the space, especially if it is a restaurant. It is easier to lease to another restaurant operator if the kitchen equipment is left in the space.

The franchisor has a vested interest in the franchise operation, in its trademark trade dress, and in its reputation.

Another item in the rider that is typically contentious with the landlord is the franchisor's ability to assign the lease to another franchisee. Most franchisors require a collateral assignment of the lease to the franchisor in case of a default by the franchisee. Many large landlords do not want a collateral assignment of the lease. Their reasons are that the lease has value only to the tenant/franchisee and no value to the assignee, such as a bank. However, landlords are becoming more accustomed to allowing a collateral assignment of the lease to the franchisor, as operation by such franchisor as the tenant under the lease is beneficial to the landlord and the franchisor is typically a stronger tenant financially. However, the rights of the franchisor to assign the lease to another franchisee are not always in landlord's best interest. Therefore, negotiating an assignment clause to another franchisee is often a major bone of contention in the negotiation of a rider. The landlord wants an operator to run the business who has experience, adequate capital, and a good reputation as a tenant rather than someone off the street with whom the franchisor happens to make a deal. When finding an assignee to operate a closed or failing franchise location in a brick-and-mortar setting, some franchisors will entertain anyone who comes in with cash to buy the franchise rights. They often do not pay attention to the overall financial ability or reputation of the new franchisee. As a side note, one area that is negotiable in the purchase of a franchise from the franchisor is in the case of a distressed location. The franchisor will often discount the franchise fee in order to keep the franchise business operating.

Even though the Franchise Agreement appears onerous, the franchisor has a vested interest in keeping the franchise operation working in good stead. The closing of a franchise store or poor quality service or product by the franchisee reflects poorly upon the franchisor. So the franchisor will often provide assistance to the franchisee outside of the Franchise Agreement terms to keep the operation going or to assist it in gaining financial strength. If the franchisor provided site approval to the franchisee, the franchisee may file a lawsuit against the franchisor for poor site selection. Therefore, if after the business opens your client comes to you with business issues, it is time to engage the franchisor in discussions to see what can be done to save the operation. If your client has extraneous issues (e.g., illness or a required relocation within the family or other such issues that prevented your client from operating the business effectively), early discussions with the franchisor will bring a happier ending than if your client neglects the business and allows it to go south. So treat the Franchise Agreement as a living document and understand it as such when negotiating. Spending too much time negotiating the Franchise Agreement will often cause the franchisor to withdraw the offer to sell a franchise to your client or will cause irreparable bad feelings before your client ever opens the doors.

Again, the FDDs with the attached Franchise Agreements are available through websites of certain states if you want to examine other what other franchisors allow in the agreement. The Secretary of States offices for California and Minnesota have good websites that provide examples of what other franchisors are agreeing to. In reviewing those agreements, it is best to find one that is in the same general business and is the same size as the franchise your client chose for its business operation.

Even though the franchisor is a large member of the square dance group, a good franchisor will help your client figure out the dance steps and make for a fun evening even if it won't engage in small-talk negotiations before the music plays. Most franchisors are structured to help your client be a successful operator. However, make sure you perform your due diligence on the franchisor to determine its reputation in the marketplace.

SIMPLE RIDER
RIDER TO LEASE AGREEMENT

THIS RIDER TO LEASE AGREEMENT (this "Rider") is made __________ __, 20___, by and between _________________________, a(n) ________________ ("Landlord"), and __________________, a(n) ___________________________ ("Tenant"), to the Lease dated __________ __, 20__ (the "Lease"), for the premises located at _________________________, which are more particularly described in the Lease ("Premises").

This Rider and the terms and conditions herein are hereby made a part of the Lease. In the event of a conflict or inconsistency between the terms and provisions of this Rider and the terms and provisions of the Lease, the terms and provisions contained in this Rider shall control. All capitalized terms herein shall have the same meanings set forth in the Lease, unless otherwise defined herein.

1. Assignment.
   a. Tenant has entered into a Franchise Agreement ("Franchise Agreement") with _________________________ (the reference to "Company" herein shall also include its successors or assigns). The Franchise Agreement prohibits any assignment or subletting of the Lease by Tenant, but does give Company, at its option, the right to require an assignment of the Lease (each a "Permitted Transfer") to a Permitted Transferee (defined below) upon delivery of written notice to Landlord and Tenant ("Assignment Notice"), but without Landlord's consent, in the event (i) the Franchise Agreement is terminated by Tenant; (ii) the Franchise Agreement is terminated by Company upon the default by Tenant under the Franchise Agreement; (iii) the Franchise Agreement expires by its own terms; (iv) Tenant decides to terminate, transfer, sell, or otherwise dispose of its leasehold interest in the Premises; or (v) Company requires assignment of the Premises due to Tenant failing to cure a material breach under the Franchise Agreement.
   b. Company's assignment rights herein shall be exercised if at all during the thirty (30) day period following the occurrence of any of the events described in (i)–(v) above but not beyond the date of expiration of the Lease. In the event Company delivers an Assignment Notice, Tenant shall and hereby does assign and transfer all of its right, title, and interest in the Lease to the Permitted Transferee identified in the Assignment Notice as of the effective date stated in the Assignment Notice ("Effective Date"). The Assignment Notice shall include the written assumption described in the paragraph below and shall be the only documentation necessary to effectuate the assignment and

assumption of the Lease, and upon receipt of the same, Landlord agrees to recognize the Permitted Transferee as the tenant under the Lease from and after the Effective Date. No assignment shall be permitted hereunder if Tenant is in default under the Lease, unless such default is cured by either Tenant or Permitted Transferee.

c. For purposes of this Rider only, following the Permitted Transfer, (i) the prior Tenant and Guarantor shall continue to remain liable for the performance of all the prior Tenant's obligations under the Lease from the Effective Date until the remaining, then-current term of the Lease expires; (ii) the Permitted Transferee and Guarantor(s) thereof shall assume in writing the performance of all obligations on the Permitted Transferee's part, as Tenant, arising or accruing under the Lease after the Effective Date; (iii) the prior Tenant shall vacate the Premises and the Permitted Transferee shall have the right to take full possession of the Premises from and after the Effective Date; and (iv) the Permitted Transferee's use of the Premises shall remain the same. In no event shall the Permitted Transferee be liable for any obligations on the prior Tenant's part arising or accruing under the Lease prior to the Effective Date.

d. Notwithstanding the definition of Permitted Transferee above, a "Permitted Transferee(s)" shall mean and include: (i) Company or any parent, subsidiary, or affiliate of Company, (ii) a surviving entity in connection with the merger, consolidation, or acquisition between Company or its affiliates with another entity, (iii) any one or more entities which control, are controlled by or are under common control with Company, which shall include any joint venture, partnership, corporation, or other entity of which Company has at least a fifty percent (50%) interest, or (iv) the purchaser of all or substantially all of Company's assets in the state where the Premises are located or all of Company's outstanding stock. In no event shall the term "Permitted Transferee" refer to an authorized franchisee of Company; any transfer to an authorized franchisee of Company shall require Landlord's prior written consent and be subject to all of the requirements of the Lease.

2. Notices. Landlord agrees to provide to Company notices of any default, breach, or non-compliance of Tenant under the Lease at the same time as any such notice is provided to Tenant. Tenant shall give Company written notice prior to exercising any early termination rights under the Lease, and Company shall have thirty (30) days from receipt of such notice to exercise its assignment rights under this Rider.

Company's notice address is as follows (such address may be changed upon delivery of written notice to Landlord):

____

____

____

Attn: ___________________________

LANDLORD	TENANT
________________________,	______________________________,
a(n) ___________________	a(n) ___________________________
By: ___________________________	By: ___________________________
Name: ___________________________	Name: ___________________________
Title: ___________________________	Title: ___________________________

COMPLEX RIDER
RIDER TO LEASE

This Rider to Lease, dated ________________, 20__, is entered into between ______________ ("Landlord") and ______________________ ("Tenant").

Recitals

A. The parties have entered into a Lease Agreement, dated , 20_, (the "Lease") pertaining to the premises located at (the "Premises").

B. Landlord acknowledges that Tenant has agreed to operate a restaurant at the Premises pursuant to Tenant's Franchise Agreement (the "Franchise Agreement") with ________________ ("Franchisor") under the name "_____________" or other name designated by Franchisor (the "Restaurant").

C. The parties desire to amend the Lease in accordance with the terms and conditions contained in this Rider to provide Franchisor the opportunity to preserve the Premises as a Franchisor-branded restaurant as provided herein.

Agreement

Landlord and Tenant agree as follows:

1. Remodeling and Decor. Landlord agrees that Tenant has the right to remodel, equip, paint and decorate the interior of the Premises and to display such proprietary marks and signs on the interior and exterior of the Premises as Tenant is reasonably required to do pursuant to the Franchise Agreement and any successor Franchise Agreement under which Tenant may operate a Restaurant on the Premises. Any remodel of the building and/or its signs shall be subject to Landlord's prior approval, which shall not be unreasonably withheld, conditioned or delayed.
2. Assignment. Tenant does not have the right to sublease or assign the Lease to any third party without Franchisor's and Landlord's written approval. Tenant has the right to assign all of its right, title and interest in the Lease to Franchisor or its affiliates, at any time during the term of the Lease, including any extensions or renewals, without first obtaining Landlord's consent. No assignment will be effective, however, until Franchisor or its designated affiliate gives Landlord written notice of its acceptance of the assignment. Franchisor or its designated affiliate will be responsible for the lease obligations incurred after the effective date of the assignment. If Franchisor elects to assume the Lease under this subparagraph or unilaterally assumes the Lease as provided for in subparagraph 3(a) or 4(a), Landlord and Tenant agree

that: (i) Tenant will remain liable for the responsibilities and obligations, including amounts owed to Landlord, prior to the date of assignment and assumption; and (ii) Franchisor will have the right to sublease the Premises to another franchisee with Landlord's prior reasonable approval, with reasonableness to be based on proposed new franchisee's related business experience and credit history, provided the franchisee meets Franchisor's then-current standards and requirements for franchisees and agrees to operate the Restaurant as a ____________ restaurant pursuant to a Franchise Agreement with Franchisor. Upon receipt by Landlord of an assumption agreement pursuant to which the assignee agrees to assume the Lease and to observe the terms, conditions and agreements on the part of Tenant to be performed under the Lease, Franchisor and its affiliates shall thereupon be released from all liability as tenant under the Lease from and after the date of assignment, without any need of a written acknowledgment of such release by Landlord.

3. Default and Notice.
    a. Landlord shall send Franchisor copies of all notices of default it gives to Tenant concurrently with giving such notices to Tenant. If Tenant fails to cure any defaults within the period specified in the Lease, Landlord shall promptly give Franchisor written notice thereof, specifying the defaults Tenant has failed to cure. Franchisor has the right to: (i) unilaterally assume the Lease if Tenant fails to cure; or (ii) cure the default or violation on behalf of Tenant without assuming the Lease. Franchisor shall have 15 days from the date Franchisor receives such notice to exercise, by written notice to Landlord and Tenant, its right for Franchisor or its designee (the "Franchisor Entity") to assume the Lease. Franchisor shall have an additional 15 days from the expiration of Tenant's cure period in which to cure the default or violation. If Franchisor cures the default or violation, any amounts incurred by Franchisor in connection with such cure shall be due and payable to Franchisor from Tenant upon demand.
    b. If the Franchisor Entity elects to assume the Lease, the Franchisor Entity shall not be required to cure defaults and/or to begin paying rent until Landlord delivers possession of the Premises to the Franchisor Entity. The Franchisor Entity shall have the right, at any time until Landlord delivers possession of the Premises, to rescind the option exercise, by written notice to Landlord.
    c. All notices to Franchisor must be sent by registered or certified mail, postage prepaid, to the following address:

        ____

        ____

        ____

        Attn: Franchise Department

Franchisor may change its address for receiving notices by giving Landlord written notice of the new address. Landlord agrees that it will notify both Tenant and Franchisor of any change in Landlord's mailing address to which notices should be sent.

4. Termination, Non-Renewal, Expiration.
   a. If the Franchise Agreement is terminated for any reason during the term of the Lease or any extension thereof, Franchisor or its designee has the right, but not the obligation, to unilaterally assume the Lease by giving Landlord written notice. Within 30 days after receipt of such notice, Landlord shall give the Franchisor Entity written notice specifying any defaults of Tenant under the Lease.
   b. If the Lease contains term renewal or extension right(s) and if Tenant allows the term to expire without exercising said right(s), Landlord shall give Franchisor written notice thereof, and a Franchisor Entity shall have the option, for thirty (30) days after receipt of said notice, to exercise the Tenant's renewal or extension right(s) on the same terms and conditions as are contained in the Lease. If a Franchisor Entity elects to exercise such right(s), it shall so notify Landlord in writing, whereupon Landlord and the Franchisor Entity shall promptly execute and deliver an agreement whereby the Franchisor Entity assumes the Lease, effective at the commencement of the extension or renewal term.
   c. Upon the expiration or termination of the Lease, Landlord will cooperate with and assist Franchisor in gaining possession of the Premises and if a Franchisor Entity does not elect to enter into a new lease for the Premises with Landlord on terms reasonably acceptable to the Franchisor Entity, Landlord will allow Franchisor to enter the Premises, without being guilty of trespass and without incurring any liability to Landlord, except for any damages caused by Franchisor's willful misconduct or gross negligence, to remove all signs, awnings, and all other items identifying the Premises as a ______________ Restaurant and to make such other modifications (such as repainting) as are reasonably necessary to protect the Franchisor marks and system. In the event Franchisor exercises its option to purchase assets of Tenant, Landlord must permit Franchisor to remove all such assets being purchased by Franchisor.
5. Additional Provisions.
   a. Landlord hereby acknowledges that the provisions of this Rider to Lease are required pursuant to the Franchise Agreement under which Tenant plans to operate its business and the Tenant would not lease the Premises without this Rider.
   b. Landlord further acknowledges that Tenant is not an agent or employee of Franchisor and the Tenant has no authority or power to act for, or to create any liability on behalf of, or to in any way bind Franchisor or any affiliate of

Franchisor, and that Landlord has entered into this Rider to Lease with full understanding that it creates no duties, obligations or liabilities of or against Franchisor or any affiliate of Franchisor, unless and until the Lease is assigned to, and accepted in writing by, Franchisor or its affiliate.

c. A Franchisor Entity may elect not to assume or be bound by the terms of any amendment to the Lease executed by Tenant without obtaining Franchisor's prior written approval, which approval shall not be unreasonably withheld or delayed.

6. Sales Reports. If requested by Franchisor, Landlord will provide Franchisor with whatever information Landlord has regarding Tenant's sales from the Restaurant.
7. Modification. No amendment or variation of the terms of this Rider is valid unless made in writing and signed by the parties and the parties have obtained the written consent of Franchisor.
8. Reaffirmation of Lease. Except as amended or modified in this Rider, all of the terms, conditions and covenants of the Lease remain in full force and effect and are incorporated by reference and made a part of this Rider as though copied herein in full. In the event of any conflict between the terms of this Rider and those in the Lease, the terms of this Rider shall control.
9. Beneficiary. Landlord and Tenant expressly agree that Franchisor is a third party beneficiary of this Rider.

IN WITNESS WHEREOF, the parties have executed this Rider as of the dates written below.

TENANT: ____________________	**LANDLORD:** ____________________
By: ____________________	By: ____________________
Printed: ____________________	Printed: ____________________
Its: ____________________	Its: ____________________

Chapter 11

The Lender

Perhaps the least welcome member of your square dance group is the lender. The old adage goes that if you don't need money, you can borrow it, and if you do need money, it is very difficult to get a loan for it. Typically, your client will be applying for a Small Business Administration ("SBA") loan to finance part of its capital and operational requirements for its business. The SBA provides guidelines for loans made by the lender with backup guarantees by the federal government. As with all governmental programs, it is heavily regulated and not always user-friendly.

Your client may have a great relationship with its local bank; however, that bank may not be the proper lender for your client's needs. Preferably, the lender needs to be in the Preferred Lenders Program (PLP) of the SBA such that the loan is guaranteed as long as your client adheres to the regulations established by the SBA. If your client's preferred bank is not in the PLP, it is best that you steer your client to a PLP lender. A PLP lender will approve the loan internally without being required to go to an outside group, and the loan will be automatically guaranteed by the SBA. The SBA has other levels of SBA lenders, but approval of the loan and the subsequent SBA guaranty may be more difficult to obtain.

The SBA has a list of approved franchisors for which it will automatically guarantee loans. The typical SBA loan is a 7(a) loan. There is another path to follow for an SBA loan, the 504 Loan program. This program lends money for real property, such as land and buildings for economic development. The 504 Loan program lends to small companies in designated development areas that are owned by women, minorities, and veterans or are located in rural areas. A 504 loan may not be used for working capital of other operation requirements. If your client fits any of these categories and does not need to borrow working capital, you should explore the 504 Loan program.

The SBA has standard operating procedures that lenders must follow for their SBA 7(a) loan portfolio. These procedures dictate how loan applications are to be submitted; how they are reviewed, approved, and structured; and how the loans are administered. Assuming that your client has set up a limited liability company for ownership of the business, the SBA will require a guarantor who owns at least 20% of the company. The SBA will want collateral assignment of all assets of the guarantor, including his house. Even if the house has little or no cash value in it, the SBA will require it to be presented as collateral of the loan. If your client's loan is up to and including $350,000, the lender must take a first lien on assets financed with the loan proceeds (your client's fixtures, furnishings, and equipment). The lender *may* take personally owned investment and residential real estate as collateral. For loans over $350,000, however, a lien on the personal residence is usually required unless the SBA considers the loan as "fully secured," meaning that the lender has taken security interests in all available fixed assets with a net book value up to the loan amount and the equity in the real estate is less than 25% of the property's fair market value. If your client has these types of fixed assets, he may not need to get an SBA loan. If the residence is owned by your client and his spouse, whether by deed or by operation of law, the spouse must agree to the assignment.

Unfortunately, if your client wants to collaterally assign "trading assets" (i.e., stocks and/or bonds), the SBA values them at only 10% of their current value for collateral purposes.

The loan process is worse than obtaining a mortgage on a house. The mortgage on a house requires a down payment and an income stream and some equity value therein. Under a 7(a) loan, the lender will look for the owner's experience, the management of the business, and, if all goes south, how to get money from the guarantor. The scrutiny required by the SBA to provide a guaranteed loan to your client is much more invasive than that required to obtain a mortgage for a residence.

The standard operating procedure set forth by the SBA requires that the lender manage the loan properly; otherwise, the SBA will pull the guarantee. Without the guaranty, the bank is highly exposed to a failing business. Remember, as many as 9 out of 10 new restaurants fail within the first year, leaving lenders exposed to bad loans. With the SBA guarantee of those loans, the bank is more likely to lend money to clients at more favorable terms. That being said, however, the SBA will only go after the guarantor after liquidation of the business. Basically, all stops must be pulled before the SBA or the lender will call in the loan. Because of all of the pledges and collateralization of your client's assets, once the business goes into bankruptcy and/or foreclosure, the results to your client can be devastating.

The bank does not want to shut down the business as long as the guarantor is there to work through the issues facing the operation. The guarantor, your client, is valuable to the lender in working through such issues. By the time the business goes south, there is never enough collateral to pay back the loan unless your client has large amounts of securities or cash. Typically operators of failing businesses will monetize all of their available assets to keep the business operation afloat and hope that it will turn around.

The lender will require collateralization of the lease, as stated in the chapter on landlords. Most landlords do not want such a collateralization because they do not want to work with a lender as a partner. The lender does not want to become a partner either; however, it does not want to lose money on the loan. Therefore, the lender will work closely with the franchisor to secure another franchisee to operate the business. Both the lender and the franchisor have a vested interest in keeping the business operational and profitable.

For an SBA loan, your client will need to provide (1) the SBA loan application; (2) a personal background and statement of personal history and a personal finance statement, all on SBA forms; (3) a projected financial statement and business plan showing your client's ability to pay back the loan; (4) an ownership affidavit; (5) your client's business certificate; (6) a loan application history; (7) at least three years of tax returns; (8) resumes for each principal; (9) the lease for the Premises; *and any other documents the lender or the SBA requires*. It seems as though your client is never finished providing information. The lender can become quite invasive in its requests for documentation regarding your client's experience and his assets, especially if your client has a marginal cash position in the business. Your client may balk at providing such information; however, delays in disclosure will only delay approval or disapproval of the loan. It is best to give the lender what it wants quickly and without much argument, if any.

Even though the lender may be in the PLP, your client must first obtain internal approvals from the lender. The lender will not automatically approve an SBA loan for your client even though the franchisor may be approved by the SBA and your client provides all of the proper documentation and assurance.

SBA 7(a) loan providers come in various sizes and shapes. Your local bank may do well for loans up to $350,000. Other SBA providers work in loans of $1 million or more and find that small loans do not fit their portfolios properly. Lenders may have had difficulties with franchisees of the franchisor in the past and are less willing to lend money to such franchisees. Find the SBA PLP lender that fits your client's financial needs.

If your client's friends at the local bank are willing to provide an SBA loan for your client, that personal relationship your client has fostered over the years will assist in the loan application process, in its approval, and in administration of the loan. However, if your client does not have a relationship with a local banker or the loan is too large for the local bank or the location of the business is not within the local bank's comfort zone (meaning physical area), the local bank may not want to participate in the SBA loan. You and your client may be searching for an SBA lender that works for the amount of the loan your client is requesting and in the physical jurisdiction in which the business is located. As with everything else, the Internet has invaded the lending market. Many lending institutions exist only on the Internet. Unfortunately, your client rarely has a personal relationship with such lenders. These lenders are often represented by local brokers or small regional offices and provide formulaic loans to applicants such that your client's needs must fit perfectly within the lender's box or the loan will be denied. Some very large banking institutions provide SBA loans, but these banks are often more institutionalized and do not offer the personal service a local banker will provide.

Fortunately, several large regional lenders have large SBA loan departments. These lenders often have regional locations in the jurisdictions in which they make loans or provide large regional offices for lending to persons such as your client. It is best that you and your client research carefully the SBA lender to whom your client desires to make application for his loan. Finding the right fit for the size and nature of the loan and business may save time and heartache throughout the process.

Unfortunately, the lender comes late to the dance. Often your client will have signed the Franchise Agreement, may have signed a lease with the landlord, and may even have negotiated with a contractor for buildout prior to applying for the loan. If your client is using a non-preferred lending provider for the SBA loan or is looking to his local banking friend for an SBA loan, he may be disappointed when either the loan is turned down or he is unable to obtain the funding necessary to build out and run his business during the early days. As soon as your client knows his capital needs, he should contact the lender and obtain preliminary approval of the loan. Another unwanted circumstance of having a loan turned down is that will affect your client's credit score. By not choosing the proper lender at the start, your client may create unfortunate and unintended consequences down the road with other lenders due to credit score degradation.

Administration of the SBA loan is dictated by the government. Many rules exist that, if not properly managed by your client and its contractor, can create problems for your client during the buildout phase of the business. Most SBA lenders will require strict adherence to the payment processing requests set forth by the lender. Such requests are approvals of the contractor, the lease, the construction progress, and just about anything else the lender can think of. All paperwork requirements, inspections, and other procedural hurdles will cause delays in payments to your client and/or to the contractor during the buildout phase. Your client will be required to provide construction draw requests on the lender's form and will be subject to inspection by lender personnel and continued scrutiny of the financial progress of the business itself. Many lenders will require a detailed breakdown of the use of funds, breaking out the various construction areas such as flooring, HVAC, architectural, equipment, kitchen equipment, manager salaries, sign costs, and any other breakdown the lender requires. The lender will typically inspect the progress of the construction after receiving each draw request from your client to make sure the work has been performed or the equipment is available to your client. Most draw requests and waivers of lien must be submitted on the lender's forms and need to be notarized. Unfortunately, this all takes time. The lender typically has third-party inspection companies that are available at only certain times, and a week to 10 days may pass after the receipt of the draw request before the inspection is made. Then the inspector will report back to the lender, the lender will examine all of the paperwork, and—lo and behold—your contractor is not getting paid within the 20 or 30 days set forth in the construction contract. These delays are why, discussed in the chapter on contractors, it is pointed out that the contractor must be flexible and be able to work with your client during the payment process.

If your client did not properly prepare a construction financial schedule with items properly allocated to the various divisions of the construction contract, the lender may deny a payment request for a line item within the construction even though the overall cost of construction has not changed. It is extremely important that your client provide the lender with a properly allocated and detailed set of costs so that the lender will not deny the draw request during construction. Your client cannot use money allocated for a manager's salary to pay the contractor for the floor.

The amount of the loan approved by the lender as compared to the total needs of your client may vary. The lender will advise your client as to the amount of money he will fund through the SBA loan. Depending on the collateral and cash position of your client, the lender may provide the 70% or even 90% of the funds necessary for the buildout and cash flow requirements necessary for your client's business during the buildout phase in first year of operation. Obviously, unless your client is well-heeled, the more money obtained by the SBA loan versus personal cash infusion is better for your client, giving him more flexibility during that first critical year of operation. The lender may come back saying that it will provide your client an 80% loan. However, it may not agree with your client as to the amount of loan necessary for buildout and startup expenses. If your client is inexperienced in the business at hand or does not have strong support from the franchisor as to cost of the buildout and the expenses necessary to make it through the first year, your client may experience a shortfall in available funds because the lender chose to underestimate the amount of overall funds required, therefore reducing the SBA loan amount. You and your client's CPA must analyze the financial requirements properly, especially against the amount set forth in the FDD, as to how much your client is really going to need through the first year of the business. The two biggest reasons your client will fail in business are lack experience and lack of proper funding.

Depending on your client's financial strength, the typical loan will be structured as interest-only for X years, typically 3 to 5 years, and then will convert to a permanent loan. The interest rate will be lower than an unsecured loan because of the SBA guarantee. It may be tied to the prime rate or to the LIBOR rate. Typically, SBA loans are tied to the prime rate at some amount over prime, typically 2% to 3% depending on the lender's risk assessment of your client. The capital requirements of the debt service should be plugged into your client's projected operational sheet to see if such debt service can be managed by the cash flow of the business. This cash flow is based on EBIDTA, as those cash requirements will need to be paid every month without fail and are not dependent on recapturing depreciation or other amortization at the end of the year via the tax returns.

Most SBA lenders are strict in the application of the loan requirements, as required by the SBA, allowing your client little room to maneuver in paying the debt service once it begins. That being said, however, lenders are loathe to become owners and/or operators. They neither have the expertise nor the desire to operate a restaurant or other franchise business in its portfolio. If your client becomes distressed in its financial operations, like the franchisor, contact the lender early to see what kind of workout arrangement is available to your client. Lenders often know of other investors and other operators and have forgiveness or tolling of debt payments at their disposal if your client is up front communicating problems with the lender. Remember, a grumpy dance participant can make for a long night.

Part Two Conclusion

As you can see from the chapter on the Franchisor and Franchise Agreement and the chapter on the lender, involvement with your client does not end upon signing the lease and making sure the loan is made. Your client will depend on you, as counselor, to provide continued oversight and advice regarding all phases of the business—from working with the franchisor and lender through working with various vendors and landlords and other national equipment and food providers. You and your client's CPA need to orchestrate all of the players at the square dance, making sure the music is played, the caller calls the dance, and your client's quadrangle dances well together. Then the franchisor may require your client to keep up with national branding, national trends, and menu changes and may make other demands. In 2016, Applebee's required its franchisees to put in wood-burning grills and make other operational changes to each location. Each franchisee was required to spend more than $40,000 to effect these changes. If a franchisor changes its logo or its internal design, the franchisee is required to foot the bill for all of these changes. The relationship between franchisor and your client and the lender is ongoing. The architect and the construction contractor typically fall by the wayside after your client opens his business. However, the four major players of the square dance quadrangle continue the dance until your client sells out, the Franchise Agreement ends and your client chooses not to renew it, or your client goes through bankruptcy.

You, as counsel to your client, should seek to continue to advise him during his tenure as a franchisee. Hopefully, the two of you will have fostered a good relationship such that he will keep you apprised of the business operation and any requests from the other players at the dance. You will want to jump in if you see an issue or an opportunity for your client or, if appropriate, advise your client to seek advice from other professionals if the issue or opportunity is beyond your scope of expertise. Even though you are not a participant on the dance floor or the stage, you can provide the cookies and punch for the square dance. Your relationship with your client may be a long and rewarding one, and you might need to step in at any time. Don't hesitate to do so, as your client's livelihood and the future of his family may depend on your expert counsel. As stated in the first chapter, you are part attorney, part negotiator, and part businessperson. Enjoy the music and the dance. It is very rewarding.

Index

L

M

N

O